W9-BWG-031

The Translator and Editor

STANLEY CORNGOLD is Professor of German and Comparative
Literature at Princeton University, where he has taught since 1966. He
is an Executive Committee Member and past President of the Kafka
Society of America as well as advisory editor of the *Journal of the Kafka
Society of America*. He is the author of *The Commentators' Despair:
The Interpretation of Kafka's* Metamorphosis, *The Fate of the Self:
German Writers and French Theory*, and *Franz Kafka: The Necessity of
Form*, as well as many articles, mainly on German literature, and the
co-author of *Borrowed Lives*. He has also edited *Ausgewählte Prosa by
Max Frisch* and co-edited *Thomas Mann: 1875–1975* and *Aspekte der
Goethezeit*.

THE METAMORPHOSIS

TRANSLATION
BACKGROUNDS AND CONTEXTS
CRITICISM

W.W. NORTON & COMPANY, INC.
also publishes

THE NORTON ANTHOLOGY OF AMERICAN LITERATURE
edited by Nina Baym et al.

THE NORTON ANTHOLOGY OF CONTEMPORARY FICTION
edited by R. V. Cassill

THE NORTON ANTHOLOGY OF ENGLISH LITERATURE
edited by M. H. Abrams et al.

THE NORTON ANTHOLOGY OF LITERATURE BY WOMEN
edited by Sandra M. Gilbert and Susan Gubar

THE NORTON ANTHOLOGY OF MODERN POETRY
edited by Richard Ellmann and Robert O'Clair

THE NORTON ANTHOLOGY OF POETRY
edited by Alexander W. Allison et al.

THE NORTON ANTHOLOGY OF SHORT FICTION
edited by R. V. Cassill

THE NORTON ANTHOLOGY OF WORLD MASTERPIECES
edited by Maynard Mack et al.

THE NORTON FACSIMILE OF
THE FIRST FOLIO OF SHAKESPEARE
prepared by Charlton Hinman

THE NORTON INTRODUCTION TO LITERATURE
edited by Carl E. Bain, Jerome Beaty, and J. Paul Hunter

THE NORTON INTRODUCTION TO THE SHORT NOVEL
edited by Jerome Beaty

THE NORTON READER
edited by Linda H. Peterson et al.

THE NORTON SAMPLER
edited by Thomas Cooley

A NORTON CRITICAL EDITION

Franz Kafka

THE METAMORPHOSIS

TRANSLATION

BACKGROUNDS AND CONTEXTS

CRITICISM

Translated and edited by

STANLEY CORNGOLD

PRINCETON UNIVERSITY

W • W • NORTON & COMPANY • *New York* • *London*

Copyright © 1996 by Stanley Corngold

THE METAMORPHOSIS by Franz Kafka,
translated by Stanley Corngold.
Translation copyright © 1972 by Stanley Corngold. Used by permission of
Bantam Books, a division of Bantam Doubleday Dell Publishing Group, Inc.

All rights reserved.
Printed in the United States of America.
First Edition.

The text of this book is composed in Electra
with the display set in Bernhard Modern.
Composition by PennSet, Inc.
Manufacturing by Courier Companies.

Library of Congress Cataloging-in-Publication Data
Kafka, Franz, 1883–1924.
[Verwandlung. English]
The metamorphosis : the translation, backgrounds and contexts,
criticism / Franz Kafka ; translated and edited by Stanley Corngold.
p.   cm. — (A Norton critical edition)
Includes bibliographical references.
I. Corngold, Stanley.   II. Title.
PT2621.A26V42613   1996
833'.912 — dc20   95-20582
ISBN 0-393-96797-2 (pbk.)

W. W. Norton & Company, Inc., 500 Fifth Avenue, New York, N.Y. 10110
W. W. Norton & Company Ltd., 10 Coptic Street, London WC1A 1PU

1 2 3 4 5 6 7 8 9 0

Contents

Preface

Franz Kafka's novella *The Metamorphosis* is perfect, even as it incessantly provokes criticism. Its perfection was noted by the Nobel Prize-winning author Elias Canetti: "In *The Metamorphosis* Kafka reached the height of his mastery: he wrote something which he could never surpass, because there is nothing which *The Metamorphosis* could be surpassed by—one of the few great, perfect poetic works of this century." But what is distinctive about such *literary* perfection is that it does not leave the reader's mind settled, satisfied, at peace with itself. Its perfection is not aesthetic. Instead, it never stops irritating the reader to produce a kind of brother or sister work in the mind that will be simpler, plainer, and altogether better-behaved, intellectually speaking, than the story itself. For this story, if Kafka is to be trusted, is not only *about* a monster; rather, it comes into the world trailing clouds of monstrosity. "What is literature?" Kafka declared. "Where does it come from? What use is it? What questionable things! Add to this questionableness the further questionableness of what you say, and what you get is a monstrosity." The monstrous aspect of the story is clear, no doubt, but where, then, is its perfection? It must be, first, in the perfection of the hopelessness that settles on Gregor Samsa and his family in the face of a nightmare they have never before seen or heard of. And it must also lie in the supreme irony with which this hopelessness is depicted, as if from the standpoint of an unnamed god who has arranged it all for his amusement.

The Metamorphosis raises such questions, certainly, but it also states facts as hard, concrete, and undeniable as the armorlike shell in which Gregor Samsa is born again one fine morning. This disparity between the underlying structure of impossibility and the wealth of atrociously detailed facts makes for the uncanny disturbance at the center of the story. Everything is in place in the family to deny the arrival of this monster in its midst. All the explanations are at hand, especially in the average, everyday awareness of Gregor himself, who thinks at various times that his metamorphosis is only a fantasy, a bad cold, a hindrance, or—as his mother puts it—a momentary absence of the real Gregor, who will surely "come back to us again." But the vermin refuses to be any of these things. It is what it materially is and does not let itself be denied so long as Gregor is alive: it is his wildly waving legs, his snap-

ping jaws, his obscene craving for decaying vegetables and dark crev-
ices, and . . . yes . . . for fiddle playing too. It is the "little red apple"
flung by his father deep into his back and left to rot and kill his son,
but it is also the acrobatic bliss that Gregor feels hanging and falling
from the ceiling when he finally lets his body do what it wants. "A little
horrible," Kafka called his story, writing to his fiancée Felice Bauer,
perhaps understating the case, and then, the next day (perhaps over-
stating it), "infinitely repulsive." But while Kafka's judgment here re-
peats the verdict of the Samsa family, the judgment of literary history
has been a different one. Readers have been drawn again and again to
this monstrosity by the desire to get it under control — to interpret it in
place of understanding it, for no one yet has so fully understood it that
it might "go away."

The fascination continues. Literally millions have read this story, so
to begin to read it now is to enter with a thrill into a community of
those who have struggled to master something that has struck them —
as the critic Theodor Adorno says — with the force of an onrushing
locomotive. Kafka collapses aesthetic distance between text and reader:
"Interpret me!" it declares. "Interpret me! . . . or be overwhelmed."
This is as it should be. "A real book," Kafka wrote, "must be the axe
for the frozen sea in us," stressing the redemptive opportunity the shock
might finally provide. It is to be hoped that the present translation of
The Metamorphosis, which tries to follow more closely Kafka's actual
idiom than previous translations, produces something of this effect.

The translation is based on Franz Kafka, "Die Verwandlung," in
Erzählungen, S. Fischer Verlag Lizenzausgabe (New York: Schocken,
1946) 71–142. A new edition of Kafka's complete works, the so-called
Manuscript Version, is nearing completion at the Research Center for
German [Exile] Literature at the University of Wuppertal in Germany.
The director of this project, Dr. Hans-Gerd Koch, has kindly made a
portion of his critical apparatus for *The Metamorphosis* available before
its appearance in print. In the section of the Norton Critical Edition
entitled "Kafka's Manuscript Revisions," I have indicated, and attempted to explain, the most significant of these changes.

The critical essays collected in this volume are meant to illustrate
some of the most interesting currents of criticism now flowing in this
lively age of literary theory. They include several post-structuralist readings, including a post-Freudian psychoanalytic study written by Professor Eric Santner of Princeton University especially for this edition.
Other essays connect *The Metamorphosis* to feminist theories and to
the concerns of cultural studies, which define the novella against Kafka's sexual and Jewish-religious background, highlighting questions of
Kafka's cultural identity. This section also contains a historical study of
the revealing details of *The Metamorphosis*'s "long journey into print."
The latter essay has been prepared by Professor Hartmut Binder, the

eminent German Kafka scholar, who was interested enough to contrib-
ute his text to this edition even before its appearance in print in
Germany.

This selection of critical materials is designed to stimulate and guide
the reader to a creative encounter with *The Metamorphosis*, and more:
it aims to suggest the richness of the modern attempt to grasp the
Schriftstellersein, the *being*-literature, to which Kafka sacrificed his personal existence.

The Text of
THE METAMORPHOSIS

Free — Write; Man does not live by bread alone.

The theme of metamorphosis is found in classical literature, most famously in the *Metamorphoses* of Ovid (43 B.C.–A.D. 17 or 18), which traces through mythology the development of the human race to its culmination in the Roman order. See below, pp. 107–8. Kafka's word for "metamorphosis"—*Verwandlung*—also means a scene change in a stage play. The English word "metamorphosis" is slightly more elevated in tone than the German, which could also arguably be translated as "The Transformation."

When Gregor Samsa[1] woke up one morning from unsettling dreams, he found himself changed in his bed into a monstrous vermin.[2] He was lying on his back as hard as armor plate, and when he lifted his head a little, he saw his vaulted brown belly, sectioned by arch-shaped ribs, to whose dome the cover, about to slide off completely, could barely cling. His many legs, pitifully thin compared with the size of the rest of him, were waving helplessly before his eyes.

"What's happened to me?" he thought. It was no dream. His room, a regular human room,[3] only a little on the small side, lay quiet between the four familiar walls. Over the table, on which an unpacked line of fabric samples was all spread out—Samsa was a traveling salesman—hung the picture which he had recently cut out of a glossy magazine and lodged in a pretty gilt frame. It showed a lady done up in a fur hat and a fur boa,[4] sitting upright and raising up against the viewer a heavy fur muff in which her whole forearm had disappeared.

Gregor's eyes then turned to the window, and the overcast weather —he could hear raindrops hitting against the metal window ledge— completely depressed him. "How about going back to sleep for a few minutes and forgetting all this nonsense," he thought, but that was completely impracticable, since he was used to sleeping on his right side and in his present state could not get into that position. No matter how hard he threw himself onto his right side, he always rocked onto his back again. He must have tried it a hundred times, closing his eyes so as not to have to see his squirming legs, and stopped only when he began to feel a slight, dull pain in his side, which he had never felt before.

"Oh God," he thought, "what a grueling job I've picked! Day in,

1. The name "Gregor Samsa" appears to derive partly from literary works Kafka had read. The hero of *The Story of Young Renate Fuchs*, by the German-Jewish novelist Jakob Wassermann (1873–1934), is a certain Gregor Samassa. The Viennese author Leopold von Sacher-Masoch (1836–1895), whose sexual imagination gave rise to the idea of masochism, is also an influence. Sacher-Masoch (note the letters Sa-Mas) wrote *Venus in Furs* (1870), a novel whose hero is named Gregor. A "Venus in furs" literally recurs in *The Metamorphosis* in the picture that Gregor Samsa has hung on his bedroom wall. See below, n. 4, and p. 165. The name Samsa also resembles Kafka in its play of vowels and consonants. See below, "Backgrounds and Contexts," p. 75.
2. Kafka uses the words *unruhige Träumen* (literally, "restless dreams"), an odd expression combining the more usual phrases "restless sleep" and "bad dreams." For a discussion of "monstrous vermin," see below, pp. 87–88 and pp. 185–90.
3. "An unusual expression, roughly analogous to 'children's room.' Gregor's nearest surroundings (in the story Gregor is doing the observing and reflecting) appear to him as something matter-of-fact and humanly normal, while this expression itself implies *his* unnaturalness as a metamorphosed animal" (Peter Beicken, *Erläuterungen und Dokumente. Franz Kafka: Die Verwandlung* [Clarifications and documents. Franz Kafka: The Metamorphosis] [Stuttgart: Reclam, 1983] 8).
4. An ornamental scarf, typically of fur or feathers, draped *snakelike* around a woman's neck. It could evoke an image of Eve before the Fall. For further discussion of this image, see below, pp. 205–6.

the need for human community

day out—on the road. The upset of doing business is much worse than the actual business in the home office, and, besides, I've got the torture of traveling, worrying about changing trains, eating miserable food at all hours, constantly seeing new faces, no relationships that last or get more intimate. To the devil with it all!" He felt a slight itching up on top of his belly; shoved himself slowly on his back closer to the bedpost, so as to be able to lift his head better; found the itchy spot, studded with small white dots which he had no idea what to make of; and wanted to touch the spot with one of his legs but immediately pulled it back, for the contact sent a cold shiver through him.

He slid back again into his original position. "This getting up so early," he thought, "makes anyone a complete idiot. Human beings have to have their sleep. Other traveling salesmen live like harem women. For instance, when I go back to the hotel before lunch to write up the business I've done, these gentlemen are just having breakfast. That's all I'd have to try with my boss; I'd be fired on the spot. Anyway, who knows if that wouldn't be a very good thing for me. If I didn't hold back for my parents' sake, I would have quit long ago, I would have marched up to the boss and spoken my piece from the bottom of my heart. He would have fallen off the desk! It is funny, too, the way he sits on the desk and talks down from the heights to the employees, especially when they have to come right up close on account of the boss's being hard of hearing. Well, I haven't given up hope completely; once I've gotten the money together to pay off my parents' debt to him—that will probably take another five or six years—I'm going to do it without fail. Then I'm going to make the big break. But for the time being I'd better get up, since my train leaves at five."

And he looked over at the alarm clock, which was ticking on the chest of drawers. "God Almighty!"[5] he thought. It was six-thirty, the hands were quietly moving forward, it was actually past the half-hour, it was already nearly a quarter to. Could it be that the alarm hadn't gone off? You could see from the bed that it was set correctly for four o'clock; it certainly had gone off, too. Yes, but was it possible to sleep quietly through a ringing that made the furniture shake? Well, he certainly hadn't slept quietly, but probably all the more soundly for that. But what should he do now? The next train left at seven o'clock; to make it, he would have to hurry like a madman, and the line of samples wasn't packed yet, and he himself didn't feel especially fresh and ready to march around. And even if he did make the train, he could not avoid getting it from the boss, because the messenger boy had been waiting at the five-o'clock train and would have long ago reported his

---

5. In Kafka's German literally "Heavenly Father," indicating that the Samsa family is Christian and almost certainly Catholic. See below, p. 19, n. 4, and p. 40, n. 9.

not showing up. He was a tool[6] of the boss, without brains or backbone. What if he were to say he was sick? But that would be extremely embarrassing and suspicious because during his five years with the firm Gregor had not been sick even once. The boss would be sure to come with the health-insurance doctor, blame his parents for their lazy son, and cut off all excuses by quoting the health-insurance doctor, for whom the world consisted of people who were completely healthy but afraid to work. And, besides, in this case would he be so very wrong? In fact, Gregor felt fine, with the exception of his drowsiness, which was really unnecessary after sleeping so late, and he even had a ravenous appetite.

Just as he was thinking all this over at top speed, without being able to decide to get out of bed—the alarm clock had just struck a quarter to seven—he heard a cautious knocking at the door next to the head of his bed. "Gregor," someone called—it was his mother—"it's a quarter to seven. Didn't you want to catch the train?" What a soft voice! Gregor was shocked to hear his own voice answering, unmistakably his own voice, true, but in which, as if from below, an insistent distressed chirping intruded, which left the clarity of his words intact only for a moment really, before so badly garbling them as they carried that no one could be sure if he had heard right. Gregor had wanted to answer in detail and to explain everything, but, given the circumstances, confined himself to saying, "Yes, yes, thanks, Mother, I'm just getting up." The wooden door must have prevented the change in Gregor's voice from being noticed outside, because his mother was satisfied with this explanation and shuffled off. But their little exchange had made the rest of the family aware that, contrary to expectations, Gregor was still in the house, and already his father was knocking on one of the side doors, feebly but with his fist.[7] "Gregor, Gregor," he called, "what's going on?" And after a little while he called again in a deeper, warning voice, "Gregor! Gregor!" At the other side door, however, his sister moaned gently, "Gregor? Is something the matter with you? Do you want anything?" Toward both sides Gregor answered: "I'm all ready," and made an effort, by meticulous pronunciation and by inserting long pauses between individual words, to eliminate everything from his voice that might betray him. His father went back to his breakfast, but his sister whispered, "Gregor, open up, I'm pleading with you." But Gregor had absolutely no intention of opening the door and complimented himself instead on the precaution he had adopted from his business trips, of locking all the doors during the night even at home.

First of all he wanted to get up quietly, without any excitement; get

6. Kafka literally writes "It [Es]" was a "tool," using for "tool" the German word *Kreatur* [creature]. Both German words introduce an atmosphere of animality—of displaced animality, for it is Gregor, after all, who is the animal.
7. See below, p. 197.

[handwritten margin note: denial of the body; original]

dressed; and, the main thing, have breakfast, and only then think about what to do next, for he saw clearly that in bed he would never think things through to a rational conclusion. He remembered how even in the past he had often felt some kind of slight pain, possibly caused by lying in an uncomfortable position, which, when he got up, turned out to be purely imaginary, and he was eager to see how today's fantasy would gradually fade away. That the change in his voice was nothing more than the first sign of a bad cold, an occupational ailment of the traveling salesman, he had no doubt in the least.

[handwritten margin note: he is not horrified!]

It was very easy to throw off the cover; all he had to do was puff himself up a little, and it fell off by itself. But after this, things got difficult, especially since he was so unusually broad. He would have needed hands and arms to lift himself up, but instead of that he had only his numerous little legs, which were in every different kind of perpetual motion and which, besides, he could not control. If he wanted to bend one, the first thing that happened was that it stretched itself out; and if he finally succeeded in getting this leg to do what he wanted, all the others in the meantime, as if set free, began to work in the most intensely painful agitation. "Just don't stay in bed being useless," Gregor said to himself.

First he tried to get out of bed with the lower part of his body, but this lower part—which by the way he had not seen yet and which he could not form a clear picture of—proved too difficult to budge; it was taking so long; and when finally, almost out of his mind, he lunged forward with all his force, without caring, he had picked the wrong direction and slammed himself violently against the lower bedpost, and the searing pain he felt taught him that exactly the lower part of his body was, for the moment anyway, the most sensitive.

He therefore tried to get the upper part of his body out of bed first and warily turned his head toward the edge of the bed. This worked easily, and in spite of its width and weight, the mass of his body finally followed, slowly, the movement of his head. But when at last he stuck his head over the edge of the bed into the air, he got too scared to continue any further, since if he finally let himself fall in this position, it would be a miracle if he didn't injure his head. And just now he had better not for the life of him lose consciousness; he would rather stay in bed.

But when, once again, after the same exertion, he lay in his original position, sighing, and again watched his little legs struggling, if possible more fiercely, with each other and saw no way of bringing peace and order into this mindless motion, he again told himself that it was impossible for him to stay in bed and that the most rational thing was to make any sacrifice for even the smallest hope of freeing himself from the bed. But at the same time he did not forget to remind himself occasionally that thinking things over calmly—indeed, as calmly as possible—was much better than jumping to desperate decisions. At such moments he fixed his eyes as sharply as possible on the window, but unfortunately there was little confidence and cheer to be gotten from the view of the morning fog, which shrouded even the other side of the narrow street. "Seven o'clock already," he said to himself as the alarm clock struck again, "seven o'clock already and still such a fog." And for a little while he lay quietly, breathing shallowly, as if expecting, perhaps, from the complete silence the return of things to the way they really and naturally were.

But then he said to himself, "Before it strikes a quarter past seven, I must be completely out of bed without fail. Anyway, by that time someone from the firm will be here to find out where I am, since the office opens before seven." And now he started rocking the complete length of his body out of the bed with a smooth rhythm. If he let himself topple out of bed in this way, his head, which on falling he planned to lift up sharply, would presumably remain unharmed. His back seemed to be hard; nothing was likely to happen to it when it fell onto the rug. His biggest misgiving came from his concern about the loud crash that was bound to occur and would probably create, if not terror, at least anxiety behind all the doors. But that would have to be risked.

When Gregor's body already projected halfway out of bed—the new method was more of a game than a struggle, he only had to keep on rocking and jerking himself along—he thought how simple everything would be if he could get some help. Two strong persons—he thought of his father and the maid—would have been completely sufficient; they would only have had to shove their arms under his arched back, in this way scoop him off the bed, bend down with their burden, and then just be careful and patient while he managed to swing himself down onto the floor, where his little legs would hopefully acquire some purpose. Well, leaving out the fact that the doors were locked, should he really call for help? In spite of all his miseries, he could not repress a smile at this thought.

He was already so far along that when he rocked more strongly he could hardly keep his balance, and very soon he would have to commit himself, because in five minutes it would be a quarter past seven—when the doorbell rang. "It's someone from the firm," he said to himself and almost froze, while his little legs only danced more quickly. For a moment everything remained quiet. "They're not going to answer," Gregor said to himself, captivated by some senseless hope. But then, of course, the maid went to the door as usual with her firm stride and opened up. Gregor only had to hear the visitor's first word of greeting to know who it was—the office manager himself. Why was only Gregor condemned to work for a firm where at the slightest omission they immediately suspected the worst? Were all employees louts without exception, wasn't there a single loyal, dedicated worker among them who, when he had not fully utilized a few hours of the morning for the firm, was driven half-mad by pangs of conscience and was actually unable to get out of bed? Really, wouldn't it have been enough to send one of the apprentices to find out—if this prying were absolutely necessary—did the manager himself have to come, and did the whole innocent family have to be shown in this way that the investigation of this suspicious affair could be entrusted only to the intellect of the manager? And more as a result of the excitement produced in Gregor by these thoughts than as a result of any real decision, he swung himself out of bed with all his might. There was a loud thump, but it was not a real crash. The fall was broken a little by the rug, and Gregor's back was more elastic than he had thought, which explained the not very noticeable muffled sound. Only he had not held his head carefully enough and hit it; he turned it and rubbed it on the rug in anger and pain.

"Something fell in there," said the manager in the room on the left. Gregor tried to imagine whether something like what had happened to him today could one day happen even to the manager; you really had to grant the possibility. But, as if in rude reply to this question, the manager took a few decisive steps in the next room and made his patent leather boots creak. From the room on the right his sister whispered, to inform Gregor, "Gregor, the manager is here." "I know," Gregor said to himself; but he did not dare raise his voice enough for his sister to hear.

"Gregor," his father now said from the room on the left, "the manager has come and wants to be informed why you didn't catch the early train. We don't know what we should say to him. Besides, he wants to speak to you personally. So please open the door. He will certainly be so kind as to excuse the disorder of the room." "Good morning, Mr. Samsa," the manager called in a friendly voice. "There's something the matter with him," his mother said to the manager while his father was still at the door, talking. "Believe me, sir, there's something the matter with him. Otherwise how would Gregor have missed a train? That boy has nothing on his mind but the business. It's almost begun to rile me that he never goes out nights. He's been back in the city for eight days now, but every night he's been home. He sits there with us at the table, quietly reading the paper or studying train schedules. It's already a distraction for him when he's busy working with his fretsaw.[8] For instance, in the span of two or three evenings he carved a little frame. You'll be amazed how pretty it is; it's hanging inside his room. You'll see it right away when Gregor opens the door. You know, I'm glad that you've come, sir. We would never have gotten Gregor to open the door by ourselves; he's so stubborn. And there's certainly something wrong

8. A saw with a long, narrow, fine-toothed blade used for cutting thin wooden boards into patterns.

with him, even though he said this morning there wasn't." "I'm coming right away," said Gregor slowly and deliberately, not moving in order not to miss a word of the conversation. "I haven't any other explanation myself," said the manager. "I hope it's nothing serious. On the other hand, I must say that we businessmen—fortunately or unfortunately, whichever you prefer—very often simply have to overcome a slight indisposition for business reasons." "So can the manager come in now?" asked his father, impatient, and knocked on the door again. "No," said Gregor. In the room on the left there was an embarrassing silence; in the room on the right his sister began to sob.

Why didn't his sister go in to the others? She had probably just got out of bed and not even started to get dressed. Then what was she crying about? Because he didn't get up and didn't let the manager in, because he was in danger of losing his job, and because then the boss would start hounding his parents about the old debts? For the time being, certainly, her worries were unnecessary. Gregor was still here and hadn't the slightest intention of letting the family down. True, at the moment he was lying on the rug, and no one knowing his condition could seriously have expected him to let the manager in. But just because of this slight discourtesy, for which an appropriate excuse would easily be found later on, Gregor could not simply be dismissed. And to Gregor it seemed much more sensible to leave him alone now than to bother him with crying and persuasion. But it was just the uncertainty that was tormenting the others and excused their behavior.

"Mr. Samsa," the manager now called, raising his voice, "what's the matter? You barricade yourself in your room, answer only 'yes' and 'no,' cause your parents serious, unnecessary worry, and you neglect—I mention this only in passing—your duties to the firm in a really shocking manner. I am speaking here in the name of your parents and of your employer and ask you in all seriousness for an immediate, clear explanation. I'm amazed, amazed. I thought I knew you to be a quiet, reasonable person, and now you suddenly seem to want to start strutting about, flaunting strange whims. The head of the firm did suggest to me this morning a possible explanation for your tardiness—it concerned the cash payments recently entrusted to you—but really, I practically gave my word of honor that this explanation could not be right. But now, seeing your incomprehensible obstinacy, I am about to lose even the slightest desire to stick up for you in any way at all. And your job is not the most secure. Originally I intended to tell you all this in private, but since you make me waste my time here for nothing, I don't see why your parents shouldn't hear too. Your performance of late has been very unsatisfactory; I know it is not the best season for doing business, we all recognize that; but a season for not doing any business, there is no such thing, Mr. Samsa, such a thing cannot be tolerated."

"But, sir," cried Gregor, beside himself, in his excitement forgetting everything else, "I'm just opening up, in a minute. A slight indisposition, a dizzy spell, prevented me from getting up. I'm still in bed. But I already feel fine again. I'm just getting out of bed. Just be patient for a minute! I'm not as well as I thought yet. But really I'm fine. How something like this could just take a person by surprise! Only last night I was fine, my parents can tell you, or wait, last night I already had a slight premonition. They must have been able to tell by looking at me. Why didn't I report it to the office! But you always think that you'll get over a sickness without staying home. Sir! Spare my parents! There's no basis for any of the accusations that you're making against me now; no one has ever said a word to me about them. Perhaps you haven't seen the last orders I sent in. Anyway, I'm still going on the road with the eight o'clock train; these few hours of rest have done me good. Don't let me keep you, sir. I'll be at the office myself right away, and be so kind as to tell them this, and give my respects to the head of the firm."

And while Gregor hastily blurted all this out, hardly knowing what he was saying, he had easily approached the chest of drawers, probably as a result of the practice he had already gotten in bed, and now he tried to raise himself up against it. He actually intended to open the door, actually present himself and speak to the manager; he was eager to find out what the others, who were now so anxious to see him, would say at the sight of him. If they were shocked, then Gregor had no further responsibility and could be calm. But if they took everything calmly, then he, too, had no reason to get excited and could, if he hurried, actually be at the station by eight o'clock. At first he slid off the polished chest of drawers a few times, but at last, giving himself a final push, he stood upright; he no longer paid any attention to the pains in his abdomen, no matter how much they were burning. Now he let himself fall against the back of a nearby chair, clinging to its slats with his little legs. But by doing this he had gotten control of himself and fell silent, since he could now listen to what the manager was saying.

"Did you understand a word?" the manager was asking his parents. "He isn't trying to make fools of us, is he?" "My God," cried his mother, already in tears, "maybe he's seriously ill, and here we are, torturing him. Grete! Grete!" she then cried. "Mother?" called his sister from the other side. They communicated by way of Gregor's room. "Go to the doctor's immediately. Gregor is sick. Hurry, get the doctor. Did you just hear Gregor talking?" "That was the voice of an animal," said the manager, in a tone conspicuously soft compared with the mother's yelling. "Anna!" "Anna!"[9] the father called through the foyer into the kitchen, clapping his hands, "get a locksmith right away!" And already the two girls were running with rustling skirts through the foyer—how

---

9. Anna is presumably the name of the maid who also does the cooking; hence she is later referred to as "the previous cook." See below, p. 24, n. 5.

could his sister have gotten dressed so quickly?—and tearing open the door to the apartment. The door could not be heard slamming; they had probably left it open, as is the custom in homes where a great misfortune has occurred.[1]

But Gregor had become much calmer. It was true that they no longer understood his words, though they had seemed clear enough to him, clearer than before, probably because his ear had grown accustomed to them. But still, the others now believed that there was something the matter with him and were ready to help him. The assurance and confidence with which the first measures had been taken did him good. He felt integrated into human society once again and hoped for marvelous, amazing feats from both the doctor and the locksmith, without really distinguishing sharply between them. In order to make his voice as clear as possible for the crucial discussions that were approaching, he cleared his throat a little—taking pains, of course, to do so in a very muffled manner, since this noise, too, might sound different from human coughing, a thing he no longer trusted himself to decide. In the next room, meanwhile, everything had become completely still. Perhaps his parents were sitting at the table with the manager, whispering; perhaps they were all leaning against the door and listening.

Gregor slowly lugged himself toward the door, pushing the chair in front of him, then let go of it, threw himself against the door, held himself upright against it—the pads on the bottom of his little legs exuded a little sticky substance—and for a moment rested there from the exertion. But then he got started turning the key in the lock with his mouth. Unfortunately it seemed that he had no real teeth—what was he supposed to grip the key with?—but in compensation his jaws, of course, were very strong; with their help he actually got the key moving and paid no attention to the fact that he was undoubtedly hurting himself in some way, for a brown liquid came out of his mouth, flowed over the key, and dripped onto the floor. "Listen," said the manager in the next room, "he's turning the key." This was great encouragement to Gregor; but everyone should have cheered him on, his father and mother too. "Go, Gregor," they should have called, "keep going, at that lock, harder, harder!" And in the delusion that they were all following his efforts with suspense, he clamped his jaws madly on the key with all the strength he could muster. Depending on the progress of the key, he danced around the lock; holding himself upright only by his mouth, he clung to the key, as the situation demanded, or pressed it down again with the whole weight of his body. The clearer click of the lock as it finally snapped back positively woke Gregor up. With a sigh of relief he said to himself, "So I didn't need the locksmith

1. A belief found among Jewish mystics, as well as in many older European cultures, holds that the doors or windows of a house in which there has been a recent death must be left open to facilitate the exit of the Angel of Death.

after all," and laid his head down on the handle in order to open wide
[one wing of the double doors].[2]

Since he had to use this method of opening the door, it was really
opened very wide while he himself was still invisible. He first had to
edge slowly around the one wing of the door, and do so very carefully
if he was not to fall flat on his back just before entering. He was still
busy with this difficult maneuver and had no time to pay attention to
anything else when he heard the manager burst out with a loud
"Oh!"—it sounded like a rush of wind—and now he could see him,
standing closest to the door, his hand pressed over his open mouth,
slowly backing away, as if repulsed by an invisible, unrelenting force.
His mother—in spite of the manager's presence she stood with her hair
still unbraided from the night, sticking out in all directions—first looked
at his father with her hands clasped, then took two steps toward Gregor,
and sank down in the midst of her skirts spreading out around her, her
face completely hidden on her breast. With a hostile expression his
father clenched his fist, as if to drive Gregor back into his room, then
looked uncertainly around the living room, shielded his eyes with his
hands, and sobbed with heaves of his powerful chest.

Now Gregor did not enter the room after all but leaned against the
inside of the firmly bolted wing of the door, so that only half his body
was visible and his head above it, cocked to one side and peeping out
at the others. In the meantime it had grown much lighter; across the
street one could see clearly a section of the endless, grayish-black building opposite—it was a hospital—with its regular windows starkly piercing the façade; the rain was still coming down, but only in large,
separately visible drops that were also pelting the ground literally one
at a time. The breakfast dishes were laid out lavishly on the table, since
for his father breakfast was the most important meal of the day, which
he would prolong for hours while reading various newspapers. On the
wall directly opposite hung a photograph of Gregor from his army days,
in a lieutenant's uniform, his hand on his sword, a carefree smile on
his lips, demanding respect for his bearing and his rank. The door to
the foyer was open, and since the front door was open too, it was
possible to see out onto the landing and the top of the stairs going
down.

"Well," said Gregor—and he was thoroughly aware of being the only
one who had kept calm—"I'll get dressed right away, pack up my samples, and go. Will you, will you please let me go? Now, sir, you see,
I'm not stubborn and I'm willing to work; traveling is a hardship, but
without it I couldn't live. Where are you going, sir? To the office? Yes?
Will you give an honest report of everything? A man might find for a
moment that he was unable to work, but that's exactly the right time

2. Literally, "the door."

to remember his past accomplishments and to consider that later on, when the obstacle has been removed, he's bound to work all the harder and more efficiently. I'm under so many obligations to the head of the firm, as you know very well. Besides, I also have my parents and my sister to worry about. I'm in a tight spot, but I'll also work my way out again. Don't make things harder for me than they already are. Stick up for me in the office, please. Traveling salesmen aren't well liked there, I know. People think they make a fortune leading the gay life. No one has any particular reason to rectify this prejudice. But you, sir, you have a better perspective on things than the rest of the office, an even better perspective, just between the two of us, than the head of the firm himself, who in his capacity as owner easily lets his judgment be swayed against an employee. And you also know very well that the traveling salesman, who is out of the office practically the whole year round, can so easily become the victim of gossip, contingencies, and unfounded accusations, against which he's completely unable to defend himself, since in most cases he knows nothing at all about them except when he returns exhausted from a trip, and back home gets to suffer on his own person the grim consequences, which can no longer be traced back to their causes. Sir, don't go away without a word to tell me you think I'm at least partly right!"

But at Gregor's first words the manager had already turned away and with curled lips looked back at Gregor only over his twitching shoulder. And during Gregor's speech he did not stand still for a minute but, without letting Gregor out of his sight, backed toward the door, yet very gradually, as if there were some secret prohibition against leaving the room. He was already in the foyer, and from the sudden movement with which he took his last step from the living room, one might have thought he had just burned the sole of his foot. In the foyer, however, he stretched his right hand far out toward the staircase, as if nothing less than an unearthly deliverance were awaiting him there.

Gregor realized that he must on no account let the manager go away in this mood if his position in the firm were not to be jeopardized in the extreme. His parents did not understand this too well; in the course of the years they had formed the conviction that Gregor was set for life in this firm; and furthermore, they were so preoccupied with their immediate troubles that they had lost all consideration for the future. But Gregor had this forethought. The manager must be detained, calmed down, convinced, and finally won over; Gregor's and the family's future depended on it! If only his sister had been there! She was perceptive; she had already begun to cry when Gregor was still lying calmly on his back. And certainly the manager, this ladies' man, would have listened to her; she would have shut the front door and in the foyer talked him out of his scare. But his sister was not there; Gregor had to handle the situation himself. And without stopping to realize that he had no idea what his new faculties of movement were, and without stopping to realize either that his speech had possibly—indeed, probably—not been understood again, he let go of the wing of the door; he shoved himself through the opening, intending to go to the manager, who was already on the landing, ridiculously holding onto the banisters with both hands; but groping for support, Gregor immediately fell down with a little cry onto his numerous little legs. This had hardly happened when for the first time that morning he had a feeling of physical well-being; his little legs were on firm ground; they obeyed him completely, as he noted to his joy; they even strained to carry him away wherever he wanted to go; and he already believed that final recovery from all his sufferings was imminent. But at that very moment, as he lay on the floor rocking with repressed motion, not far from his mother and just opposite her, she, who had seemed so completely self-absorbed, all at once jumped up, her arms stretched wide, her fingers spread, crying, "Help, for God's sake, help!" held her head bent as if to see Gregor better, but inconsistently darted madly backward instead; had forgotten that the table laden with the breakfast dishes stood behind her; sat down on it hastily, as if her thoughts were elsewhere, when she reached it; and did not seem to notice at all that near her the big coffeepot had been knocked over and coffee was pouring in a steady stream onto the rug.

"Mother, Mother," said Gregor softly and looked up at her. For a minute the manager had completely slipped his mind; on the other hand at the sight of the spilling coffee he could not resist snapping his jaws several times in the air. At this his mother screamed once more, fled from the table, and fell into the arms of his father, who came rushing up to her. But Gregor had no time now for his parents; the manager was already on the stairs; with his chin on the banister, he was taking a last look back. Gregor was off to a running start, to be as sure as possible of catching up with him; the manager must have suspected something like this, for he leaped down several steps and disappeared; but still he shouted "Agh," and the sound carried through the whole staircase. Unfortunately the manager's flight now seemed to confuse his father completely, who had been relatively calm until now, for instead of running after the manager himself, or at least not hindering Gregor in his pursuit, he seized in his right hand the manager's cane, which had been left behind on a chair with his hat and overcoat, picked up in his left hand a heavy newspaper from the table, and stamping his feet, started brandishing the cane and the newspaper to drive Gregor back into his room. No plea of Gregor's helped, no plea was even understood; however humbly he might turn his head, his father merely stamped his feet more forcefully. Across the room his mother had thrown open a window in spite of the cool weather, and leaning out, she buried her face, far outside the window, in her hands. Between the alley and the staircase a strong draft was created, the window curtains blew in, the newspapers on the table rustled, single sheets fluttered across the floor. Pitilessly his father came on, hissing like a wild man. Now Gregor had not had any practice at all walking in reverse; it was really very slow going. If Gregor had only been allowed to turn around, he could have gotten into his room right away, but he was afraid to make his father impatient by this time-consuming gyration, and at any minute the cane in his father's hand threatened to come down on his back or his head with a deadly blow. Finally, however, Gregor had no choice, for he noticed with horror that in reverse he could not even keep going in one direction; and so, incessantly throwing uneasy side-glances at his father, he began to turn around as quickly as possible, in reality turning only very slowly. Perhaps his father realized his good intentions, for he did not interfere with him; instead, he even now and then directed the maneuver from afar with the tip of his cane. If only his father did not keep making this intolerable hissing sound! It made Gregor lose his head completely. He had almost finished the turn when—his mind continually on this hissing—he made a mistake and even started turning back around to his original position. But when he had at last successfully managed to get his head in front of the opened door, it turned out that his body was too broad to get through as it was. Of course in his father's present state of mind it did not even remotely occur to him to open the other wing of the door in order to give Gregor enough room to pass through. He had only the fixed idea that Gregor must return to his room as quickly as possible. He would never have allowed the complicated preliminaries Gregor needed to go through in order to stand up on one end and perhaps in this way fit through the door. Instead he drove Gregor on, as if there were no obstacle, with exceptional loudness; the voice behind Gregor did not sound like that of only a single father; now this was really no joke anymore, and Gregor forced himself—come what may—into the doorway. One side of his body rose up, he lay lop-sided in the opening, one of his flanks was scraped raw, ugly blotches marred the white door, soon he got stuck and could not have budged any more by himself, his little legs on one side dangled tremblingly in midair, those on the other were painfully crushed against the floor—when from behind his father gave him a hard shove, which was truly his salvation, and bleeding profusely, he flew far into his room. The door was slammed shut with the cane, then at last everything was quiet.

II

It was already dusk when Gregor awoke from his deep, comalike sleep. Even if he had not been disturbed, he would certainly not have woken up much later, for he felt that he had rested and slept long enough, but it seemed to him that a hurried step and a cautious shutting of the door leading to the foyer had awakened him. The light of the electric street-lamps lay in pallid streaks on the ceiling and on the upper parts of the furniture, but underneath, where Gregor was, it was dark. Groping clumsily with his antennae, which he was only now beginning to appreciate, he slowly dragged himself toward the door to see what had been happening there. His left side felt like one single long, unpleasantly tautening scar, and he actually had to limp on his two rows of legs. Besides, one little leg had been seriously injured in the course of the morning's events—it was almost a miracle that only one had been injured—and dragged along lifelessly.

Only after he got to the door did he notice what had really attracted him—the smell of something to eat. For there stood a bowl filled with fresh milk, in which small slices of white bread were floating. He could almost have laughed for joy, since he was even hungrier than he had been in the morning, and he immediately dipped his head into the milk, almost to over his eyes. But he soon drew it back again in disappointment, not only because he had difficulty eating on account of the soreness in his left side—and he could eat only if his whole panting body cooperated—but because he didn't like the milk at all, although it used to be his favorite drink, and that was certainly why his sister had put it in the room; in fact, he turned away from the bowl almost with repulsion and crawled back to the middle of the room.

In the living room, as Gregor saw through the crack in the door, the gas had been lit, but while at this hour of the day his father was in the habit of reading the afternoon newspaper in a loud voice to his mother and sometimes to his sister too, now there wasn't a sound. Well, perhaps this custom of reading aloud, which his sister was always telling him and writing him about, had recently been discontinued altogether. But in all the other rooms too it was just as still, although the apartment certainly was not empty. "What a quiet life the family has been leading," Gregor said to himself, and while he stared rigidly in front of him into the darkness, he felt very proud that he had been able to provide such a life in so nice an apartment for his parents and his sister. But what now if all the peace, the comfort, the contentment were to come to a horrible end? In order not to get involved in such thoughts, Gregor decided to keep moving, and he crawled up and down the room.

During the long evening, first one of the side doors and then the other was opened a small crack and quickly shut again; someone had probably had the urge to come in and then had had second thoughts. Gregor now settled into position right by the living-room door, determined somehow to get the hesitating visitor to come in, or at least to find out who it might be; but the door was not opened again, and Gregor waited in vain. In the morning, when the doors had been locked, everyone had wanted to come in; now that he had opened one of the doors and the others had evidently been opened during the day, no one came in, and now the keys were even inserted on the outside.

It was late at night when the light finally went out in the living room, and now it was easy for Gregor to tell that his parents and his sister had stayed up so long, since, as he could distinctly hear, all three were now retiring on tiptoe. Certainly no one would come in to Gregor until the morning; and so he had ample time to consider undisturbed how best to rearrange his life. But the empty high-ceilinged room in which he was forced to lie flat on the floor made him nervous, without his being able to tell why—since it was, after all, the room in which he had lived for the past five years—and turning half unconsciously and not without a slight feeling of shame, he scuttled under the couch where, although his back was a little crushed and he could not raise his head any more, he immediately felt very comfortable and was only sorry that his body was too wide to go completely under the couch.

There he stayed the whole night, which he spent partly in a sleepy trance, from which hunger pangs kept waking him with a start, partly in worries and vague hopes, all of which, however, led to the conclusion that for the time being he would have to lie low and, by being patient and showing his family every possible consideration, help them bear the inconvenience which he simply had to cause them in his present condition.

Early in the morning—it was still almost night—Gregor had the opportunity of testing the strength of the resolutions he had just made, for his sister, almost fully dressed, opened the door from the foyer and looked in eagerly. She did not see him right away, but when she caught sight of him under the couch—God, he had to be somewhere, he couldn't just fly away—she became so frightened that she lost control of herself and slammed the door shut again. But, as if she felt sorry for her behavior, she immediately opened the door again and came in on tiptoe, as if she were visiting someone seriously ill or perhaps even a stranger. Gregor had pushed his head forward just to the edge of the couch and was watching her. Would she notice that he had left the milk standing, and not because he hadn't been hungry, and would she bring in a dish of something he'd like better? If she were not going to do it of her own free will, he would rather starve than call it to her attention, although, really, he felt an enormous urge to shoot out from under the couch, throw himself at his sister's feet, and beg her for something good to eat. But his sister noticed at once, to her astonishment, that the bowl was still full, only a little milk was spilled around it; she picked it up immediately—not with her bare hands, of course, but with a rag—and carried it out. Gregor was extremely curious to know what she would bring him instead, and he racked his brains on the subject. But he would never have been able to guess what his sister, in the goodness of her heart, actually did. To find out his likes and dislikes, she brought him a wide assortment of things, all spread out on an old newspaper: old, half-rotten vegetables; bones left over from the evening meal, caked with congealed white sauce; some raisins and almonds; a piece of cheese, which two days before Gregor had declared inedible; a plain slice of bread, a slice of bread and butter, and one with butter and salt. In addition to all this she put down some water in the bowl apparently permanently earmarked for Gregor's use. And out of a sense of delicacy, since she knew that Gregor would not eat in front of her, she left hurriedly and even turned the key, just so that Gregor should know that he might make himself as comfortable as he wanted. Gregor's legs began whirring now that he was going to eat. Besides, his bruises must have completely healed, since he no longer felt any handicap, and marveling at this he thought how, over a month ago, he had cut his finger very slightly with a knife and how this wound was still hurting him only the day before yesterday. "Have I become less sensitive?" he thought, already sucking greedily at the cheese, which had immediately and forcibly attracted him ahead of all the other dishes. One right after the other, and with eyes streaming with tears of contentment, he devoured the cheese, the vegetables, and the sauce; the fresh foods, on the other hand, he did not care for; he couldn't even stand their smell and even dragged the things he wanted to eat a bit farther away. He had finished with everything long since and was just lying lazily at the same spot when his sister slowly turned the key as a sign for him to withdraw. That immediately startled him, although he was almost asleep, and he scuttled under the couch again. But it took great self-control for him to stay under the couch even for the short time his sister was in the room, since his body had become a little bloated from the heavy meal, and in his cramped position he could hardly breathe. In between slight attacks of suffocation he watched with bulging eyes as his unsuspecting sister took a broom and swept up, not only his leavings, but even the foods which Gregor had left completely untouched—as if they too were no longer usable—and dumping everything hastily into a pail, which she covered with a wooden lid, she carried everything out. She had hardly turned her back when Gregor came out from under the couch, stretching and puffing himself up.

This, then, was the way Gregor was fed each day, once in the morning, when his parents and the maid[3] were still asleep, and a second time in the afternoon after everyone had had dinner, for then his parents took a short nap again, and the maid could be sent out by his sister on some errand. Certainly they did not want him to starve either, but perhaps they would not have been able to stand knowing any more about his meals than from hearsay, or perhaps his sister wanted to spare

---

3. Presumably a new maid, a girl of sixteen; the former maid, Anna, left on the very first day of Gregor's metamorphosis. See below, p. 19.

them even what was possibly only a minor torment, for really, they were suffering enough as it was.

Gregor could not find out what excuses had been made to get rid of the doctor and the locksmith on that first morning, for since the others could not understand what he said, it did not occur to any of them, not even to his sister, that he could understand what they said, and so he had to be satisfied, when his sister was in the room, with only occasionally hearing her sighs and appeals to the saints.[4] It was only later, when she had begun to get used to everything—there could never, of course, be any question of a complete adjustment—that Gregor sometimes caught a remark which was meant to be friendly or could be interpreted as such. "Oh, he liked what he had today," she would say when Gregor had tucked away a good helping, and in the opposite case, which gradually occurred more and more frequently, she used to say, almost sadly, "He's left everything again."

But if Gregor could not get any news directly, he overheard a great deal from the neighboring rooms, and as soon as he heard voices, he would immediately run to the door concerned and press his whole body against it. Especially in the early days, there was no conversation that was not somehow about him, if only implicitly. For two whole days there were family consultations at every mealtime about how they should cope; this was also the topic of discussion between meals, for at least two members of the family were always at home, since no one probably wanted to stay home alone and it was impossible to leave the apartment completely empty. Besides, on the very first day the maid—it was not completely clear what and how much she knew of what had happened—had begged his mother on bended knees to dismiss her immediately; and when she said goodbye a quarter of an hour later, she thanked them in tears for the dismissal, as if for the greatest favor that had ever been done to her in this house, and made a solemn vow, without anyone asking her for it, not to give anything away to anyone.

Now his sister, working with her mother, had to do the cooking too; of course that did not cause her much trouble, since they hardly ate anything. Gregor was always hearing one of them pleading in vain with one of the others to eat and getting no answer except, "Thanks, I've had enough," or something similar. They did not seem to drink anything either. His sister often asked her father if he wanted any beer and gladly offered to go out for it herself; and when he did not answer, she said, in order to remove any hesitation on his part, that she could also send the janitor's wife to get it, but then his father finally answered with a definite "No," and that was the end of that.

In the course of the very first day his father explained the family's

---

4. Further evidence of the Samsas' probable Catholicism.

financial situation and prospects to both the mother and the sister. From time to time he got up from the table to get some kind of receipt or notebook out of the little strongbox he had rescued from the collapse of his business five years before. Gregor heard him open the complicated lock and secure it again after taking out what he had been looking for. These explanations by his father were to some extent the first pleasant news Gregor had heard since his imprisonment. He had always believed that his father had not been able to save a penny from the business, at least his father had never told him anything to the contrary, and Gregor, for his part, had never asked him any questions. In those days Gregor's sole concern had been to do everything in his power to make the family forget as quickly as possible the business disaster which had plunged everyone into a state of total despair. And so he had begun to work with special ardor and had risen almost overnight from stock clerk to traveling salesman, which of course had opened up very different money-making possibilities, and in no time his successes on the job were transformed, by means of commissions, into hard cash that could be plunked down on the table at home in front of his astonished and delighted family. Those had been wonderful times, and they had never returned, at least not with the same glory, although later on Gregor earned enough money to meet the expenses of the entire family and actually did so. They had just gotten used to it, the family as well as Gregor, the money was received with thanks and given with pleasure, but no special feeling of warmth went with it any more. Only his sister had remained close to Gregor, and it was his secret plan that she, who, unlike him, loved music and could play the violin movingly, should be sent next year to the Conservatory, regardless of the great expense involved, which could surely be made up for in some other way. Often during Gregor's short stays in the city, the Conservatory would come up in his conversations with his sister, but always merely as a beautiful dream which was not supposed to come true, and his parents were not happy to hear even these innocent allusions; but Gregor had very concrete ideas on the subject and he intended solemnly to announce his plan on Christmas Eve.

Thoughts like these, completely useless in his present state, went through his head as he stood glued to the door, listening. Sometimes out of general exhaustion he could not listen any more and let his head bump carelessly against the door, but immediately pulled it back again, for even the slight noise he made by doing this had been heard in the next room and made them all lapse into silence. "What's he carrying on about in there now?" said his father after a while, obviously turning toward the door, and only then would the interrupted conversation gradually be resumed.

Gregor now learned in a thorough way—for his father was in the habit of often repeating himself in his explanations, partly because he himself had not dealt with these matters for a long time, partly, too, because his mother did not understand everything the first time around—that in spite of all their misfortunes a bit of capital, a very little bit, certainly, was still intact from the old days, which in the meantime had increased a little through the untouched interest. But besides that, the money Gregor had brought home every month—he had kept only a few dollars for himself—had never been completely used up and had accumulated into a tidy principal. Behind his door Gregor nodded emphatically, delighted at this unexpected foresight and thrift. Of course he actually could have paid off more of his father's debt to the boss with this extra money, and the day on which he could have gotten rid of his job would have been much closer, but now things were undoubtedly better the way his father had arranged them.

Now this money was by no means enough to let the family live off the interest; the principal was perhaps enough to support the family for one year, or at the most two, but that was all there was. So it was just a sum that really should not be touched and that had to be put away for a rainy day; but the money to live on would have to be earned. Now his father was still healthy, certainly, but he was an old man who had not worked for the past five years and who in any case could not be expected to undertake too much; during these five years, which were the first vacation of his hard-working yet unsuccessful life, he had gained a lot of weight and as a result had become fairly sluggish. And was his old mother now supposed to go out and earn money, when she suffered from asthma, when a walk through the apartment was already an ordeal for her, and when she spent every other day lying on the sofa under the open window, gasping for breath? And was his sister now supposed to work—who for all her seventeen years was still a child and whom it would be such a pity to deprive of the life she had led until now, which had consisted of wearing pretty clothes, sleeping late, helping in the house, enjoying a few modest amusements, and above all playing the violin? At first, whenever the conversation turned to the necessity of earning money, Gregor would let go of the door and throw himself down on the cool leather sofa which stood beside it, for he felt hot with shame and grief.

Often he lay there the whole long night through, not sleeping a wink and only scrabbling on the leather for hours on end. Or, not balking at the huge effort of pushing an armchair to the window, he would crawl up to the window sill and, propped up in the chair, lean against the window, evidently in some sort of remembrance of the feeling of freedom he used to have from looking out the window. For, in fact, from day to day he saw things even a short distance away less and less distinctly; the hospital opposite, which he used to curse because he saw so much of it, was now completely beyond his range of vision, and if he had not been positive that he was living in Charlotte Street—a quiet but still very much a city street—he might have believed that he was looking out of his window into a desert where the gray sky and the gray earth were indistinguishably fused. It took his observant sister only twice to notice that his armchair was standing by the window, for her to push the chair back to the same place by the window each time she had finished cleaning the room, and from then on she even left the inside casement of the window open.

If Gregor had only been able to speak to his sister and thank her for everything she had to do for him, he could have accepted her services more easily; as it was, they caused him pain. Of course his sister tried to ease the embarrassment of the whole situation as much as possible, and as time went on, she naturally managed it better and better, but in time Gregor, too, saw things much more clearly. Even the way she came in was terrible for him. Hardly had she entered the room than she would run straight to the window without taking time to close the door—though she was usually so careful to spare everyone the sight of Gregor's room—then tear open the casements with eager hands, almost as if she were suffocating, and remain for a little while at the window even in the coldest weather, breathing deeply. With this racing and crashing she frightened Gregor twice a day; the whole time he cowered under the couch, and yet he knew very well that she would certainly have spared him this if only she had found it possible to stand being in a room with him with the window closed.

One time—it must have been a month since Gregor's metamorphosis, and there was certainly no particular reason any more for his sister to be astonished at Gregor's appearance—she came a little earlier than usual and caught Gregor still looking out the window, immobile and so in an excellent position to be terrifying. It would not have surprised Gregor if she had not come in, because his position prevented her from immediately opening the window, but not only did she not come in, she even sprang back and locked the door; a stranger might easily have thought that Gregor had been lying in wait for her, wanting to bite her. Of course Gregor immediately hid under the couch, but he had to wait until noon before his sister came again, and she seemed much more uneasy than usual. He realized from this that the sight of him was still repulsive to her and was bound to remain repulsive to her in the future, and that she probably had to overcome a lot of resistance not to run away at the sight of even the small part of his body that jutted out from under the couch. So, to spare her even this sight, one day he carried the sheet on his back to the couch—the job took four hours—and arranged it in such a way that he was now completely covered up and his sister could not see him even when she stooped. If she had considered this sheet unnecessary, then of course she could have removed it, for it was clear enough that it could not be for his own pleasure that

Gregor shut himself off altogether, but she left the sheet the way it was, and Gregor thought that he had even caught a grateful look when one time he cautiously lifted the sheet a little with his head in order to see how his sister was taking the new arrangement.

During the first two weeks, his parents could not bring themselves to come in to him, and often he heard them say how much they appreciated his sister's work, whereas until now they had frequently been annoyed with her because she had struck them as being a little useless. But now both of them, his father and his mother, often waited outside Gregor's room while his sister straightened it up, and as soon as she came out she had to tell them in great detail how the room looked, what Gregor had eaten, how he had behaved this time, and whether he had perhaps shown a little improvement. His mother, incidentally, began relatively soon to want to visit Gregor, but his father and his sister at first held her back with reasonable arguments to which Gregor listened very attentively and of which he whole-heartedly approved. But later she had to be restrained by force, and then when she cried out, "Let me go to Gregor, he is my unfortunate boy! Don't you understand that I have to go to him?" Gregor thought that it might be a good idea after all if his mother did come in, not every day of course, but perhaps once a week; she could still do everything much better than his sister, who, for all her courage, was still only a child and in the final analysis had perhaps taken on such a difficult assignment only out of childish flightiness.

Gregor's desire to see his mother was soon fulfilled. During the day Gregor did not want to show himself at the window, if only out of consideration for his parents, but he couldn't crawl very far on his few square yards of floor space, either; he could hardly put up with just lying still even at night; eating soon stopped giving him the slightest pleasure, so, as a distraction, he adopted the habit of crawling crisscross over the walls and the ceiling. He especially liked hanging from the ceiling; it was completely different from lying on the floor; one could breathe more freely; a faint swinging sensation went through the body; and in the almost happy absent-mindedness which Gregor felt up there, it could happen to his own surprise that he let go and plopped onto the floor. But now, of course, he had much better control of his body than before and did not hurt himself even from such a big drop. His sister immediately noticed the new entertainment Gregor had discovered for himself—after all, he left behind traces of his sticky substance wherever he crawled—and so she got it into her head to make it possible for Gregor to crawl on an altogether wider scale by taking out the furniture which stood in his way—mainly the chest of drawers and the desk. But she was not able to do this by herself; she did not dare ask her father for help; the maid would certainly not have helped her, for although this girl, who was about sixteen, was bravely sticking it out after the previous cook[5] had left, she had asked for the favor of locking herself in the kitchen at all times and of only opening the door on special request. So there was nothing left for his sister to do except to get her mother one day when her father was out. And his mother did come, with exclamations of excited joy, but she grew silent at the door of Gregor's room. First his sister looked to see, of course, that everything in the room was in order; only then did she let her mother come in. Hurrying as fast as he could, Gregor had pulled the sheet down lower still and pleated it more tightly—it really looked just like a sheet accidently thrown over the couch. This time Gregor also refrained from spying from under the sheet; he renounced seeing his mother for the time being and was simply happy that she had come after all. "Come on, you can't see him," his sister said, evidently leading her mother in by the hand. Now Gregor could hear the two frail women moving the old chest of drawers—heavy for anyone—from its place and his sister insisting on doing the harder part of the job herself, ignoring the warnings of her mother, who was afraid that she would overexert herself. It went on for a long time. After struggling for a good quarter of an hour, his mother said that they had better leave the chest where it was, because, in the first place, it was too heavy, they would not finish before his father came, and with the chest in the middle of the room, Gregor would be completely barricaded; and, in the second place, it was not at all certain that they were doing Gregor a favor by removing his furniture. To her the opposite seemed to be the case; the sight of the bare wall was heartbreaking; and why shouldn't Gregor also have the same feeling, since he had been used to his furniture for so long and would feel abandoned in the empty room. "And doesn't it look," his mother concluded very softly—in fact she had been almost whispering the whole time, as if she wanted to avoid letting Gregor, whose exact whereabouts she did not know, hear even the sound of her voice, for she was convinced that he did not understand the words—"and doesn't it look as if by removing his furniture we were showing him that we have given up all hope of his getting better and are leaving him to his own devices without any consideration? I think the best thing would be to try to keep the room exactly the way it was before, so that when Gregor comes back to us again, he'll find everything unchanged and can forget all the more easily what's happened in the meantime."

When he heard his mother's words, Gregor realized that the monotony of family life, combined with the fact that not a soul had addressed a word directly to him, must have addled his brain in the course of the past two months, for he could not explain to himself in any other way how in all seriousness he could have been anxious to have his

5. Presumably the new maid, who replaced Anna, the maid of all work who also did the cooking—here called "the previous cook."

room cleared out. Had he really wanted to have his warm room, comfortably fitted with furniture that had always been in the family, changed into a cave, in which, of course, he would be able to crawl around unhampered in all directions but at the cost of simultaneously, rapidly, and totally forgetting his human past? Even now he had been on the verge of forgetting, and only his mother's voice, which he had not heard for so long, had shaken him up. Nothing should be removed; everything had to stay; he could not do without the beneficial influence of the furniture on his state of mind; and if the furniture prevented him from carrying on this senseless crawling around, then that was no loss but rather a great advantage.

But his sister unfortunately had a different opinion; she had become accustomed, certainly not entirely without justification, to adopt with her parents the role of the particularly well-qualified expert whenever Gregor's affairs were being discussed; and so her mother's advice was now sufficient reason for her to insist, not only on the removal of the chest of drawers and the desk, which was all she had been planning at first, but also on the removal of all the furniture with the exception of the indispensable couch. Of course it was not only childish defiance and the self-confidence she had recently acquired so unexpectedly and at such a cost that led her to make this demand; she had in fact noticed that Gregor needed plenty of room to crawl around in; and on the other hand, as best she could tell, he never used the furniture at all. Perhaps, however, the romantic enthusiasm of girls her age, which seeks to indulge itself at every opportunity, played a part, by tempting her to make Gregor's situation even more terrifying in order that she might do even more for him. Into a room in which Gregor ruled the bare walls all alone, no human being beside Grete was ever likely to set foot.

And so she did not let herself be swerved from her decision by her mother, who, besides, from the sheer anxiety of being in Gregor's room, seemed unsure of herself, soon grew silent, and helped her daughter as best she could to get the chest of drawers out of the room. Well, in a pinch Gregor could do without the chest, but the desk had to stay. And hardly had the women left the room with the chest, squeezing against it and groaning, than Gregor stuck his head out from under the couch to see how he could feel his way into the situation as considerately as possible. But unfortunately it had to be his mother who came back first, while in the next room Grete was clasping the chest and rocking it back and forth by herself, without of course budging it from the spot. His mother, however, was not used to the sight of Gregor, he could have made her ill, and so Gregor, frightened, scuttled in reverse to the far end of the couch but could not stop the sheet from shifting a little at the front. That was enough to put his mother on the alert. She stopped, stood still for a moment, and then went back to Grete.

Although Gregor told himself over and over again that nothing spe-

cial was happening, only a few pieces of furniture were being moved,
he soon had to admit that this coming and going of the women, their
little calls to each other, the scraping of the furniture along the floor
had the effect on him of a great turmoil swelling on all sides, and as
much as he tucked in his head and his legs and shrank until his belly
touched the floor, he was forced to admit that he would not be able to
stand it much longer. They were clearing out his room; depriving him
of everything that he loved; they had already carried away the chest of
drawers, in which he kept the fretsaw and other tools; were now budging the desk firmly embedded in the floor, the desk he had done his
homework on when he was a student at business college, in high
school, yes, even in public school—now he really had no more time to
examine the good intentions of the two women, whose existence, besides, he had almost forgotten, for they were so exhausted that they
were working in silence, and one could hear only the heavy shuffling
of their feet.

And so he broke out—the women were just leaning against the desk
in the next room to catch their breath for a minute—changed his course
four times, he really didn't know what to salvage first, then he saw
hanging conspicuously on the wall, which was otherwise bare already,
the picture of the lady all dressed in furs, hurriedly crawled up on it
and pressed himself against the glass, which gave a good surface to stick
to and soothed his hot belly. At least no one would take away this
picture while Gregor completely covered it up. He turned his head
toward the living-room door to watch the women when they returned.

They had not given themselves much of a rest and were already
coming back; Grete had put her arm around her mother and was
practically carrying her. "So what should we take now?" said Grete
and looked around. At that her eyes met Gregor's as he clung to the
wall. Probably only because of her mother's presence she kept her self-
control, bent her head down to her mother to keep her from looking
around, and said, though in a quavering and thoughtless voice: "Come,
we'd better go back into the living room for a minute." Grete's intent
was clear to Gregor, she wanted to bring his mother into safety and
then chase him down from the wall. Well, just let her try! He squatted
on his picture and would not give it up. He would rather fly in Grete's
face.

But Grete's words had now made her mother really anxious; she
stepped to one side, caught sight of the gigantic brown blotch on the
flowered wallpaper, and before it really dawned on her that what she
saw was Gregor, cried in a hoarse, bawling voice: "Oh, God, Oh,
God!"; and as if giving up completely, she fell with outstretched arms
across the couch and did not stir. "You, Gregor!" cried his sister with
raised fist and piercing eyes. These were the first words she had addressed directly to him since his metamorphosis. She ran into the next

room to get some kind of spirits to revive her mother; Gregor wanted to help too—there was time to rescue the picture—but he was stuck to the glass and had to tear himself loose by force; then he too ran into the next room, as if he could give his sister some sort of advice, as in the old days; but then had to stand behind her doing nothing while she rummaged among various little bottles; moreover, when she turned around she was startled, a bottle fell on the floor and broke, a splinter of glass wounded Gregor in the face, some kind of corrosive medicine flowed around him; now without waiting any longer, Grete grabbed as many little bottles as she could carry and ran with them inside to her mother; she slammed the door behind her with her foot. Now Gregor was cut off from his mother, who was perhaps near death through his fault; he could not dare open the door if he did not want to chase away his sister, who had to stay with his mother; now there was nothing for him to do except wait; and tormented by self-reproaches and worry, he began to crawl, crawled over everything, walls, furniture, and ceiling, and finally in desperation, as the whole room was beginning to spin, fell down onto the middle of the big table.

A short time passed; Gregor lay there prostrate; all around, things were quiet, perhaps that was a good sign. Then the doorbell rang. The maid, of course, was locked up in her kitchen, and so Grete had to answer the door. His father had come home. "What's happened?" were his first words; Grete's appearance must have told him everything. Grete answered in a muffled voice, her face was obviously pressed against her father's chest: "Mother fainted, but she's better now. Gregor's broken out." "I knew it," his father said. "I kept telling you, but you women don't want to listen." It was clear to Gregor that his father had put the worst interpretation on Grete's all-too-brief announcement and assumed that Gregor was guilty of some outrage. Therefore Gregor now had to try to calm his father down, since he had neither the time nor the ability to enlighten him. And so he fled to the door of his room and pressed himself against it for his father to see, as soon as he came into the foyer, that Gregor had the best intentions of returning to his room immediately and that it was not necessary to drive him back; if only the door were opened for him, he would disappear at once.

But his father was in no mood to notice such subtleties; "Ah!" he cried as he entered, in a tone that sounded as if he were at once furious and glad. Gregor turned his head away from the door and lifted it toward his father. He had not really imagined his father looking like this, as he stood in front of him now; admittedly Gregor had been too absorbed recently in his newfangled crawling to bother as much as before about events in the rest of the house and should really have been prepared to find some changes. And yet, and yet—was this still his father? Was this the same man who in the old days used to lie wearily buried in bed when Gregor left on a business trip; who greeted him on his return in the evening, sitting in his bathrobe in the armchair, who actually had difficulty getting to his feet but as a sign of joy only lifted up his arms; and who, on the rare occasions when the whole family went out for a walk, on a few Sundays in June and on the major holidays, used to shuffle along with great effort between Gregor and his mother, who were slow walkers themselves, always a little more slowly than they, wrapped in his old overcoat, always carefully planting down his crutch-handled cane, and, when he wanted to say something, nearly always stood still and assembled his escort around him? Now, however, he was holding himself very erect, dressed in a tight-fitting blue uniform with gold buttons, the kind worn by messengers at banking concerns; above the high stiff collar of the jacket his heavy chin protruded; under his bushy eyebrows his black eyes darted bright, piercing glances; his usually rumpled white hair was combed flat, with a scrupulously exact, gleaming part. He threw his cap—which was adorned with a gold monogram, probably that of a bank—in an arc across the entire room onto the couch, and with the tails of his long uniform jacket slapped back, his hands in his pants pockets, went for Gregor with a sullen look on his face. He probably did not know himself what he had in mind; still he lifted his feet unusually high off the floor, and Gregor staggered at the gigantic size of the soles of his boots. But he did not linger over this, he had known right from the first day of his new life that his father considered only the strictest treatment called for in dealing with him. And so he ran ahead of his father, stopped when his father stood still, and scooted ahead again when his father made even the slightest movement. In this way they made more than one tour of the room, without anything decisive happening; in fact the whole movement did not even have the appearance of a chase because of its slow tempo. So Gregor kept to the floor for the time being, especially since he was afraid that his father might interpret a flight onto the walls or the ceiling as a piece of particular nastiness. Of course Gregor had to admit that he would not be able to keep up even this running for long, for whenever his father took one step, Gregor had to execute countless movements. He was already beginning to feel winded, just as in the old days he had not had very reliable lungs. As he now staggered around, hardly keeping his eyes open in order to gather all his strength for the running; in his obtuseness not thinking of any escape other than by running; and having almost forgotten that the walls were at his disposal, though here of course they were blocked up with elaborately carved furniture full of notches and points—at that moment a lightly flung object hit the floor right near him and rolled in front of him. It was an apple; a second one came flying right after it; Gregor stopped dead with fear; further running was useless, for his father was determined to bombard him. He had filled his pockets from the fruit bowl on the buffet and was now pitching one apple after another, for the time being without taking good aim. These little red apples rolled around on the floor as if electrified, clicking into each another. One apple, thrown weakly, grazed Gregor's back and slid off harmlessly. But the very next one that came flying after it literally forced its way into Gregor's back;[6] Gregor tried to drag himself away, as if the startling, unbelievable pain might disappear with a change of place; but he felt nailed to the spot and stretched out his body in a complete confusion of all his senses. With his last glance he saw the door of his room burst open as his mother rushed out ahead of his screaming sister, in her chemise, for his sister had partly undressed her while she was unconscious in order to let her breathe more freely; saw his mother run up to his father and on the way her unfastened petticoats slide to the floor one by one; and saw as, stumbling over the skirts, she forced herself onto his father, and embracing him, in complete union with him—but now Gregor's sight went dim—her hands clasping his father's neck, begged for Gregor's life.

III

Gregor's serious wound, from which he suffered for over a month—the apple remained imbedded in his flesh as a visible souvenir since no one dared to remove it—seemed to have reminded even his father that Gregor was a member of the family, in spite of his present pathetic and repulsive shape, who could not be treated as an enemy; that, on the contrary, it was the commandment of family duty to swallow their disgust and endure him, endure him and nothing more.

And now, although Gregor had lost some of his mobility probably for good because of his wound, and although for the time being he needed long, long minutes to get across his room, like an old war veteran—crawling above ground was out of the question—for this deterioration of his situation he was granted compensation which in his view was entirely satisfactory: every day around dusk the living-room door—which he was in the habit of watching closely for an hour or two beforehand—was opened, so that, lying in the darkness of his room, invisible from the living room, he could see the whole family sitting at the table under the lamp and could listen to their conversation, as it were with general permission; and so it was completely different from before.

Of course these were no longer the animated conversations of the old days, which Gregor used to remember with a certain nostalgia in small hotel rooms when he'd had to throw himself wearily into the damp bedding. Now things were mostly very quiet. Soon after supper his father would fall asleep in his armchair; his mother and sister would caution each other to be quiet; his mother, bent low under the light,

6. See "Kafka's Manuscript Revisions," below, pp. 46–47.

sewed delicate lingerie for a clothing store; his sister, who had taken a job as a salesgirl, was learning shorthand and French in the evenings in order to attain a better position some time in the future. Sometimes his father woke up, and as if he had absolutely no idea that he had been asleep, said to his mother, "Look how long you're sewing again today!" and went right back to sleep, while mother and sister smiled wearily at each other.

With a kind of perverse obstinacy his father refused to take off his official uniform even in the house;[7] and while his robe hung uselessly on the clothes hook, his father dozed, completely dressed, in his chair, as if he were always ready for duty and were waiting even here for the voice of his superior. As a result his uniform, which had not been new to start with, began to get dirty in spite of all the mother's and sister's care, and Gregor would often stare all evening long at this garment, covered with stains and gleaming with its constantly polished gold buttons, in which the old man slept most uncomfortably and yet peacefully.

As soon as the clock struck ten, his mother tried to awaken his father with soft encouraging words and then persuade him to go to bed, for this was no place to sleep properly, and his father badly needed his sleep, since he had to be at work at six o'clock. But with the obstinacy that had possessed him ever since he had become a messenger, he always insisted on staying at the table a little longer, although he invariably fell asleep and then could be persuaded only with the greatest effort to exchange his armchair for bed. However much mother and sister might pounce on him with little admonitions, he would slowly shake his head for a quarter of an hour at a time, keeping his eyes closed, and would not get up. Gregor's mother plucked him by the sleeves, whispered blandishments into his ear, his sister dropped her homework in order to help her mother, but all this was of no use. He only sank deeper into his armchair. Not until the women lifted him up under his arms did he open his eyes, look alternately at mother and

---

7. In the version of *The Metamorphosis* which Kafka oversaw and published in his lifetime, he so punctuated the sentence that it would have to be translated differently—indeed, in two different ways. One way of reading says, "With a kind of perverse obstinacy, his father refused also to take off his official uniform in the house." This would make the point that among the various forms of obstinate behavior the father displays at home, refusing to take off his uniform is one of them. But the sentence can also be translated as follows: "With a kind of perverse obstinacy, his father refused to take off his official uniform in the house as well." About this interpretation of the sentence, critic Eric Santner comments: "The ambiguity of Kafka's diction makes possible the reading that the father has refused to remove his uniform not just at home but in public as well." Santner then develops this point by speculating that Mr. Samsa's "recent 'investiture' with a kind of official status and authority, low though it might be, might, in other words, be a sham." This observation contributes importantly to Santner's reading of *The Metamorphosis* as the representation of a crisis in the constitution of authority. See below, pp. 195–210, esp. 201.

    Interestingly enough, despite the claim to authenticity made by the so-called Manuscript Version of Kafka's complete works, recently published in Germany, the crucial sentence is printed in the normalized way: the editors place the comma in a position to produce the more "sensible" reading that the translation, above, reflects.

sister, and usually say, "What a life. So this is the peace of my old age." And leaning on the two women, he would get up laboriously, as if he were the greatest weight on himself, and let the women lead him to the door, where, shrugging them off, he would proceed independently, while Gregor's mother threw down her sewing, and his sister her pen, as quickly as possible so as to run after his father and be of further assistance.

Who in this overworked and exhausted family had time to worry about Gregor any more than was absolutely necessary? The household was stinted more and more; now the maid was let go after all;[8] a gigantic bony cleaning woman with white hair fluttering about her head came mornings and evenings to do the heaviest work; his mother took care of everything else, along with all her sewing. It even happened that various pieces of family jewelry, which in the old days his mother and sister had been overjoyed to wear at parties and celebrations, were sold, as Gregor found out one evening from the general discussion of the prices they had fetched. But the biggest complaint was always that they could not give up the apartment, which was much too big for their present needs, since no one could figure out how Gregor was supposed to be moved. But Gregor understood easily that it was not only consideration for him which prevented their moving, for he could easily have been transported in a suitable crate with a few air holes; what mainly prevented the family from moving was their complete hopelessness and the thought that they had been struck by a misfortune as none of their relatives and acquaintances had ever been hit. What the world demands of poor people they did to the utmost of their ability; his father brought breakfast for the minor officials at the bank, his mother sacrificed herself to the underwear of strangers, his sister ran back and forth behind the counter at the request of the customers; but for anything more than this they did not have the strength. And the wound in Gregor's back began to hurt anew when mother and sister, after getting his father to bed, now came back, dropped their work, pulled their chairs close to each other and sat cheek to cheek; when his mother, pointing to Gregor's room, said, "Close that door, Grete"; and when Gregor was back in darkness, while in the other room the women mingled their tears or stared dry-eyed at the table.

Gregor spent the days and nights almost entirely without sleep. Sometimes he thought that the next time the door opened he would take charge of the family's affairs again, just as he had done in the old days; after this long while there again appeared in his thoughts the boss and the manager, the salesmen and the trainees, the handyman who was so dense, two or three friends from other firms, a chambermaid in a provincial hotel—a happy fleeting memory—a cashier in a millinery

---

8. Presumably the new maid, the girl of sixteen.

store, whom he had courted earnestly but too slowly—they all appeared, intermingled with strangers or people he had already forgotten; but instead of helping him and his family, they were all inaccessible, and he was glad when they faded away. At other times he was in no mood to worry about his family, he was completely filled with rage at his miserable treatment, and although he could not imagine anything that would pique his appetite, he still made plans for getting into the pantry to take what was coming to him, even if he wasn't hungry. No longer considering what she could do to give Gregor a special treat, his sister, before running to business every morning and afternoon, hurriedly shoved any old food into Gregor's room with her foot; and in the evening, regardless of whether the food had only been toyed with or—the most usual case—had been left completely untouched, she swept it out with a swish of the broom. The cleaning up of Gregor's room, which she now always did in the evenings, could not be done more hastily. Streaks of dirt ran along the walls, fluffs of dust and filth lay here and there on the floor. At first, whenever his sister came in, Gregor would place himself in those corners which were particularly offending, meaning by his position in a sense to reproach her. But he could probably have stayed there for weeks without his sister's showing any improvement; she must have seen the dirt as clearly as he did, but she had just decided to leave it. At the same time she made sure—with an irritableness that was completely new to her and which had in fact infected the whole family—that the cleaning of Gregor's room remain her province. One time his mother had submitted Gregor's room to a major housecleaning, which she managed only after employing a couple of pails of water—all this dampness, of course, irritated Gregor too and he lay prostrate, sour and immobile, on the couch—but his mother's punishment was not long in coming. For hardly had his sister noticed the difference in Gregor's room that evening than, deeply insulted, she ran into the living room and, in spite of her mother's imploringly uplifted hands, burst out in a fit of crying, which his parents—his father had naturally been startled out of his armchair—at first watched in helpless amazement; until they too got going; turning to the right, his father blamed his mother for not letting his sister clean Gregor's room; but turning to the left, he screamed at his sister that she would never again be allowed to clean Gregor's room; while his mother tried to drag his father, who was out of his mind with excitement, into the bedroom; his sister, shaken with sobs, hammered the table with her small fists; and Gregor hissed loudly with rage because it did not occur to any of them to close the door and spare him such a scene and a row.

But even if his sister, exhausted from her work at the store, had gotten fed up with taking care of Gregor as she used to, it was not necessary at all for his mother to take her place and still Gregor did not have to be neglected. For now the cleaning woman was there. This old widow,

who thanks to her strong bony frame had probably survived the worst
in a long life, was not really repelled by Gregor. Without being in the
least inquisitive, she had once accidentally opened the door of Gregor's
room, and at the sight of Gregor—who, completely taken by surprise,
began to race back and forth although no one was chasing him—she
had remained standing, with her hands folded on her stomach, marveling. From that time on she never failed to open the door a crack
every morning and every evening and peek in hurriedly at Gregor. In
the beginning she also used to call him over to her with words she
probably considered friendly, like, "Come over here for a minute, you
old dung beetle!" or "Look at that old dung beetle!" To forms of address
like these Gregor would not respond but remained immobile where he
was, as if the door had not been opened. If only they had given this
cleaning woman orders to clean up his room every day, instead of
letting her disturb him uselessly whenever the mood took her. Once,
early in the morning—heavy rain, perhaps already a sign of approaching
spring, was beating on the window panes—Gregor was so exasperated
when the cleaning woman started in again with her phrases that he
turned on her, of course slowly and decrepitly, as if to attack. But the
cleaning woman, instead of getting frightened, simply lifted up high a
chair near the door, and as she stood there with her mouth wide open,
her intention was clearly to shut her mouth only when the chair in her
hand came crashing down on Gregor's back. "So, is that all there is?"
she asked when Gregor turned around again, and she quietly put the
chair back in the corner.

Gregor now hardly ate anything anymore. Only when he accidentally
passed the food laid out for him would he take a bite into his mouth
just for fun, hold it in for hours, and then mostly spit it out again. At
first he thought that his grief at the state of his room kept him off food,
but it was the very changes in his room to which he quickly became
adjusted. His family had gotten into the habit of putting in this room
things for which they could not find any other place, and now there
were plenty of these, since one of the rooms in the apartment had been
rented to three boarders. These serious gentlemen—all three had long
beards, as Gregor was able to register once through a crack in the
door—were obsessed with neatness, not only in their room, but since
they had, after all, moved in here, throughout the entire household and
especially in the kitchen. They could not stand useless, let alone dirty
junk. Besides, they had brought along most of their own household
goods. For this reason many things had become superfluous, and
though they certainly weren't salable, on the other hand they could not
just be thrown out. All these things migrated into Gregor's room. Likewise the ash can and the garbage can from the kitchen. Whatever was
not being used at the moment was just flung into Gregor's room by
the cleaning woman, who was always in a big hurry; fortunately Gregor

generally saw only the object involved and the hand that held it. Maybe the cleaning woman intended to reclaim the things as soon as she had a chance or else to throw out everything together in one fell swoop, but in fact they would have remained lying wherever they had been thrown in the first place if Gregor had not squeezed through the junk and set it in motion, at first from necessity, because otherwise there would have been no room to crawl in, but later with growing pleasure, although after such excursions, tired to death and sad, he did not budge again for hours.

Since the roomers sometimes also had their supper at home in the common living room, the living-room door remained closed on certain evenings, but Gregor found it very easy to give up the open door, for on many evenings when it was opened he had not taken advantage of it, but instead, without the family's noticing, had lain in the darkest corner of his room. But once the cleaning woman had left the living-room door slightly open, and it also remained opened a little when the roomers came in in the evening and the lamp was lit. They sat down at the head of the table where in the old days his father, his mother, and Gregor had eaten, unfolded their napkins, and picked up their knives and forks. At once his mother appeared in the doorway with a platter of meat, and just behind her came his sister with a platter piled high with potatoes. A thick vapor steamed up from the food. The roomers bent over the platters set in front of them as if to examine them before eating, and in fact the one who sat in the middle, and who seemed to be regarded by the other two as an authority, cut into a piece of meat while it was still on the platter, evidently to find out whether it was tender enough or whether it should perhaps be sent back to the kitchen. He was satisfied, and mother and sister, who had been watching anxiously, sighed with relief and began to smile.

The family itself ate in the kitchen. Nevertheless, before going into the kitchen, his father came into this room and, bowing once, cap in hand, made a turn around the table. The roomers rose as one man and mumbled something into their beards. When they were alone again, they ate in almost complete silence. It seemed strange to Gregor that among all the different noises of eating he kept picking up the sound of their chewing teeth, as if this were a sign to Gregor that you needed teeth to eat with and that even with the best make of toothless jaws you couldn't do a thing. "I'm hungry enough," Gregor said to himself, full of grief, "but not for these things. Look how these roomers are gorging themselves, and I'm dying!"

On this same evening—Gregor could not remember having heard the violin during the whole time—the sound of violin playing came from the kitchen. The roomers had already finished their evening meal, the one in the middle had taken out a newspaper, given each of the two others a page, and now, leaning back, they read and smoked. When the violin began to play, they became attentive, got up, and went on tiptoe to the door leading to the foyer, where they stood in a huddle. They must have been heard in the kitchen, for his father called, "Perhaps the playing bothers you, gentlemen? It can be stopped right away." "On the contrary," said the middle roomer. "Wouldn't the young lady like to come in to us and play in here where it's much roomier and more comfortable?" "Oh, certainly," called Gregor's father, as if he were the violinist. The boarders went back into the room and waited. Soon Gregor's father came in with the music stand, his mother with the sheet music, and his sister with the violin. Calmly his sister got everything ready for playing; his parents—who had never rented out rooms before and therefore behaved toward the roomers with excessive politeness—did not even dare sit down on their own chairs; his father leaned against the door, his right hand inserted between two buttons of his uniform coat, which he kept closed; but his mother was offered a chair by one of the roomers, and since she left the chair where the roomer just happened to put it, she sat in a corner to one side.

His sister began to play. Father and mother, from either side, attentively followed the movements of her hands. Attracted by the playing, Gregor had dared to come out a little further and already had his head in the living room. It hardly surprised him that lately he was showing so little consideration for the others; once such consideration had been his greatest pride. And yet he would never have had better reason to keep hidden; for now, because of the dust which lay all over his room and blew around at the slightest movement, he too was completely covered with dust; he dragged around with him on his back and along his sides fluff and hairs and scraps of food; his indifference to everything was much too deep for him to have gotten on his back and scrubbed himself clean against the rug, as once he had done several times a day. And in spite of his state, he was not ashamed to inch out a little farther on the immaculate living-room floor.

Admittedly no one paid any attention to him. The family was completely absorbed by the violin-playing; the roomers, on the other hand, who at first had stationed themselves, hands in pockets, much too close behind his sister's music stand, so that they could all have followed the score, which certainly must have upset his sister, soon withdrew to the window, talking to each other in an undertone, their heads lowered, where they remained, anxiously watched by his father. It now seemed only too obvious that they were disappointed in their expectation of hearing beautiful or entertaining violin-playing, had had enough of the whole performance, and continued to let their peace be disturbed only out of politeness. Especially the way they all blew the cigar smoke out of their nose and mouth toward the ceiling suggested great nervousness. And yet his sister was playing so beautifully. Her face was inclined to one side, sadly and probingly her eyes followed the lines of music.

Gregor crawled forward a little farther, holding his head close to the floor, so that it might be possible to catch her eye. Was he an animal, that music could move him so? He felt as if the way to the unknown nourishment he longed for were coming to light. He was determined to force himself on until he reached his sister, to pluck at her skirt, and to let her know in this way that she should bring her violin into his room, for no one here appreciated her playing the way he would appreciate it. He would never again let her out of his room—at least not for as long as he lived; for once, his nightmarish looks would be of use to him; he would be at all the doors of his room at the same time and hiss and spit at the aggressors; his sister, however, should not be forced to stay with him, but would do so of her own free will; she should sit next to him on the couch, bending her ear down to him, and then he would confide to her that he had had the firm intention of sending her to the Conservatory, and that, if the catastrophe had not intervened, he would have announced this to everyone last Christmas—certainly Christmas had come and gone?—without taking notice of any objections. After this declaration his sister would burst into tears of emotion, and Gregor would raise himself up to her shoulder and kiss her on the neck which, ever since she started going out to work, she kept bare, without a ribbon or collar.

"Mr. Samsa!" the middle roomer called to Gregor's father and without wasting another word pointed his index finger at Gregor, who was slowly moving forward. The violin stopped, the middle roomer smiled first at his friends, shaking his head, and then looked at Gregor again. Rather than driving Gregor out, his father seemed to consider it more urgent to start by soothing the roomers although they were not at all upset, and Gregor seemed to be entertaining them more than the violin-playing. He rushed over to them and tried with outstretched arms to drive them into their room and at the same time with his body to block their view of Gregor. Now they actually did get a little angry—it was not clear whether because of his father's behavior or because of their dawning realization of having had without knowing it such a next-door neighbor as Gregor. They demanded explanations from his father; in their turn they raised their arms, plucked excitedly at their beards, and, dragging their feet, backed off toward their room. In the meantime his sister had overcome the abstracted mood into which she had fallen after her playing had been so suddenly interrupted; and all at once, after holding violin and bow for a while in her slackly hanging hands and continuing to follow the score as if she were still playing, she pulled herself together, laid the instrument on the lap of her mother—who was still sitting in her chair, fighting for breath, her lungs violently heaving—and ran into the next room, which the roomers, under pressure from her father, were nearing more quickly than before. One could see the covers and bolsters on the beds, obeying his sister's practiced hands, fly up and arrange themselves. Before the boarders had reached the room, she had finished turning down the beds and had slipped out. Her father seemed once again to be gripped by his perverse obstinacy to such a degree that he completely forgot any respect still due his tenants. He drove them on and kept on driving until, already at the bedroom door, the middle boarder stamped his foot thunderingly and thus brought him to a standstill. "I herewith declare," he said, raising his hand and casting his eyes around for Gregor's mother and sister too, "that in view of the disgusting conditions prevailing in this apartment and family"—here he spat curtly and decisively on the floor—"I give notice as of now. Of course I won't pay a cent for the days I have been living here, either; on the contrary, I shall consider taking some sort of action against you with claims that—believe me—will be easy to substantiate." He stopped and looked straight in front of him, as if he were expecting something. And in fact his two friends at once chimed in with the words, "We too give notice as of now." Thereupon he grabbed the doorknob and slammed the door with a bang.

Gregor's father, his hands groping, staggered to his armchair and collapsed into it; it looked as if he were stretching himself out for his usual evening nap, but the heavy drooping of his head, as if it had lost all support, showed that he was certainly not asleep. All this time Gregor had lain quietly at the spot where the roomers had surprised him. His disappointment at the failure of his plan—but perhaps also the weakness caused by so much fasting—made it impossible for him to move. He was afraid with some certainty that in the very next moment a general debacle would burst over him, and he waited. He was not even startled by the violin as it slipped from under his mother's trembling fingers and fell off her lap with a reverberating clang.

"My dear parents," said his sister and by way of an introduction pounded her hand on the table, "things can't go on like this. Maybe you don't realize it, but I do. I won't pronounce the name of my brother in front of this monster, and so all I say is: we have to try to get rid of it. We've done everything humanly possible to take care of it and to put up with it; I don't think anyone can blame us in the least."

"She's absolutely right," said his father to himself. His mother, who still could not catch her breath, began to cough dully behind her hand, a wild look in her eyes.

His sister rushed over to his mother and held her forehead. His father seemed to have been led by Grete's words to more definite thoughts, had sat up, was playing with the cap of his uniform among the plates which were still lying on the table from the roomers' supper, and from time to time looked at Gregor's motionless form.

"We must try to get rid of it," his sister now said exclusively to her father, since her mother was coughing too hard to hear anything. "It will be the death of you two, I can see it coming. People who already have to work as hard as we do can't put up with this constant torture at home, too. I can't stand it anymore either." And she broke out crying so bitterly that her tears poured down onto her mother's face, which she wiped off with mechanical movements of her hand.

"Child," said her father kindly and with unusual understanding, "but what can we do?"

Gregor's sister only shrugged her shoulders as a sign of the bewildered mood that had now gripped her as she cried, in contrast with her earlier confidence.

"If he could understand us," said her father, half questioning; in the midst of her crying Gregor's sister waved her hand violently as a sign that that was out of the question.

"If he could understand us," his father repeated and by closing his eyes, absorbed his daughter's conviction of the impossibility of the idea, "then maybe we could come to an agreement with him. But the way things are————"

"It has to go," cried his sister. "That's the only answer, Father. You just have to try to get rid of the idea that it's Gregor. Believing it for so long, that is our real misfortune. But how can it be Gregor? If it were Gregor, he would have realized long ago that it isn't possible for human beings to live with such a creature, and he would have gone away of his own free will. Then we wouldn't have a brother, but we'd be able to go on living and honor his memory. But as things are, this animal persecutes us, drives the roomers away, obviously wants to occupy the whole apartment and for us to sleep in the gutter. Look, Father," she suddenly shrieked, "he's starting in again!" And in a fit of terror that was completely incomprehensible to Gregor, his sister abandoned even her mother, literally shoved herself off from her chair, as if she would rather sacrifice her mother than stay near Gregor, and rushed behind her father, who, upset only by her behavior, also stood up and half-lifted his arms in front of her as if to protect her.

But Gregor had absolutely no intention of frightening anyone, let alone his sister. He had only begun to turn around in order to trek back to his room; certainly his movements did look peculiar, since his ailing condition made him help the complicated turning maneuver along with his head, which he lifted up many times and knocked against the floor. He stopped and looked around. His good intention seemed to have been recognized; it had only been a momentary scare. Now they all watched him, silent and sad. His mother lay in her armchair, her legs stretched out and pressed together, her eyes almost closing from exhaustion; his father and his sister sat side by side, his sister had put her arm around her father's neck.

Now maybe they'll let me turn around, Gregor thought and began his labors again. He could not repress his panting from the exertion, and from time to time he had to rest. Otherwise no one harassed him;

he was left completely on his own. When he had completed the turn, he immediately began to crawl back in a straight line. He was astonished at the great distance separating him from his room and could not understand at all how, given his weakness, he had covered the same distance a little while ago almost without realizing it. Constantly intent only on rapid crawling, he hardly noticed that not a word, not an exclamation from his family interrupted him. Only when he was already in the doorway did he turn his head—not completely, for he felt his neck stiffening; nevertheless he still saw that behind him nothing had changed except that his sister had gotten up. His last glance ranged over his mother, who was now fast asleep.

He was hardly inside his room when the door was hurriedly slammed shut, firmly bolted, and locked. Gregor was so frightened at the sudden noise behind him that his little legs gave way under him. It was his sister who had been in such a hurry. She had been standing up straight, ready and waiting, then she had leaped forward nimbly, Gregor had not even heard her coming, and she cried "Finally!" to her parents as she turned the key in the lock.

"And now?" Gregor asked himself, looking around in the darkness. He soon made the discovery that he could no longer move at all. It did not surprise him; rather, it seemed unnatural that until now he had actually been able to propel himself on these thin little legs. Otherwise he felt relatively comfortable. He had pains, of course, throughout his whole body, but it seemed to him that they were gradually getting fainter and fainter and would finally go away altogether. The rotten apple in his back and the inflamed area around it, which were completely covered with fluffy dust, already hardly bothered him. He thought back on his family with deep emotion and love. His conviction that he would have to disappear was, if possible, even firmer than his sister's. He remained in this state of empty and peaceful reflection until the tower clock struck three in the morning. He still saw that outside the window everything was beginning to grow light. Then, without his consent, his head sank down to the floor, and from his nostrils streamed his last weak breath.

When early in the morning the cleaning woman came—in sheer energy and impatience she would slam all the doors so hard although she had often been asked not to, that once she had arrived, quiet sleep was no longer possible anywhere in the apartment—she did not at first find anything out of the ordinary on paying Gregor her usual short visit. She thought that he was deliberately lying motionless, pretending that his feelings were hurt; she credited him with unlimited intelligence. Because she happened to be holding the long broom, she tried from the doorway to tickle Gregor with it. When this too produced no results, she became annoyed and jabbed Gregor a little, and only when she had shoved him without any resistance to another spot did she begin to take notice. When she quickly became aware of the true state of things, she opened her eyes wide, whistled softly, but did not dawdle; instead, she tore open the door of the bedroom and shouted at the top of her voice into the darkness: "Come and have a look, it's croaked; it's lying there, dead as a doornail!"

The couple Mr. and Mrs. Samsa sat up in their marriage bed and had a struggle overcoming their shock at the cleaning woman before they could finally grasp her message. But then Mr. and Mrs. Samsa hastily scrambled out of bed, each on his side, Mr. Samsa threw the blanket around his shoulders, Mrs. Samsa came out in nothing but her nightgown; dressed this way, they entered Gregor's room. In the meantime the door of the living room had also opened, where Grete had been sleeping since the roomers had moved in; she was fully dressed, as if she had not been asleep at all; and her pale face seemed to confirm this. "Dead?" said Mrs. Samsa and looked inquiringly at the cleaning woman, although she could scrutinize everything for herself and could recognize the truth even without scrutiny. "I'll say," said the cleaning woman, and to prove it she pushed Gregor's corpse with her broom a good distance sideways. Mrs. Samsa made a movement as if to hold the broom back but did not do it. "Well," said Mr. Samsa, "now we can thank God!" He crossed himself,[9] and the three women followed his example. Grete, who never took her eyes off the corpse, said, "Just look how thin he was. Of course he didn't eat anything for such a long time. The food came out again just the way it went in." As a matter of fact, Gregor's body was completely flat and dry; this was obvious now for the first time, really, since the body was no longer raised up by his little legs and nothing else distracted the eye.

"Come in with us for a little while, Grete," said Mrs. Samsa with a melancholy smile, and Grete, not without looking back at the corpse, followed her parents into their bedroom. The cleaning woman shut the door and opened the window wide. Although it was early in the morning, there was already some mildness mixed in with the fresh air. After all, it was already the end of March.

The three boarders came out of their room and looked around in astonishment for their breakfast; they had been forgotten. "Where's breakfast?" the middle roomer grumpily asked the cleaning woman. But she put her finger to her lips and then hastily and silently beckoned the boarders to follow her into Gregor's room. They came willingly and then stood, their hands in the pockets of their somewhat shabby jackets, in the now already very bright room, surrounding Gregor's corpse.

At that point the bedroom door opened, and Mr. Samsa appeared in his uniform, his wife on one arm, his daughter on the other. They all

9. Final evidence of the Samsas' probable Catholicism.

looked as if they had been crying; from time to time Grete pressed her face against her father's sleeve.

"Leave my house immediately," said Mr. Samsa and pointed to the door, without letting go of the women. "What do you mean by that?" said the middle roomer, somewhat nonplussed, and smiled with a sugary smile. The two others held their hands behind their back and incessantly rubbed them together, as if in joyful anticipation of a big argument, which could only turn out in their favor. "I mean just what I say," answered Mr. Samsa and with his two companions marched in a straight line toward the roomer. At first the roomer stood still and looked at the floor, as if the thoughts inside his head were fitting themselves together in a new order. "So, we'll go, then," he said and looked up at Mr. Samsa as if, suddenly overcome by a fit of humility, he were asking for further permission even for this decision. Mr. Samsa merely nodded briefly several times, his eyes wide open. Thereupon the roomer actually went immediately into the foyer, taking long strides; his two friends had already been listening for a while, their hands completely still, and now they went hopping right after him, as if afraid that Mr. Samsa might get into the foyer ahead of them and interrupt the contact with their leader. In the foyer all three took their hats from the coatrack, pulled their canes from the umbrella stand, bowed silently, and left the apartment. In a suspicious mood which proved completely unfounded, Mr. Samsa led the two women out onto the landing; leaning over the banister, they watched the three roomers slowly but steadily going down the long flight of stairs, disappearing on each landing at a particular turn of the stairway and a few moments later emerging again; the farther down they got, the more the Samsa family's interest in them wore off, and when a butcher's boy with a carrier on his head came climbing up the stairs with a proud bearing, toward them and then up on past them, Mr. Samsa and the women quickly left the banister and all went back, as if relieved, into their apartment.

They decided to spend this day resting and going for a walk; they not only deserved a break in their work, they absolutely needed one. And so they sat down at the table and wrote three letters of excuse, Mr. Samsa to the management of the bank, Mrs. Samsa to her employer, and Grete to the store owner. While they were writing, the cleaning woman came in to say that she was going, since her morning's work was done. The three letter writers at first simply nodded without looking up, but as the cleaning woman still kept lingering, they looked up, annoyed. "Well?" asked Mr. Samsa. The cleaning woman stood smiling in the doorway, as if she had some great good news to announce to the family but would do so only if she were thoroughly questioned. The little ostrich feather which stood almost upright on her hat and which had irritated Mr. Samsa the whole time she had been with them swayed lightly in all directions. "What do you want?" asked Mrs. Samsa, who inspired the most respect in the cleaning woman. "Well," the cleaning woman answered, and for good-natured laughter could not immediately go on, "look, you don't have to worry about getting rid of the stuff next door. It's already been taken care of." Mrs. Samsa and Grete bent down over their letters, as if to continue writing; Mr. Samsa, who noticed that the cleaning woman was now about to start describing everything in detail, stopped her with a firmly outstretched hand. But since she was not going to be permitted to tell her story, she remembered that she was in a great hurry, cried, obviously insulted, "So long, everyone," whirled around wildly, and left the apartment with a terrible slamming of doors.

"We'll fire her tonight," said Mr. Samsa, but did not get an answer from either his wife or his daughter, for the cleaning woman seemed to have ruined their barely regained peace of mind. They got up, went to the window, and stayed there, holding each other tight. Mr. Samsa turned around in his chair toward them and watched them quietly for a while. Then he called, "Come on now, come over here. Stop brooding over the past. And have a little consideration for me, too." The women obeyed him at once, hurried over to him, fondled him, and quickly finished their letters.

Then all three of them left the apartment together, something they had not done in months, and took the trolley into the open country on the outskirts of the city. The car, in which they were the only passengers, was completely filled with warm sunshine. Leaning back comfortably in their seats, they discussed their prospects for the time to come, and it seemed on closer examination that these weren't bad at all, for all three positions—about which they had never really asked one another in any detail—were exceedingly advantageous and especially promising for the future. The greatest immediate improvement in their situation would come easily, of course, from a change in apartments; they would now take a smaller and cheaper apartment, but one better situated and in every way simpler to manage than the old one, which Gregor had picked for them. While they were talking in this vein, it occurred almost simultaneously to Mr. and Mrs. Samsa, as they watched their daughter getting livelier and livelier, that lately, in spite of all the troubles which had turned her cheeks pale, she had blossomed into a good-looking, shapely girl. Growing quieter and communicating almost unconsciously through glances, they thought that it would soon be time, too, to find her a good husband. And it was like a confirmation of their new dreams and good intentions when at the end of the ride their daughter got up first and stretched her young body.

Kafka's Manuscript Revisions

[4, 15] are just having breakfast.
The MS continues with the phrase "and yawning discuss the world political situation." Kafka subsequently crossed it out, not least, presumably, because it jars ludicrously with the habits of "harem women." And Gregor, who despite his weird looks, still is responsible for reporting the story, must not be allowed to sound silly, at the risk of alienating the reader's credulity.

[6, 21] get out of bed
The MS has *herauskommen*, which Kafka thereafter changed to *hinauskommen*. Both words are translated as "get out," but the first verb, *herauskommen*, situates the speaker at the place where the action originates, namely, the speaker's body, as his body moves outward into its environing world. On the other hand, *hinauskommen* situates the speaker at some distance from the immediate situation: he is already outside, in the world; hence, he is reporting on Gregor's movements as an objective observer. Kafka's preference for *hinauskommen* appears to be motivated by the desire to lend objectivity to Gregor's report of things. Gregor suffers his situation passively and at the same time appears to give a report on it: hence, he is already at some remove from himself.

[6, 31] its width
The pronoun in the MS can be translated as "his." Its replacement by the impersonal pronoun "its" is highly suggestive. With this change, Kafka conveys Gregor's distance from (and amazement toward) this new body, which is still an "it" and not yet "his," not yet a certain feature of his identity.

[7, 13–14] rocking the complete length of his body out of the bed
The same narrative strategy as described in revision [6, 21], above, very likely compelled Kafka to substitute *hinausschaukeln* for the original *herausschaukeln*, where *schaukeln* means "to rock [one's body]."

[7, 27] bend down with their burden
The MS shows that Kafka backed around in mid-sentence to add this phrase, which emphasizes the heavy materiality of Gregor's body.

[8, 12] than he had thought
In the MS these words have been added: "and finally fortunately landed all at once on the floor." This phrase survives, slightly altered, even in the first printed version: "and finally he had landed on the floor, fortunately in the horizontal position." Thereupon, Kafka eliminated it. The reason is apparent: the words that follow this phrase speak of a "muffled sound" and refer the reader to the preceding "crash." The reader, like Gregor, is kept in the realm of surmise and inference with respect to the capacities of his body. Like Gregor, we can only judge from certain signs (muffled sounds and crashes) that Gregor's body has indeed landed on the carpet with a fair amount of success. Kafka continually wants to stress the strangeness of Gregor's body even—and especially—*for Gregor*. Its nature is something he still has to figure out by trial and error.

[9, 1–2] "I'm coming right away," said Gregor
In the MS Kafka wrote, "Karl" for "Gregor," evidently thinking of Karl Rossmann, the hero of his (unfinished) novel *Der Verschollene* (*The Boy Who Sank Out of Sight*, a.k.a. *Amerika*), which Kafka was writing in the same period as *The Metamorphosis*.

[9, 9] In the room on the left
Kafka originally wrote, "From out of the room." The reason for this change appears to be the same as the one already identified. See revisions [6, 21] and [7, 13–14], above, p. 43. The preposition which Kafka chose—namely, "in"—situates the reporter at the scene of the event though he is also outside it, detached from his own merely subjective impression of the event; thus the change of preposition lends truth and objectivity to his report.

[10, 30] clinging to its slats
In his MS, Kafka chose the verb *ergreifen* ("to seize hold of") in order to describe the bug's hold on the chair, then rejected it for the verb *festhalten*, meaning "to cling to." This decision is illuminated by Kafka's use of the verb "cling to" to describe his own relation to his writing desk, namely, "Since the existence of the writer is truly dependent upon his desk and if he wants to keep madness at bay, he must never go far from his desk, he must cling to it with his teeth" (*Letters to Friends*, 335 [Translation modified]). See below, p. 100.

[11, 26] he had no real teeth
For "had," in the MS, Kafka originally wrote, "*hätte*," using the subjunctive. The subjunctive conveys the sense that the fact reported—Gregor's teeth are missing—is itself only a hypothesis and may not be true. In replacing the verb with the indicative *hatte*, Kafka appears to remove any suggestion of doubt as to the reality of this (negative) feature

of Gregor's physique. Gregor's report must be a report of what is truly the case.

[11, 40] the whole weight of his body

For "weight," Kafka literally wrote the word "*Last*," or "burden." This is the same word he used earlier [7] to describe the body that "two strong persons" would have to "scoop up" and "bend down with" in order to lift Gregor off the bed. In the MS Kafka did at first literally write the word *Gewicht* (weight) before rejecting it for *Last* (burden). The latter word specifies the weight as enormous. The MS also reveals that Kafka at first had Gregor "tugging" on the key (Kafka used a form of the verb *ziehen*); but by finally having Gregor "cling" to it, or, more literally, "hang himself on" to it, Kafka conveys the huge, desperate, life-or-death stakes of the effort. The same motive presumably prompted him to replace the expression *ließ dann wieder sein* (let go) with *drückte nieder* (pressed down). Gregor is now shown to be unrelenting in applying his monstrous body to the task of turning the key.

[11, 41] positively woke Gregor up

The MS gives the version "woke him up positively [or 'literally' or 'truly'] from his eager absorption in his work [*Arbeitseifer*]." It seems clear why Kafka rejected this phrase. Who could supply the formulation that Gregor had been "eagerly absorbed in his work"? Only someone, really, who wasn't Gregor, because if Gregor had been truly absorbed in his work, he would hardly have been able to report his state of mind *in the instant of being wrenched from it,* hardly been able to give a name immediately to what had so completely, mindlessly absorbed him. Kafka requires that the flow of information be confined to what Gregor is capable of reporting and naming in the instant.

[12, 24–25] building

Kafka started to write, "hospital," instead of "building," then preferred to have Gregor catch sight of some sort of building and then only subsequently identify it as a hospital. This change responds to the same principle discussed in the revision [11, 41], above. Gregor as reporter must not be allowed to exhibit too much totalizing presence of mind. The illusion must be maintained that our perspective on these events is defined by Gregor's angle of vision, a vision correct within the limits of perception.

[12, 33] demanding respect

Kafka originally added the words "from the viewer," then removed them, presumably because of the too peculiar effect arising for the reader, who, upon asking the question "Which viewer then?" would realize that the viewer is now Gregor the bug. We would then have the image of Gregor demanding respect from the bug he has become. Here the humor verges on ridicule.

[13, 24] And during Gregor's speech
In place of "Gregor," the original text has "Georg," the name of Kafka's deceased younger brother and the hero of Kafka's great breakthrough story, "The Judgment," which he completed in the early morning of September 23, 1912, two months or so before he wrote this line. The heroes of the three stories that Kafka proposed publishing under a single, unifying title, *The Sons*—namely, "The Judgment," *The Metamorphosis*, and "The Stoker" (the first chapter of Kafka's "America-novel," *The Boy Who Sank Out of Sight*)—all haunt this text. Kafka made the proposal to publish *The Sons* to his publisher Kurt Wolff in April 1913. See below, p. 173.

[13, 35–36] was set for life in this firm
The MS says "had a lifetime job (*Lebensstellung*)." Kafka then replaced this phrase with one that translates literally as "was provided for [or 'taken care of'] for life in this firm." Unfortunately, the latter expression sounds awkward in the English translation, and so I have given the word "set" instead of "provided for." But it is good to keep the latter phrase in mind, which Kafka chose and which brings to the surface an unconscious anticipation of the question that will soon beset the Samsa household (and anybody else concerned): namely, who is going to take care of this monster?

[14, 16] Gregor
In the MS Kafka again wrote, "Karl," thinking of Karl Rossmann, the hero of *Der Verschollene* (*The Boy Who Sank Out of Sight* a.k.a. *Amerika*], which Kafka was writing at the same time as composing *The Metamorphosis*.

[14, 38] picked up
Kafka originally used the neutral verb "took (*nahm*)," then substituted *holte*, here translated as "picked up" but which means literally "went to fetch." The word Kafka finally used sounds a lot more menacing, especially to a child, because the sort of thing that traditionally gets "fetched" in a household is a stick, a strap, the police, or the Devil.

[15, 23] Gregor
Kafka again began writing "Karl," then corrected this name of the hero of a different work to "Gregor."

[15, 28–29] the voice . . . a single father
See below, pp. 200–201. Kafka originally wrote, "only a father," then felt it important to introduce the word "single"—"only a single father." The original version appears to suggest that while the voice that Gregor hears is intolerably loud, the voice of even "a" (that is to say, "any") father would be loud enough and bad enough. This is a point that might have been plain enough in Kafka's family but not in every read-

er's, so the revised version makes the point universal: the exceptional loudness of Mr. Samsa's voice contrasts with his ordinary voice as the voice of *many* fathers contrasts with that of only *one*. The effect of Mr. Samsa's voice on Gregor is part of a phenomenon general throughout the story: in his buglike state, Gregor is acutely, even excessively sensitive to the treatment he receives from his father, especially when it is harsh.

Cf. revision [27, 32], p. 51, below, and, further, the behavior of the little apples flung by Gregor's father [29]: "But the very next one that came flying after it literally forced its way into Gregor's back; Gregor began to drag himself away, as if the startling, unbelievable pain might disappear with a change of place. . . ."

[15, 32] soon he got stuck
Instead of "he," Kafka originally wrote, "Gregor." But the name acts as an interruption in the flow of swift actions and sensations. The rush of behavior that effectively annihilates Gregor as a personality is better preserved without the introduction of his name.

[16, 26] there wasn't a sound
The MS has these words following: "The cook, who [being] otherwise occupied in the kitchen with preparations for supper, as powerfully with"—words which Kafka eliminated presumably because doing so allowed him to dwell on the topic of reading aloud, which interested him enormously (see the following sentence). He was to read this very story *The Metamorphosis* aloud, in public, to friends (see below, p. 172), and dreamed of reciting in its entirety *The Sentimental Education* (1869), a long novel by the great French writer Gustave Flaubert (1821–1880), namely, "As a child . . . I liked to dream of reciting, before a huge, crowded auditorium . . . the complete *Education sentimentale*, uninterruptedly, for as many days and nights as were required, in French, of course (oh dear, my accent!), and the walls would reverberate!" (*Letters to Felice* 86. Translation modified). Kafka expressed this thought while composing the final pages of *The Metamorphosis.*

[16, 32] provide
The MS begins with the word "offer, bid" (*bieten*), which it then changes to "provide" (*verschaffen*). "Offer" is obviously the more generous action—suggesting, even, that under the right circumstances it might be refused by the persons to whom the offer is made without offense to the offering party, whose action could seem innocent and open-handed. "Provide," on the other hand, especially in the German, suggests an object produced by labor and exertion, one that is much more likely to oblige the taker into a position of humility. "Provide" reflects a note of aggressive pride in Gregor's sense of accomplishment.

[16, 43–44] the doors had been locked
Kafka originally wrote, "when he had locked all the doors." Kafka's first choice is indeed less good for reasons of accuracy (in his vermin shape, Gregor certainly did not lock the doors that morning). And, moreover, the new decision, which suppresses the identity of the person who locks the door, interestingly suggests that Gregor may have been locked into, i.e., caged in, his own room right from the start, so that Gregor's metamorphosis can now begin to seem less a radical transformation than a realization, like the punishments meted out in Dante's *Inferno*, of the animal Gregor has always been. By rewriting this sentence, Kafka deprives Gregor of even so much control and mastery as is implied by the ability to rule over the locks on his doors. See the scene when Gregor's room is firmly bolted and locked from the outside [39].

[17, 5] no one would come in
Kafka originally wrote, "no one is coming [in]" or "no one will come [in]," situating the narrative standpoint inside Gregor's head. Then, in the final text, he moved the narrative standpoint away from Gregor to a standpoint that could be Gregor's but could also be that of an impersonal, third-person narrator. This is the narrative device called "indirect free speech," in which a narrator so intimately espouses the thoughts of a character that it is impossible to tell which of these "persons" is responsible for having them.

[17, 32–33] left the milk standing
In the MS, Kafka originally had Grete observe that Gregor "had not drunk the milk." In the final version, Kafka appears to be reluctant to attribute to Grete the degree of empathetic feeling that would allow her to identify with Gregor actually drinking. The formulation he chose is colder, more neutral.

[17, 38] his sister
The MS reads "the dear girl," a tone identifying the speaker as Gregor—who is befuddled, for it is doubtful that Grete is "a dear girl"—rather than the narrator, who we assume is clear-sighted. "His sister" is something that both Gregor and the narrator could say: hence the word choice shows Kafka keeping to his principle of narrative congruence, keeping the reader uncertain about which of these two authorities supports the various claims making up the story.

[17, 41] carried it out.
Here, too, as in several previous examples, Kafka changed the adverb of direction from *heraus* to *hinaus*. This change seems motivated by his desire to lend the objectivity of impersonal narration to Gregor's report of things, keeping the perspectives of the two authorities congruent.

[18, 2] evening meal
Kafka originally wrote, "*Nachtessen*," a word in German more like "supper"; then he appeared to want to elevate the tone in order to heighten the social station of the Samsa family, in accordance with the ancient principle of tragedy that makes brutal events more dignified and worthy of attention the higher the social station of the characters they befall.

[18, 33] carried everything out
Again, Kafka changed the verb prefix from *heraus* to *hinaus*, presumably in order to give the narration the authority of a standpoint consistent with, but detached from, Gregor's own.

[19, 30] in this house
Kafka originally wrote the phrase *bei dieser Herrschaft* ["at these employers"], which, taken literally, means something rather grandiose, approximately, "under such seigniory." But his next impulse was, as always, to reject such irony. Moreover, it is not only irony that's at stake here but a dangerous pulling apart of the narrating voice and the voice of the character. As a rule, Kafka seeks to hold these voices together.

[20, 12–13] the business disaster which had plunged everyone into a state of total despair
Kafka originally wrote, "the disaster which had absolutely destroyed so many plans and hopes," but, to judge from the narrative, he had not yet concretely imagined these plans and hopes. Several sentences later, Kafka does take up this challenge and invents the important idea that Gregor had plans for his sister's education.

[20, 41–42] obviously turning toward the door
The MS shows that at first Kafka did not introduce this indication, then interpolated the important fact that Mr. Samsa continues to watch the door of Gregor's room with some concern lest Gregor "break out."

[21, 37] scrabbling
In the journal *Die weißen Blätter* (October 1915), in which the first printed version of *The Metamorphosis* appeared, Gregor is described as "staring" [*starrte*], not "scrabbling" [*scharrte*], for hours on end. Kafka subsequently corrected this version for the first book publication of the story, which is the basis of the Norton translation. "Scrabbling" is also what Kafka's badgerlike hero does throughout the great, unfinished story "The Burrow." Interestingly, the word "scrabble" [*scharren*] is etymologically related to the word "write" [*schreiben*], both verbs deriving from the Indo-European root *sker*. Kafka associated lying on his sofa with his nightly preparations to write.

[22, 8] If Gregor had only been able to speak
For "Gregor," Kafka initially wrote, "Karl," again thinking of Karl Ross-

mann, the hero of the (unfinished) novel *Der Verschollene* (*The Boy Who Sank Out of Sight* a.k.a. *Amerika*), which Kafka was writing at the same time as *The Metamorphosis*.

[22, 22] possible to stand
The text raises the impossibility of "spending time" (sich *aufhalten*) with Gregor in a room with closed windows. The MS speaks originally of the impossibility of "putting up with" or "enduring" (*aushalten*) Gregor under such circumstances, but it expresses this thought in an ungrammatical sentence. So strong, however, was the association in Kafka's mind of the anguish of "enduring" Gregor—stronger at first than that of just "spending time" with him—that it momentarily took precedence over grammar. But then the sentence had to be changed.

[22, 28–29] It would not have surprised Gregor
Kafka originally wrote, "It would indeed have been understandable for Gregor" but then substituted a phrase emphasizing Gregor's capacity for passive surprise over his ability to conceptualize his situation.

[23, 6–7] they appreciated his sister's work
Kafka originally wrote, "they admired his sister," then changed the phrase to "they admired his sister's work," then finally chose an expression suggesting a cooler appreciation of her efforts. The Samsas seem hardly capable of admiring their own children; indeed, in this situation, it is understandable that they would find little to admire.

[23, 9–10] waited outside Gregor's room
In place of "Gregor," the original text has "Georg," the name of Kafka's deceased younger brother and the hero of Kafka's great breakthrough story, "The Judgment," which he completed in the early morning of September 23, 1912, around two months before he wrote this line.

[23, 13] a little improvement
At this point, the MS reads: "His father then regularly . . . [broken off] with a quavering voice his mother asked questions: Grete, I'm pleading with you, first wash off your hands, then you can tell us." Kafka thereafter crossed these words out as, perhaps, too trifling, too cozy, too anecdotal. Furthermore, if, as the next sentence indicates, Gregor's mother wants to go to him, then she should not be allowed to express her disgust of Gregor so casually. The mother is, finally, a marginal figure, and Kafka wishes to limit our experience of her (see revision **[24, 38]**, below, p. 51). On the heightening of the Samsas' social status, see revision **[18, 2]**, above, p. 49.

[23, 19] I have to go to him?"
Following these words, the MS has "then a great many things indeed urged Gregor to come to her aid and certainly his appear . . . would have." But Kafka is not yet ready to have Gregor burst out of his room.

[23, 23] taken on such a difficult assignment
In the MS, Kafka wrote, "dared so much," and thereafter evidently
grasped the living truth that the daily care of a family invalid cannot
be compassed under the head of a dare or an adventure: the crucial
point is the heaviness of a constant, a seemingly perpetual task.

[23, 31–32] hanging from the ceiling
A second book edition of *The Metamorphosis* appeared in Leipzig in
1918, containing several variants. It is difficult to decide whether Kafka
had a hand in these changes. In one instance, the preposition found
in the first book edition—*an*, meaning "at"—has been changed to *auf*,
meaning "upon." *An* suggests that Gregor was hanging on to some
point on the ceiling; *auf* pictures Gregor flat out hanging from the
ceiling and reads like an improvement.

[24, 38] in the meantime."
At this point in the MS, Kafka wrote the words "Come, Grete, let's put
the chest of drawers back in its original place." His elision of these lines
is consistent with his practice of eliminating speeches by Gregor's
mother.

[25, 25] by tempting her
The MS has the qualifier "of course unintentionally." Kafka deleted
this phrase, presumably because it conflicts with the "enthusiasm" [*der
schwärmerische Sinn*] at first attributed to Grete, a word which in
German connotes intention or purpose.

[25, 32] to get the chest of drawers out of the room
Kafka revised the nominalized verb from *Herausschaffen* to *Hinaus-
schaffen*, consistent with his narrative strategy of lending objectivity to
the standpoint of the narrator.

[26, 23] soothed his hot belly
The MS shows that Kafka debated between the verbs "cooled" [*kühlte*]
and "did good/soothed" [*wohltat*] and chose the second, which contains
the more explicit sexual connotation.

[26, 42] as if giving up completely
Kafka originally added onto this phrase the dramatic qualifier "and as
if it [the situation] were now entering into the depths [of her]" *or* "and
as if things were now falling into an abyss." He then proposed "and as
if she were toppling into an abyss," before finally deciding to eliminate
any such phrase.

[27, 32] and pressed himself against it
Kafka originally wrote the phrase "got his body into the erect position
[*richtete sich auf*] as fast as he could," then rejected it, perhaps remem-
bering that he had written earlier how difficult it was for Gregor to

raise himself up against the chest of drawers [10] or stand erect against the inside of the door to his room [11–12]. Interestingly, this action reappears a page later [28], where it is attributed to the father. There, he is seen "holding himself very erect," as if, in Kafka's mind, only the father were capable of this potent gesture, and so the phrase *richtete sich auf* must be saved for him. (I owe this perception to Eric Patton.)

[29, 14] embracing him
The MS has "embracing him wildly," which Kafka then eliminated, consistent with his principle of minimizing pathos.

[30, 24–25] the greatest effort
In the midst of composing this sentence, Kafka wrote, in place of the word "effort" [*Mühe*], the "word" *Büch*—which, of course, isn't, properly speaking, a word but only the fragment of a word, *Bücher*, meaning "books." So we have this remarkable emanation from Kafka's "graphic unconscious"—the idea that his father could be persuaded to exchange his armchair for his bed only by means of the greatest "books."

Two thoughts of Kafka seem to come together here (keep in mind the probable date of composition of this sentence: December 1, 1912). The first thought is that with the aid of his books, and only with their aid, Kafka could move his father into another position—one more favorable to himself. In Kafka's breakthrough story "The Judgment," completed on the night of September 22–23, 1912, the hero, the son Georg Bendemann, in a gesture of self-assertion, carries his infantilized father to bed. Secondly, the thought was unquestionably on Kafka's mind that he should soon be able to influence his father by presenting him with a copy of his first published book, *Meditation* (*Betrachtung*). Kafka had begun writing *The Metamorphosis* on November 17, 1912, only two weeks before beginning to correct proofs of this book. Then, a week into the writing of *The Metamorphosis*, he had announced to Felice Bauer the coming appearance of *Meditation*. Finally, on December 10, 1912, three days after completing *The Metamorphosis*, he received a copy of *Meditation* in the mail.

On that day or the next, Kafka very likely showed *Meditation* to his father. Did his father then respond to this gift in the way that Kafka describes him as traditionally responding to his published books? In his *Letter to His Father*, Kafka wrote, "My vanity and my ambition suffered from your way of greeting my books that became famous between us: 'Put it on my bedside table'" (implication: Mr. Kafka would read a page of it before falling asleep; moreover, Franz would be denied audience with his father at the moment of his father's immediate reaction to it) (*Letter to His Father* [*Brief an den Vater*], trans. Ernst Kaiser and Eithne Wilkins [New York: Schocken, 1966] 87 (Translation modified). But Kafka longed literally to persuade his father by means of his books. On the same page of *Letter to His Father*, he wrote: "My writing was all about you; all I did there, after all, was to bemoan what I could not bemoan upon your breast. It was an intentionally long-drawn-out leave-taking from you, yet, although it was enforced by you, it did take its course in the direction determined by me." Hence, the likely association in his mind, during the writing of *The Metamorphosis*, of an "effort" [*Mühe*], "enforced" by his father, to produce "books" [*Bücher*].

[32, 2–3] but instead of helping him and his family,
After these words, Kafka's MS contains this sentence: "they all began, the whole night through/night after night, to genuflect around him, it was impossible to say anything to them," but Kafka eliminated this image, presumably on grounds of its comic extravagance.

[32, 11] into Gregor's room
Another instance where Kafka revised the adverb or verbal prefix—*herein*—to *hinein*, in order to make the report of the action originate from a standpoint farther away from the person occupying the room—i.e., farther away from Gregor's subject-position—but consistent with it.

[32, 13] swept it out
Another instance of Kafka's revising the prefix of the verb from *heraus* to *hinaus*, in order to lend distance to the standpoint of the narrator.

[33, 4] completely taken by surprise
Gregor's being taken by surprise and becoming so agitated upon being observed might seem an excessive, overdetermined reaction, but here Kafka's original formulation helps us to understand what is at stake. Before writing this phrase, Kafka originally described Gregor "as often recently crouching/camping/squatting [*hockte*] on the picture of the lady." The embarrassed sexuality of Gregor's relation to his pinup is evident.

[33, 8] peek in
Here, again, Kafka changed the position of the narrator reporting this action to one at a distance from, but consistent with, that of the subject, Gregor.

[33, 11] "Look at that old dung beetle!"
Kafka originally wrote, "Did he have a bad day today, our old dung beetle." Perhaps Kafka's sense of rigor ruled out the muddled effect of the cleaning woman's trivial, everyday attribution to the animal of a human soul, like a pet owner's to his pet, when Gregor does in fact have a human soul. The tone of the sentence is contradicted, moreover, by the fact that the cleaning woman "credited him with unlimited intelligence" [39].

[33, 19] decrepitly,
Kafka originally wrote "limping," but rejected it, preferring a word

that does not characterize his advance so particularly—and hence so comically.

[33, 23] came crashing down on Gregor's back.
In the MS, Kafka added, "to crush him to bits," then crossed it out, presumably as too graphically violent.

[33, 31] putting in
An example of Kafka's substitution of the prefix *hinein* for *herein* in the verb, producing the effect of distanced, hence objective, reportage.

[33, 35–36] was able to register once through a crack in the door—
Kafka's MS added, "they ate at noon in the common living room," but he rejected this for introducing, at the least, the stylistic fault of having to repeat the word "room" excessively.

[34, 3] to throw out everything together in one fell swoop,
The MS added "nonetheless [however] this did not happen"—a vague phrase, which Kafka eliminated.

[34, 34] It seemed strange to Gregor
Thinking of the hero of his novel-in-progress *The Boy Who Sank Out of Sight*, Kafka wrote the name "Karl" for "Gregor." The reminiscence is understandable, since *The Boy Who Sank Out of Sight* contains rather elaborately detailed descriptions of meals. For example, in the third chapter, "A Country House near New York," Karl, who is little interested in the things being eaten, endures a long dinner, where two older male authority figures dominate.

[35, 44] Her face
At this point, Kafka wrote, "Gregor thought," then eliminated it, in accord with his narrative principle of indirect free style. The report of Grete's face that follows is made from a standpoint that is interchangeably Gregor's and that of an impersonal narrator.

[36, 13] bending her ear down to him,
This is the only place in the MS where Kafka reversed the usual procedure informing his revisions. He substituted the verb prefix *herunter*—one that places the source of the report of the action in or beside Gregor—for the original verb prefix *hinunter*—one that places the source of the report of the action at a distance from Gregor. The substitution makes good sense because the incestuous fantasy is being elaborated by Gregor.

[36, 18] his sister would burst into tears
After "sister," Kafka originally wrote, "without consideration," a phrase that would then belong to Gregor's train of thought. But Kafka rejected this qualifier, as perhaps too flagrantly ironical. For on the previous page [35], it was Gregor who was described memorably as being "with-

out consideration": "It hardly surprised him that lately he was showing so little consideration for the others; once such consideration had been his greatest pride." If Gregor had used this phrase in the MS for Grete, we would now have Gregor too ironically projecting his greatest defect as a valuable attribute of his sister.

[37, 3] gripped by his perverse obstinacy
In the MS, Kafka added, "which could only be a phenomenon of old age," then struck it out, for it is inconsistent with his picture of the father, however old, as harboring an at least virtual vitality.

[37, 43] "We must try to get rid of it,"
Kafka wrote in the MS, "We must try to get rid of him," but then made this change of pronoun sealing Gregor's fate as an insect, an It, eligible for the harshest treatment.

[38, 17] "That's the only answer, Father.
In the MS, Kafka added: "I'll run away from home if it stays here any longer. I thought," then rejected these lines. Gregor's sister, who is here engaged in sentencing him to death, must not be allowed to seem too flighty.

[39, 19] "And now?"
Kafka originally wrote, "Where am I supposed to go now?" But the sentence makes little sense, even as an expression of Gregor's despair. Ever since his change, except for his two excursions into the living room, he has gone nowhere except up and down the floor, walls, and ceiling of his room.

[40, 15] "Dead?" said Mrs. Samsa
For Mrs. Samsa, Kafka wrote, "Mother," then corrected himself. From the bottom of p. 39 on, it is clear that the narrative perspective has changed: it is cleansed of any participation of Gregor's view of things. Gregor, of course, would perceive his mother as "Mother" and certainly not as "Mrs. Samsa." But now Gregor is dead, and the narrative resorts entirely to the view of an impersonal narrator.

[40, 19] Mrs. Samsa made a movement
Again Kafka, consistent with his narrative practice throughout the story up until Gregor's death, wrote, "Mother," for Mrs. Samsa but then corrected himself.

[40, 20] "Well," said Mr. Samsa,
In the same spirit, Kafka wrote, "Father," for Mr. Samsa, then corrected himself.

[40, 24] the way it went in."
Here, too, as in many previous passages, Kafka changed the prefix of the participle to show that the standpoint from which the report is made

is consistent with Gregor's but not to be associated exclusively with it. What Grete says should not suggest her imaginative intimacy with Gregor's situation: hence, the change.

[40, 28–29] said Mrs. Samsa with a melancholy smile,
Here, too, in the MS, Kafka persisted in calling Mrs. Samsa "Mother," then corrected himself.

[41, 9] answered Mr. Samsa
Again, Kafka momentarily called Mr. Samsa "Father."

[41, 14–15] Mr. Samsa merely nodded
Kafka began to write "Fa" for Mr. Samsa, then checked the impulse.

[41, 19–20] interrupt the contact with their leader.
Before finding this formulation, Kafka wrote, "and then they'd be cut off/locked out [abgesperrt] from their friend." Kafka must have smiled before beginning to cross out what he had written: he intended to note the two roomers' fear of being cut off from their leader, but what he said could also refer to their fear of being *locked out* of the room of their "friend" Gregor.

[41, 23] out onto the landing;
Again, Kafka substituted the adverbial prefix *hinaus* for *heraus*, wanting to keep the standpoint of the narrator distanced from the subject occupying the scene.

[41, 35] Mr. Samsa to the management of the bank, Mrs. Samsa to her employer,
Kafka crossed out the more intimate appellations "Father" and "Mother," which would evoke Gregor's point of view.

[41, 37] to say that she was going,
Kafka originally wrote, "to take her leave," but perhaps this struck his ear, with its high style, as evoking a too pat finality—as if, with the death of Gregor, the cleaning woman, too, could now take leave of the story world (forever).

[42, 11] whirled around wildly,
Kafka originally added, "like a top," then eliminated this choice, consistent with his aversion to ornamental figures. See below, pp. 82–83.

[42, 23] into the open country
Kafka wrote at first: "to the most beautiful public park in the city," but then rejected the phrase. Even as a reflection of the point of view of the Samsa family, it could be too kitschy. But more important for Kafka is not to take up again the indirect free style that had earlier merged one distinctive personal viewpoint—namely, Gregor's—with that of the narrator.

[**42**, 27–28] these weren't bad at all,
The same consideration seems to have led Kafka to revise his first choice: "weren't all that bad." Especially in the German, the MS evokes the speech patterns of the Samsas and not that of the more "civilized" narrator.

[**42**, 28] all three positions—
Again, Kafka rejected his first choice: "all three jobs." This is the word that the Samsas would have used among themselves.

[**42**, 40] a good husband.
Kafka originally wrote, "a nice-looking and rich bridegroom," then rejected it as presumably mimicking too closely the familiar diction of the Samsas.

BACKGROUNDS AND CONTEXTS

FRANZ KAFKA

From Wedding Preparations in the Country†

And besides, can't I do it the way I always did as a child when dangerous matters were involved. I don't even have to go to the country myself, it isn't necessary. I'll send [only] my clothed body. [So I shall send this clothed body.] If it staggers to the door on the way out of my room, the staggering will indicate not fear but its nullity. It is also not a sign of excitement if it stumbles on the stairs, if it goes to the country sobbing, and eats its dinner there in tears. For I, I am meanwhile lying in my bed, all covered up with a yellow-brown blanket, exposed to the breeze that blows in through the barely opened window.

* * *

As I lie in bed I assume the shape of a big beetle, a stag beetle or a June beetle, I think.

* * * The form of a big beetle, yes. Then I would pretend it were a matter of hibernating, and I would press my little legs against my bulging body. And I whisper a few words. These are instructions to my sad body, which stands close beside me, bent over. Soon I have finished, it bows, it goes swiftly, and it will do everything the best way possible while I rest.

Letters and Diaries

To Max Brod[1]

October 8, 1912

Dearest Max,

After I had been writing well during the night from Sunday to Monday—I could have gone on writing through the night, and all day, and

---

† Franz Kafka, "Hochzeitsvorbereitungen auf dem Lande," in *Hochzeitsvorbereitungen auf dem Lande und andere Prosa aus dem Nachlaß*, ed. Max Brod (Frankfurt a.M.: Fischer, 1953) 11–12 (translated by the editor of this Norton Critical Edition). This is an unfinished novel, fragments of which survive; Kafka began writing it in 1907, at the age of twenty-four. Words in brackets appear in the text of "Hochzeitsvorbereitungen auf dem Lande," "Fassung [version] A," in Franz Kafka, *Beschreibungen eines Kampfes und andere Schriften aus dem Nachlaß*, nach der Kritischen Ausgabe, ed. Hans-Gerd Koch (Frankfurt a.M.: Fischer Taschenbuch Verlag, 1994) 18.

1. Franz Kafka, *Briefe, 1902–1924*, ed. Max Brod (Frankfurt a.M.: Fischer, 1958) 107–9 (translated by the editor of this Norton Critical Edition). Max Brod (1884–1968) was Kafka's close friend and literary executor and himself a prolific writer.

all night and all day, and finally flown away—and certainly could have
written well today too—one page, really only the last dying breath of
yesterday's ten, is actually finished—I have to stop for the following
reason: My brother-in-law, the factory owner—something which I, in
my happy absent-mindedness [glückliche Zerstreutheit],[2] had hardly
paid attention to—went away early this morning on a business trip that
will last ten days to two weeks. While he is away, the factory is really
entirely in the hands of the manager; and no employer, least of all one
so nervous as my father, would doubt that the most complete fraud is
now being perpetrated in the factory. By the way, I also think so, not
so much, of course, because of worry about the money but because of
ignorance and pangs of conscience. But, finally, even someone not
involved, so far as I can imagine such a person, couldn't doubt very
much that my father's fears are justified, even though I may also not
forget that in the last analysis I cannot see at all why a factory manager
from Germany, even during the absence of my brother-in-law, to whom
he is vastly superior in all technical and organizational questions,
should not be able to keep things running in the same orderly way as
before, since, after all, we are human beings and not thieves. * * *

When I maintained to you once recently that nothing from the outside could disturb my writing (I wasn't boasting, of course; just consol-
ing myself), I was thinking only of how my mother whimpers to me
almost every evening that I really should have a look at the factory once
in a while for my father's peace of mind and how, for his part too, my
father has said the same thing, only much nastier, with looks and in
other indirect ways. Pleading with me and reproaching me in this way
isn't, of course, for the most part, something stupid, since a supervision
of my brother-in-law would certainly do him and the factory a lot of
good; only—and in this lay the undeniable stupidity of all this talk—I
can't carry through this sort of a supervision even in my most lucid
moments.

But it's not a question of this for the next two weeks, when all that
is needed is for any pair of eyes, even if only mine, to wander about
over the factory. And one can't have the slightest objection to their
making this demand precisely of me, for in everyone's opinion I am
mainly responsible [bear the most guilt, trage . . . die Hauptschuld] for
founding the factory—to me, of course, it seems that I must have been
dreaming when I took over this responsibility [debt, Schuld]—and besides there is no one here besides me who could go to the factory, since
my parents, whose going is out of the question anyway for other reasons,
are right now in the middle of their busiest season (the business also
seems to be doing better in the new locale), and today, for example,
my mother didn't even come home for lunch.

2. "Happy absent-mindedness" is Kafka's phrase to describe Gregor Samsa hanging from the
   ceiling of his room [23].

And so, when this evening my mother started in again with the old complaint and, besides referring to my father's getting embittered and sick on account of me [through my fault, *durch meine Schuld*], also brought up this new argument of my brother-in-law's business trip and the complete abandonment of the factory, and when my younger sister too, who at other times does after all back me up with the true feeling that has recently gone over from me to her, in the same breath abandoned me,[3] with a monstrous lack of judgment, right in front of my mother, and when a wave of bitterness—I don't know if it was only gall—went through my whole body, I saw with perfect clarity that the only alternatives I now had were either waiting until everyone had gone to bed and then jumping out of the window or of going to the factory and sitting in my brother-in-law's office every day for the next two weeks. The first would make it possible for me to cast off all responsibility both for interrupting my writing and for abandoning the factory, the second would certainly interrupt my writing—I can't just rub fourteen nights' sleep out of my eyes—and leave me, if I had enough strength of will and hope, with the prospect of perhaps being able to begin again in two weeks where I left off today.

And so I didn't jump out of the window, and even the temptation of turning this letter into a letter of farewell (my ideas for it are running in a different direction) is not very strong. I stood at the window for a long time and pressed myself against the pane, and several times I felt like frightening the toll collector on the bridge with my fall. But the whole time I felt myself too solid for this decision to dash myself to pieces on the pavement to penetrate me to the right, crucial depth. It also seemed to me that staying alive—even when one talks of nothing, nothing, but an interruption—interrupts my writing less than my death, and that between the beginning of my novel[4] and its continuation in two weeks, I shall somehow move about at the heart of my novel and live in it right in the factory, right in the face of my contented parents.

I put the whole story before you, my dearest Max, not perhaps for judgment, for you really can't pass judgment on it, but since I had firmly resolved to jump without a letter of farewell—before the end one is surely allowed to be tired—I wanted, since I am going to walk back into my room again as its occupant, to write you instead a long letter of meeting again, and here it is. And now a final kiss and good night, so that tomorrow I can be boss of a factory, as they want.

Your Franz

3. Grete's abandonment of Gregor at the close of *The Metamorphosis* provokes his death.
4. This is the novel that Kafka called *Der Verschollene* [*The Boy Who Sank Out of Sight*], more familiar under the title that Max Brod gave to it: *Amerika*. It was never finished. It appeared in English as *Amerika: A Novel*, trans. Edwin Muir and Willa Muir (New York: Schocken, 1962).

Tuesday, half-past one o'clock, October 1912
And yet—something I may not conceal either—now that it is morning, I hate them all, each in turn, and think that during these two weeks I shall hardly manage words of greeting for them. But hate—and this will once more go against me—surely belongs more outside the window than quietly sleeping in bed. I am far less sure than I was last night.[5]

To Felice Bauer[6]

November 17, 1912
Dearest, * * * I was simply too miserable to get out of bed. It also seemed to me that last night my novel[7] got much worse, and I lay in the lowest depths. * * * I'll write you again today, even though I still have to run around a lot and shall write down a short story that occurred to me during my misery in bed and oppresses me with inmost intensity.[8]

To Felice Bauer[9]

Night of November 17–18, 1912
Dearest, it is now 1:30 in the morning, the story I proclaimed is a long way from being finished, not a line of the novel has been written today, I am going to bed with little enthusiasm. If only I had the night free and without lifting pen from paper could write right through it till morning! That would be a lovely night.

To Felice Bauer[1]

November 18, 1912
I was just sitting down to yesterday's story with an infinite longing to pour myself into it, obviously stimulated by my despair. Harassed by so

5. Note by Max Brod (translated by the editor): "Without my friend's knowledge, I brought a copy of his letter (without the N.B.) to the attention of his mother, as I was seriously afraid for Franz's life. His mother's reply, as well as further facts important for a judgment of the situation which supplement the *Letter to His Father*, are found on page 113 of my biography." See Max Brod, *Franz Kafka—A Biography*, trans. G. Humphreys Roberts (New York: Schocken, 1947) 91–93. Julie Kafka's reply was full of concern.
6. *Briefe an Felice*, ed. Erich Heller and Jürgen Born (Frankfurt a.M.: Fischer, 1967) 101–2. (All extracts from this volume of letters have been translated by the editor of this Norton Critical Edition, who has consulted *Letters to Felice*, trans. James Stern and Elizabeth Duckworth [New York: Schocken, 1973].) Felice Bauer (1887–1960) was Kafka's fiancée in the year 1914 (the engagement was dissolved) and then again in 1917 (the engagement was again dissolved). During this time, she lived in Berlin and worked as executive secretary of a manufacturer of dictating machines; she was also active in social work. Kafka described her once as a "happy, healthy, self-confident girl." After their relationship ended, Felice married and had two children. She lived with her family in Switzerland and then in the United States until her death.
7. *The Boy Who Sank Out of Sight*.
8. This is the first mention of *The Metamorphosis*.
9. *Briefe an Felice* 102.
1. Ibid. 105.

much, uncertain of you, completely incapable of coping with the office, in view of the novel's being at a standstill for a day with a wild desire to continue the new, equally cautionary story, for several days and nights worrisomely close to complete insomnia, and with some less important but still upsetting and irritating things in my head—in a word, when I went for my evening walk today, which is already down to half an hour, * * * I firmly decided that my only salvation was to write to a man in Silesia whom I got to know fairly well this summer and who, for entire long afternoons, tried to convert me to Jesus.

To Felice Bauer[2]

November 23, 1912

It is very late at night. I have put aside my little story, on which I really haven't done anything at all for two evenings now and which in the stillness is beginning to develop into a bigger story. Give it to you to read? How shall I do that, even if it were already finished? It is written quite illegibly, and even if that weren't an obstacle—for up until now I certainly haven't spoiled you with beautiful handwriting—I still don't want to send you anything to read. I want to read it aloud to you. Yes, that would be fine, to read this story aloud to you and be forced to hold your hand, for the story is a little horrible. It is called *The Metamorphosis*, it would give you a real scare * * * . I am too depressed now, and perhaps I shouldn't have written to you at all. But today the hero of my little story also had a very bad time, and yet this is only the latest rung of his misfortune, which is now becoming permanent.

To Felice Bauer[3]

November 24, 1912

What sort of exceptionally repulsive story is this, which I am now once again putting aside in order to refresh myself with thoughts of you. It has already advanced a bit past the half-way mark, and on the whole I am not dissatisfied with it; but it is infinitely repulsive; and such things, you see, rise up from the same heart in which you dwell and which you put up with as your dwelling place. But don't be unhappy about this, for who knows, the more I write and the more I free myself, the purer and more worthy of you I may become, but no doubt there is still a lot more of me to be gotten rid of, and the nights can never be long enough for this business which, incidentally, is extremely voluptuous.

2. Ibid. 116.
3. Ibid. 117.

To Felice Bauer[4]

November 24, 1912

Now that I've mentioned the trip to Kratzau, I can't get this annoying thought out of my head. My little story would certainly have been finished tomorrow, but now I have to leave at 6 tomorrow evening, arrive at Reichenberg at 10, and go on to Kratzau at 7 the next morning to appear in court.

To Felice Bauer[5]

November 25, 1912

Well, today, dearest, I have to put aside my story, which I didn't work on today nearly as much as yesterday, and on account of the damned Kratzau trip shelve it for a day or two. I'm so unhappy about this, even if, as I hope, the story won't suffer too much, though I still need another 3–4 evenings to finish it. By not "suffering too much," I mean that the story is, unfortunately, already damaged by my method of working on it. This kind of story should be written with at most one interruption, in two ten-hour bouts: then it would have the natural thrust and charge it had in my head last Sunday. But I don't have twice ten hours at my disposal. So one has to try to do the best one can, since the best has been denied to one. What a pity that I can't read it to you—a great pity—for example, every Sunday morning. Not in the afternoon, I wouldn't have time then, that's when I have to write to you.

To Felice Bauer[6]

November 26, 1912

It was a horrible trip, dearest. * * * One should never travel: better be insubordinate at the office if there's work to be done at home that requires all one's strength. This eternal worry, which, incidentally, I still have now, that the trip will harm my little story, that I won't be able to write any more, etc.

To Felice Bauer[7]

November 27, 1912

I sit here all alone in the night, and, as today and yesterday, haven't written particularly well—the story lurches forward rather drearily and monotonously, and the requisite clarity illuminates it only for moments. * * * Now, however, I was firmly determined to use [the Christmas vacation] just for my novel and perhaps even to finish it. Today, when

4. Ibid. 122.
5. Ibid. 125.
6. Ibid. 130.
7. Ibid. 135.

the novel has lain quiet for over a week—and the new story, though
nearing its end, has been trying to convince me for the past two days
that I have gotten stuck—I really should have to keep to that decision
even more firmly.

To Felice Bauer[8]

December 1, 1912

After concluding the struggle with my little story—a third section,
however, quite definitely * * * the last, has begun to take shape—I
must absolutely say good night to you, dearest.

To Felice Bauer[9]

December 1, 1912

Just a few words, it's late, very late, and tomorrow there's a lot of
work to be done; I've finally caught fire a bit with my little story, my
heart wants to drive me with its beating further into it. However, I must
try to get myself out of it as best I can, and since this will be hard work,
and it will be hours before I get to sleep. I must hurry to bed. * * *
Dearest, I wish I could still say something amusing, but nothing occurs
to me naturally; furthermore, on the last page of my story open before
me all 4 characters are crying or at any rate are in a most mournful
mood.

To Felice Bauer[1]

December 3, 1912

I really should have kept on writing all night long. It would have
been my duty, for I'm right at the end of my little story, and uniformity
and the fire of consecutive hours would do this ending an unbelievable
amount of good. Who knows, besides, whether I shall still be able to
write tomorrow after the reading,[2] which I'm cursing now. Nevertheless—I'm stopping, I won't risk it. As a result of my writing, which
I haven't been doing by any means for long with this sort of coherence
and regularity, I have turned from being a by no means exemplary but
in some ways still quite useful employee * * * into a horror for my
boss. My desk in the office was certainly never orderly, but now it is
piled high with a chaotic heap of papers and files. I have a rough idea
of whatever lies on top, but I suspect nothing down below except ter-
rors. Sometimes I think I can almost hear myself being ground to bits
by my writing, on the one hand, and by the office, on the other. Then,

8. Ibid. 145.
9. Ibid. 147.
1. Ibid. 153.
2. Kafka was going to read aloud his story "The Judgment" at an evening event devoted to
Prague writers.

again, there are times when I keep them both relatively well-balanced, especially when at home I've written badly, but I'm afraid I am gradually losing this ability (I don't mean of writing badly).

To Felice Bauer[3]

Night of December 4–5, 1912

Oh dearest, infinitely beloved, it is really too late now for my little story, just as I feared it would be; it will stare up at the sky unfinished until tomorrow night.

To Felice Bauer[4]

Presumably during the night of December 5–6, 1912

Cry, dearest, cry, the time for crying has come! The hero of my little story died a little while ago. If it is of any comfort to you, learn now that he died peaceably enough and reconciled with everything. The story itself is not yet completely finished: I'm no longer in the right mood for it now, and I am leaving the ending for tomorrow. It is also already very late, and I had enough to do to get over yesterday's disturbance.[5] It's a pity that in many passages of the story my states of exhaustion and other interruptions and extraneous worries are clearly inscribed; it could certainly have been done more purely: this can be seen precisely from the charming pages. That is exactly this persistently nagging feeling: I myself, I, with the creative powers that I feel in me, quite apart from their strength and endurance, could in more favorable circumstances of life have achieved a purer, more compelling, better organized work than the one which now exists. It is the one feeling that no amount of reason can dissuade me of, despite the fact, of course, that it is none other than reason that is right—which says that, just as there are no circumstances other than real ones, one cannot take any other ones into account, either. However that may be, I hope to finish the story tomorrow and the day after tomorrow throw myself back onto the novel.[6]

To Felice Bauer[7]

December 6–7, 1912

Dearest, listen now: my little story is finished, but today's ending does not make me happy at all; it really could have been better, no doubt about that.

3. *Briefe an Felice* 155.
4. Ibid. 160.
5. Presumably his reading "The Judgment" aloud at the Prague authors' evening.
6. *The Boy Who Sank Out of Sight.*
7. *Briefe an Felice* 163.

To Felice Bauer[8]

March 1, 1913

Just a few words, dearest. A lovely evening at Max's. I read myself into a frenzy with my story. Then we let ourselves go and laughed a lot.

Diary[9]

October 20, 1913

I have been reading *The Metamorphosis* at home, and I find it bad.

Diary[1]

January 19, 1914

Great antipathy to *The Metamorphosis*. Unreadable ending. Imperfect almost to the core. It would have been much better if I had not been interrupted at the time by the business trip.

To Grete Bloch[2]

April 21, 1914

Whether you might look forward to the "story" [*The Metamorphosis*]? I don't know, you did not like "The Stoker."[3] Still the "story" is looking forward to you, there's no doubt about that. Incidentally, the heroine's name is Grete, and she does not dishonor you, at least not in the first part. Later on, though, when the torment becomes too great, she gives up and starts a life of her own, abandoning the one who needs her. An old story, by the way, more than a year old; at that time I hadn't begun to appreciate the name Grete and learned to do so only in the course of writing the story.

Diary[4]

August 6, 1914

From the standpoint of literature my fate is very simple. The sense for the representation of my dreamlike inner life has rendered everything else trivial, and it has withered in a terrible way and does not

---

8. Ibid. 320.
9. *Tagebücher*, ed. Max Brod (Frankfurt a.M.: Fischer, 1951) 323 (translated by the editor of this Norton Critical Edition). The student may consult *The Diaries of Franz Kafka, 1910–1913*, trans. Joseph Kresh (New York: Schocken, 1948), and *The Diaries of Franz Kafka, 1914–1923*, trans. Martin Greenberg (New York: Schocken, 1949).
1. Ibid. 351.
2. *Briefe an Felice* 561. Grete Bloch (1892–1943?) was a Berlin friend of Felice Bauer; Kafka got to know her in Prague in 1913, when she came to act as an intermediary in their troubled relationship. She was probably murdered in a Nazi concentration camp.
3. The first chapter of Kafka's unfinished, "unfortunate" novel *The Boy Who Sank Out of Sight*, published separately to critical acclaim.
4. *Tagebücher* 420.

stop withering. Nothing else can ever satisfy me. But my strength for that representation is not to be counted on, perhaps it has already vanished forever, perhaps it actually will come over me once again; the circumstances of my life by no means favor its return. And so I waver, fly incessantly to the summit of the mountain but can keep myself on top for hardly a moment. Others waver too, but in lesser regions, with greater powers; if they threaten to fall, they are caught up by the kinsman who walks beside them for this purpose. But I waver on the heights; it is not a death, alas, but the eternal torments of dying.

To Kurt Wolff Publishing Company[5]

Dear Sir, You recently wrote that Ottomar Starke is going to do an illustration for the title page of *The Metamorphosis*. Now I have had a slight * * * probably wholly unnecessary shock. It occurred to me that Starke * * * might want, let us say, to draw the insect itself. Not that, please, not that! I don't want to restrict his authority but only to make this request from my own naturally better knowledge of the story. The insect itself cannot be drawn. It cannot even be shown at a distance. * * * If I might make suggestions for an illustration I would choose such scenes as the parents and the office manager in front of the closed door or, even better, the parents and the sister in the room with the lights on, while the door to the totally dark adjoining room is open.

To Felice Bauer[6]

October 7, 1916

Dearest, * * * Incidentally, won't you tell me what I really am? In the latest issue of the *Neue Rundschau*, *The Metamorphosis* is mentioned and rejected on reasonable grounds; then there are these lines, more or less: "There is something *ur*-German about K's art of narration."[7] In Max's essay, on the other hand, "K's narratives are among the most Jewish documents of our time." A painful case. Am I a circus rider on 2 horses? Unfortunately, I'm not a rider, but lie prostrate on the ground.

---

5. *Franz Kafka, Briefe* 135–36 (translated by the editor of this Norton Critical Edition).
6. *Briefe an Felice* 719–20.
7. The *Neue Rundschau* was an influential literary journal, a weekly edited in Vienna by the novelist Robert Musil (1880–1939). *Ur* is a prefix meaning "originally" or "primordially."

To Felice Bauer[8]

December 7, 1916

Incidentally, in Prague I also remembered Rilke's words.[9] After some very kind things about "The Stoker" he said that neither in *The Metamorphosis* nor in "In the Penal Colony" had the same rigor [*Konsequenz*] been achieved. This remark is not immediately understandable, but it is perceptive.

Letter to His Father[1]

November 1919

[Kafka imagines his father speaking to him].

You have in fact gotten it into your head to live completely off me. I admit that we are fighting with each other, but there are two kinds of fighting. The chivalrous fight, where the powers of independent opponents compete with each other: each is his own man, loses on his own, wins on his own. And the fight of the vermin, which not only stings but also sucks blood for its self-preservation. That is after all what the real professional soldier is, and that's what you are. You are unfit for life; but in order to be able to settle down in it comfortably, without worries and without self-reproaches, you prove that I took all your fitness for life out of you and put it into my pocket. What does it matter to you now if you're unfit for life: it's my responsibility. But you calmly stretch yourself out and let yourself be dragged body and soul through life by me.

Letter to Elli Hermann[2]

Fall 1921

What Swift means [by the sentence "Parents are the last of all others to be trusted with the education of their own children"][3] is:
Every typical family at first represents only an animal connection, to

8. *Briefe an Felice* 744.
9. Rainer Maria Rilke (1875–1926), perhaps the greatest German lyric poet of the twentieth century and author of the modernist novel *The Notebooks of Malte Laurids Brigge* (1910). He was born in Prague but wrote mostly in Germany, France, and Switzerland. He was an admirer of Kafka's work. Cf. *Letters to Felice* 577. An acquaintance of Rilke, Lou Albert-Lasard (1891–1969), an eminent portrait painter, declared that Rilke had read *The Metamorphosis* aloud to her (*Wege mit Rilke* [Frankfurt a.M.: Fischer, 1952] 43). Cf. *Briefe an Felice* 744.
1. "Brief an den Vater," in *Hochzeitsvorbereitungen auf dem Lande* 221–22 (translated by the editor of this Norton Critical Edition).
2. Franz Kafka, *Briefe* 344–45 (translated by the editor of this Norton Critical Edition). Elli (Gabriele) Hermann (b. 1889) was Kafka's oldest sister. In October 1941, together with her husband and children, she was deported by the Nazis to the Lodz ghetto, where she subsequently perished.
3. Jonathan Swift, *Gulliver's Travels* ("A Voyage to Lilliput," Part I, Chap. 6) (London: Methuen, 1960) 48. Swift (1667–1745) was a great Anglo-Irish satirical writer.

a certain extent a single organism, a single bloodstream. Thus, thrown back only upon itself, it cannot get beyond itself; it cannot create a new human being only from itself; if it tries to do so through family education, it is a kind of spiritual incest.

The family, then, is an organism, but an extremely complicated and unstable one; like every organism it too continually strives for equilibrium. To the extent that this striving for equilibrium goes on between parents and children, * * * it is called education. Why it is called that is incomprehensible, for there is no trace here of real education, that is, the calm, selflessly-loving unfolding of the abilities of a developing human being or even the calm tolerance of its independent unfolding. Rather, it is precisely only the mostly convulsive attempt of an animal organism to achieve equilibrium one that for many years at least has been condemned to the most acute instability and which in distinction to the individual human animal can be called the family animal.

The reason for the absolute impossibility of immediately achieving a just equilibrium (and only a just equilibrium is a true equilibrium, only it can endure) within this family animal is the unequal rank of its parts, that is, the monstrous dominance of the parent pair over the children for many years. As a result, while their children are growing up, the parents arrogate to themselves the sole prerogative of representing the family not only to the outside world but also within the inner spiritual organization: thus they deprive their children, step by step, of the right to their own personality and from then on can make them incapable of ever asserting this right in a healthy way, a misfortune which can later befall the parents not much less gravely than the children.

The essential difference between real education and family education is that the first is a human affair, the second a family affair. In the human world every individual has his place or at least the possibility of being destroyed in his own fashion, but in a family in the clutches of the parents, only quite particular kinds of individuals have a place —those who conform to quite particular demands and furthermore to the deadlines imposed by the parents. If they don't conform, they are not, say, cast out—that would be very fine, but it is impossible, for after all we are dealing with an organism—but are instead cursed or devoured or both. This devouring doesn't happen physically as in the case of the old archetype of the parent in Greek mythology (Kronos, who gobbled up his sons—that most honest of fathers), but perhaps Kronos preferred his method to the usual ones precisely out of pity for his children.

Letter to Max Brod[4]

July 5, 1922

I am, to put it first quite generally, afraid of the trip. * * * But it is not fear of the trip itself. * * * Rather, it is the fear of change, fear of attracting the attention of the gods to myself by an act great for my condition.

When during last night's sleepless night I let everything run back and forth again and again between my aching temples, I once more became aware of what I had almost forgotten in the relative calm of the past days—what a weak or even nonexistent ground I live on, over a darkness out of which the dark power emerges when it wills and, without bothering about my stammering, destroys my life. Writing maintains me, but isn't it more correct to say that it maintains this sort of life? Of course I don't mean by this that my life is better when I don't write. Rather it is much worse then and wholly intolerable and must end in madness. But that [is true], of course, only under the condition that I, as is actually the case, even when I don't write, am a writer; and a writer who doesn't write is, to be sure, a monster [*Unding*] asking for madness.

But what is it to be a writer? Writing is a sweet, wonderful reward, but its price? During the night the answer was transparently clear to me: it is the reward for service to the devil. This descent to the dark powers, this unbinding of spirits by nature bound, dubious embraces and whatever else may go on below, of which one no longer knows anything above ground, when in the sunlight one writes stories. Perhaps there is another kind of writing, I only know this one; in the night, when anxiety does not let me sleep, I know only this. And what is devilish in it seems to me quite clear. It is vanity and the craving for enjoyment, which is forever whirring around one's own form or even another's—the movement then multiplies itself, it becomes a solar system of vanities—and enjoys it. What a naive person sometimes wishes: "I would like to die and watch the others cry over me," is what such a writer constantly experiences: he dies (or he does not live) and continually cries over himself. From this comes a terrible fear of death, which does not have to manifest itself as the fear of death but can also emerge as the fear of change * * *.

The reasons for his fear of death can be divided into two main groups. First, he is terribly afraid of dying because he hasn't yet lived. By this I don't mean that to live, wife and child and field and cattle are necessary. What is necessary for life is only the renunciation of self-delight: to move into the house instead of admiring it and decking it with wreathes. Countering this, one could say that that is fate and put into no man's hands. But then why does one feel remorse, why doesn't

4. *Briefe* 383–86.

the remorse stop? To make oneself more beautiful, more tasty? That too. But why, over and beyond this, in such nights, is the keyword always: I could live, but I do not.

The second main reason—perhaps there is only the one, at the moment I can't quite tell the two apart—is the consideration: "What I have played at will really happen. I have not ransomed myself by writing. All my life I have been dead, and now I shall really die. My life was sweeter than that of the others, my death will be that much more terrible. The writer in me of course will die at once, for such a figure has no basis, has no substance, isn't even of dust; it is only a little bit possible in the maddest earthly life, it is only a construction of the craving for enjoyment. This is the writer. But I myself cannot live on, as indeed I have not lived, I have remained clay, I have not turned the spark into a fire but used it only for the illumination of my corpse." It will be a peculiar burial: the writer, hence, a thing without existence, consigns the old corpse, corpse from the beginning, to the grave. I am enough of a writer to want to enjoy it with all my senses, in total self-forgetfulness—not wakefulness, self-forgetfulness is the first prerequisite of literature—or what amounts to the same thing, to want to tell the story of it, but that won't happen any more. But why do I speak only of real dying? It is after all the same thing in life. I sit here in the comfortable position of the writer, ready for anything beautiful, and must watch idly—for what can I do besides write—as my real self, this poor defenseless being (the writer's existence is an argument against the soul, for the soul has evidently abandoned the real self, but has only become a writer, has not been able to get any further; ought its parting from the self be able to weaken the soul so much?) for any old reason, now, for a little trip * * * , is pinched, thrashed, and almost ground to bits by the devil. What right have I to be shocked, I who was not at home, when the house suddenly collapses; for do I know what preceded the collapse, didn't I wander off, abandoning the house to all the powers of evil?

GUSTAV JANOUCH

From Conversations with Kafka†

I took the English book out of my pocket and laid it on the bedcover in front of Kafka. * * * When I said that Garnett's[1] book imitated the

---

† From *Conversations with Kafka*, trans. Goronwy Rees (New York: New Directions, 1971) 22, 31–32 (translation modified by the editor of this Norton Critical Edition). Reprinted by permission of the New Directions Publishing Corporation and Andre Deutsch Ltd. Copyright © 1968 by S. Fischer Verlag, GmbH, Frankfurt am Main.
1. David Garnett, *Lady into Fox* (London: Chatto & Windus, 1922).

method of *The Metamorphosis*, he gave a tired smile, and with a faint, disclaiming movement of his hand said: "Oh no! He didn't get that from me. It's in the times. We both copied it from that. Animals are closer to us than human beings. That is the bars of the cage. We find relations easier with animals than with men."

*   *   *

My friend Alfred Kämpf * * * admired Kafka's story *The Metamorphosis*. He described the author as "a new, more profound and therefore more significant Edgar Allan Poe."

During a walk with Franz Kafka on the Altstädter Ring I told him about his new admirer of his, but aroused neither interest nor understanding. On the contrary, Kafka's expression showed that any discussion of his book was distasteful to him. I, however, was filled with a craving for discoveries, and so I was tactless.

"The hero of the story is called Samsa," I said. "It sounds like a cryptogram for Kafka. Five letters in each word. The S in the word Samsa has the same position as the K in the word Kafka. The A . . ."

Kafka interrupted me.

"It is not a cryptogram. Samsa is not merely Kafka, and nothing else. *The Metamorphosis* is not a confession, although it is—in a certain sense—an indiscretion."

"I know nothing about that."

"Is it perhaps delicate and discreet to talk about the bedbugs in one's own family?"

"It isn't usual in good society."

"You see what bad manners I have."

Kafka smiled. He wished to dismiss the subject. But I did not wish to.

"It seems to me that the distinction between good and bad manners hardly applies here," I said. *"The Metamorphosis* is a terrible dream, a terrible conception."

Kafka stood still.

"The dream reveals the reality, which conception lags behind. That is the horror of life—the terror of art. But now I must go home."

He took a curt farewell.

Had I driven him away?

I felt ashamed.

CRITICISM

STANLEY CORNGOLD

Kafka's *The Metamorphosis*:
Metamorphosis of the Metaphor†

What *is* literature? Where does it come from? What use is it? What questionable things! Add to this questionableness the further questionableness of what
you say, and what you get is a monstrosity.

FRANZ KAFKA, Dearest Father

To judge from its critical reception, Franz Kafka's *The Metamorphosis* (*Die Verwandlung*) is the most haunting and universal of all his
stories, and yet Kafka never claimed for it any special distinction. He
never, for example, accorded it the importance he reserved for "The
Judgment," a work it resembles but which it surpasses in depth and
scope.[1] On the morning of September 23, 1912, after the night he spent
composing "The Judgment," Kafka, with a fine elation, wrote in his
diary: "Only *in this way* can writing be done, only with such coherence,
with such a complete opening out of the body and the soul" (DI 276).
But throughout the period of the composition of *The Metamorphosis*—
from November 17 to December 7, 1912—and until the beginning of
the new year, his diary does not show an entry of any kind; and when
it resumes on February 11, 1913, it is with an interpretation not of *The
Metamorphosis* but of "The Judgment." The diary does finally acknowledge the new story, almost a year after its composition, with this remark:
"I have been reading *The Metamorphosis* at home, and I find it bad" [69].

Kafka was especially disappointed with the conclusion of the story.
On January 19, 1914, he wrote, "Great antipathy to *The Metamorphosis*.
Unreadable ending" [69], and he blamed the botched conclusion on
a business trip he was obliged to make just as he was well advanced
into the piece. His annoyance and remorse at having to interrupt his
work is vivid in the letters written at the time to his fiancée, Felice
Bauer. These letters reveal Kafka's moods all during the composition
of the story—moods almost entirely negative. The story originates "during my misery in bed and oppresses me with inmost intensity" [*inner-
lichst bedrängt*]" ([64] (BF 102). The tonality of the piece appears again
as "despair" [64] and "monotony" [66]. On November 23 the story is

† Adapted from *Franz Kafka: The Necessity of Form*, (Ithaca: Cornell, 1988) 47–80 (1970, rev.
1986). Used by permission of the publisher, Cornell University Press. Copyright © 1988 by
Cornell University. Norton Critical Edition page numbers appear in brackets.
1. Elias Canetti wrote: "In *The Metamorphosis* Kafka reached the height of his mastery: he wrote
something which he could never surpass, because there is nothing which *The Metamorphosis*
could be surpassed by—one of the few great, perfect poetic works of this century" (*Der andere
Prozeß: Kafkas Briefe an Felice* [Munich: Hanser, 1969], pp. 22–23).

said to be "a little horrible [*fürchterlich*]" (BF 116) [65]; a day later, "exceptionally repulsive" [65]. A trace of liking and concern for *The Metamorphosis* appears in a later letter: "It's a pity that in many passages of the story my states of exhaustion and other interruptions and extraneous worries are clearly inscribed [*eingezeichnet*]; it could certainly have been done more purely [*reiner*]; this can be seen precisely from the charming [*süße*] pages" (BF 160) [68]. But by this time Kafka has begun to consider *The Metamorphosis* more and more an interruption of the writing of the uncompleted novel that was to become *Amerika*. Finally, on the morning of December 7, he states the complaint that will recur: "My little story is finished, but today's ending does not make me happy at all; it really could have been better, no doubt about that" [68].

Kafka's own sense of *The Metamorphosis* compels us to consider the work essentially unfinished. The interruptions that set in so frequently past the midpoint of the story tend to shift the weight of its significance back toward its beginning. This view draws support from other evidence establishing what might be termed the general and fundamental priority of the beginning in Kafka's works. One thinks of the innumerable openings to stories scattered throughout the diaries and notebooks, suddenly appearing and as swiftly vanishing, leaving undeveloped the endless dialectical structures they contain. On October 16, 1921, Kafka explicitly invoked "the misery of having perpetually to begin, the lack of the illusion that anything is more than, or even as much as, a beginning" (DII 193). For Dieter Hasselblatt, Kafka's prose "is in flight from the beginning, it does not strive toward the end: *initiofugal*, not final. And since it takes the impulse of its progression from what is set forth or what is just present at the outset, it cannot be completed. The end, the conclusion, is unimportant compared to the opening situation."[2]

One is directed, it would seem, by these empirical and theoretical considerations to formulate the overwhelming question of *The Metamorphosis* as the question of the meaning of its beginning. What fundamental intention inspires the opening sentence: "When Gregor Samsa woke up one morning from unsettling dreams, he found himself changed in his bed into a monstrous vermin [*ungeheueres Ungeziefer*]" (M 3; E 71) [3]? We shall do well to keep in mind, in the words of Edward Said, "the identity [of the beginning] as *radical* starting point; the intransitive and conceptual aspect, that which has no object but its own constant clarification."[3] Much of the action of *The Metamorphosis* consists of Kafka's attempt to come to terms with its beginning.

2. Dieter Hasselblatt, *Zauber und Logik: Eine Kafka Studie* (Cologne: Verlag Wissenschaft und Politik), p. 61.
3. Edward Said, "Beginnings," *Salmagundi*, Fall 1968, p. 49.

The opening recounts the transformation of a man into a monstrous, verminous bug; in the process, it appears to accomplish still another change: it metamorphoses a common figure of speech. This second transformation emerges in the light of the hypothesis proposed in 1947 by Günther Anders: "Kafka's sole point of departure is . . . *ordinary language*. . . . More precisely: *he draws from the resources on hand, the figurative nature [Bildcharakter], of language.* He takes metaphors at their word [*beim Wort*]. For *example*: Because Gregor Samsa wants to live as an artist [i.e. as a *Luftmensch*—one who lives on air, lofty and free-floating], in the eyes of the highly respectable, hard-working world he is a 'nasty bug [*dreckiger Käfer*]': and so in *The Metamorphosis* he wakes up as a beetle whose ideal of happiness is to be sticking to the ceiling." For Anders, *The Metamorphosis* originates in the transformation of a familiar metaphor into a fictional being having the literal attributes of this figure. The story develops as aspects of the metaphor are enacted in minute detail. Anders's evidence for this view is furnished partly by his total understanding of Kafka: "What Kafka describes are . . . existing things, the world, as it appears to the stranger (namely strange)." Anders further adduces examples of everyday figures of speech which, taken literally, inspire stories and scenes in Kafka. "Language says, 'To feel it with your own body [*Am eignen Leibe etwas erfahren*]' when it wants to express the reality of experience. This is the basis of Kafka's *In the Penal Colony*, in which the criminal's punishment is not communicated to him by word of mouth, but is instead scratched into his body with a needle."[4]

Anders's hypothesis has been taken up in Walter Sokel's studies of *The Metamorphosis*. The notion of the "extended metaphor," which Sokel considers in an early essay to be "significant" and "interesting" though "insufficient as a total explanation of *The Metamorphosis*,"[5] re-emerges in his *Writer in Extremis* as a crucial determinant of Expressionism: "The character Gregor Samsa has been transformed into a metaphor that states his essential self, and this metaphor in turn is treated like an actual fact. Samsa does not call himself a cockroach; instead he wakes up to find himself one." Expressionistic prose, for Sokel, is defined precisely by such "extended metaphors, metaphoric visualizations of emotional situations, uprooted from any explanatory context."[6] In *Franz Kafka: Tragik und Ironie*, the factual character of the Kafkan metaphor is emphasized: "In Kafka's work, as in the dream,

4. Günther Anders, *Kafka—Pro und Contra* (Munich: Beck, 1951), pp. 40–41, 20, 41. For an English version (not a literal translation), see Günther Anders, *Franz Kafka*, trans. A. Steer and A. K. Thorlby (London: Bowes & Bowes, 1960). The translations here are mine.
5. Walter Sokel, "Kafka's 'Metamorphosis': Rebellion and Punishment," *Monatshefte 40* (April–May 1956): 203.
6. Walter Sokel, *The Writer in Extremis: Expressionism in Twentieth-Century Literature* (Stanford, Calif.: Stanford University Press, 1959), pp. 47, 46.

symbol is fact. . . . A world of pure significance, of naked expression, is represented deceptively as a sequence of empirical facts."[7] Finally, in his *Franz Kafka*, Sokel states the most advanced form of his understanding of Kafka's literalization of the metaphor:

> German usage applies the term *Ungeziefer* (vermin) to persons considered low and contemptible, even as our usage of "cockroach" describes a person deemed a spineless and miserable character. The traveling salesman Gregor Samsa, in Kafka's *Metamorphosis*, is "like a cockroach" because of his spineless and abject behavior and parasitic wishes. However, Kafka drops the word "like" and has the metaphor become reality when Gregor Samsa wakes up finding himself turned into a giant vermin. With this metamorphosis, Kafka reverses the original act of metamorphosis carried out by thought when it forms metaphor; for metaphor is always "metamorphosis." Kafka transforms metaphor back into his fictional reality, and this counter-metamorphosis becomes the starting point of his tale.[8]

The sequence of Sokel's reflections on Anders's hypothesis contains an important shift of emphasis. Initially, the force of *The Metamorphosis* is felt to lie in the choice and "extension" (dramatization) of the powerful metaphor. To support his view, Sokel cites Johannes Urzidil's recollection of a conversation with Kafka: "Once Kafka said to me: 'To be a poet means to be strong in metaphors. The greatest poets were always the most metaphorical ones. They were those who recognized the deep mutual concern, yes, even the identity of things between which nobody noticed the slightest connection before. It is the range and the scope of the metaphor which makes one a poet.' "[9] But in his later work Sokel locates the origin of Kafka's "poetry" not in the metamorphosis of reality accomplished by the metaphor but in the "counter-metamorphosis" accomplished by the transformation of the metaphor. Kafka's "taking over" figures from ordinary speech enacts a second metaphorization (*metapherá* = "a transfer")—one that concludes in the literalization and hence the metamorphosis of the metaphor.[1] This point once made, the genuine importance of Kafka's remarks to Urzidil stands revealed through their irony. In describing the poet as one "strong in metaphors," Kafka is describing writers other than himself; for he is the writer par excellence who came to detect in metaphorical language a crucial obstacle to his own enterprise.

Kafka's critique of the metaphor begins early, in the phantasmagoric

7. Walter Sokel, *Franz Kafka: Tragik und Ironie, Zur Struktur seiner Kunst* (Frankfurt am Main: Fischer Taschenbuch, 1983), p. 110.
8. Walter Sokel, *Franz Kafka* (New York: Columbia University Press, 1966), p. 5.
9. Walter Sokel, "Kafka's 'Metamorphosis,'" 205. John [sic] Urzidil, "Recollections," in *The Kafka Problem*, ed. Angel Flores (New York: Octagon, 1963), p. 22.
1. Anders, *Kafka*, p. 42.

story "Description of a Struggle" (1904–5). The first-person narrator addresses the supplicant—another persona of the author—with exaggerated severity:

> Now I realize, by God, that I guessed from the very beginning the state you are in. Isn't it something like a fever, a seasickness on land, a kind of leprosy? Don't you feel that it's this very feverishness which is preventing you from being properly satisfied with the genuine [*wahrhaftigen*] names of things, and that now, in your frantic haste, you're just pelting them with any old [*zufällige*] names? You can't do it fast enough. But hardly have you run away from them when you've forgotten the names you gave them. The poplar in the fields, which you've called the "Tower of Babel" because you didn't want to know it was a poplar, sways again without a name, so you have to call it "Noah in his cups." [DS 60]

The weight of these accusations falls on the character who is dissatisfied with the "genuine" names of things and substitutes metaphors for them. His action is doubly arbitrary. First, the motive that prompts him to rename things—the act that generates figures—is arbitrary. His metaphors are the contingent product of a fever; or worse, they arise from deliberate bad faith, the refusal to accept the conventional bond of word and thing. Second, not a single one of his metaphors is any good, none leaves a permanent trace.

But what is also striking about this passage is its critique of "ordinary" as well as figurative names. With the irony of overstatement, the accusatory speaker calls the conventional link of name and thing "genuine," despite the fact that he does not appear to have at his disposal any such genuine names to identify the affliction of the supplicant. The speaker suffers from the same unhappy necessity of designating things by an enchainment of "any old" metaphors—such as "fever," "seasickness on dry land," "a kind of leprosy." Because (as Derrida says) "language is fundamentally metaphorical," figuring, in Heidegger's phrase, the "significations to which words accrue" as the significations within words, a critique of metaphor amounts logically to a critique of naming.[2] The exact difference between ordinary names and figurative names cannot be specified. Kafka's speaker, while seeing no advantage in replacing names with the figures of poetic language, at the same time cannot enact naming except by associating metaphors. Metaphors falsify, and they also invade "genuine" names.[3]

2. Jacques Derrida, "Violence et Métaphysique," *L'ecriture et la différence* (Paris: Seuil, 1967), p. 137; Martin Heidegger, "Den Bedeutungen wachsen Worte zu," in *Sein und Zeit* (Tübingen: Klostermann, 1963), p. 161.
3. This suspicious critique of metaphor is proto-Expressionist. It will be taken up again and again by Expressionist writers—e.g., Carl Einstein, writing retrospectively: "Metaphor and metaphoricity refer to more than an isolated literary process; they characterize a general mood and attitude. In the metaphor one avoids repeating facts and weakens contact with reality. Meta-

In a diary entry for December 27, 1911, Kafka recorded his despair of a particular attempt at metaphor. "An incoherent assumption is thrust like a board between the actual feeling and the metaphor of the description" (DI 201). Kafka had begun this diary entry confidently, claiming to have found an image analogous to a moral sentiment. "My feeling when I write something that is wrong might be depicted as follows": A man stands before two holes in the ground, one to the right and one to the left; he is waiting for something that can rise up only out of the hole to the right. Instead, apparitions rise, one after the other, from the left; they try to attract his attention and finally even succeed in covering up the right-hand hole. At this stage of the construction, the materiality of the image predominates; as it is developed, however, so is the role of the spectator, who scatters these apparitions upward and in all directions in the hope "that after the false apparitions have been exhausted, the true will finally appear." But precisely at the point of conjuring up "truthful apparitions," the metaphorist feels most critically the inadequacy of this figurative language: "How weak this picture is." And he concludes with the complaint that between his sentiment and figurative language there is no true coherence (though he cannot, predictably, say this without having recourse to a figure of speech). Now what is crucial here is that an image that is mainly material has failed to represent the sentiment of writing; and though it has been replaced by one that introduces the consciousness of an observer, between the moral sentiment of writing and an act of perception there is also no true connection. If the writer finds it difficult to construct metaphors for "a feeling of falsity," how much greater must be his difficulty in constructing figures for genuine feelings, figures for satisfying the desire "to write all my anxiety entirely out of me, write it into the depths of the paper just as it comes out of the depths of me, or write it down in such a way that I could draw what I have written into me completely" (DI 173).

Kafka's awareness of the limitations of metaphorical language continues to grow. The desire to represent a state of mind directly in language—in a form consubstantial with that consciousness—and hence to create symbols cannot be gratified. "For everything outside the phenomenal world, language can only be used allusively [as an allusion, *andeutungsweise*] but never even approximately in a comparative way [as a simile, *vergleichsweise*], since, corresponding as it does to the phenomenal world, it is concerned only with property and its relations" (DF 40; H 45). But try as language will to reduce itself to its allusive function, it continues to be dependent on the metaphor, on developing states of mind by means of material analogues. On December 6, 1921,

---

phoricity is justified by the illusion of arbitrarily creating something new at every moment. The literati lost a sense of factual events and trusted in the empty power of their words" (*Die Fabrikationen der Fiktionen*, ed. Sibylle Penkert [Hamburg: Rowohlt, 1973], p. 283).

Kafka wrote: "Metaphors are one among many things which make me despair of writing. Writing's lack of independence of the world, its dependence on the maid who tends the fire, on the cat warming itself by the stove; it is even dependent on the poor old human being warming himself by the stove. All these are independent activities ruled by their own laws; only writing is helpless, cannot live in itself, is a joke and a despair" (DII 200–201). Indeed, the question arises of what truth even a language determinedly nonsymbolic—in Kafka's words, "allusive"—could possess. The parable employs language allusively, but in the powerful fable "On Parables" Kafka writes: "All these parables really set out to say merely that the incomprehensible is incomprehensible, and we know that already" (GW 258). At this point, it is clear, the literary enterprise is seen in its radically problematical character. The growing desperation of Kafka's critique of metaphorical language leads to the result—in the words of Maurice Blanchot—that at this time of Kafka's life "the exigency of the truth of this other world [of sheer inwardness determined on salvation] henceforth surpasses in his eyes the exigency of the work of art."[4] This situation suggests not the renunciation of writing but only the clearest possible awareness of its limitations, an awareness that emerges through Kafka's perplexity before the metaphor in the work of art and his despair of escaping it.

Kafka's "counter-metamorphosis" of the metaphor in *The Metamorphosis* is inspired by his fundamental objection to the metaphor. His purpose is accomplished—so Anders and Sokel propose—through the literalization of the metaphor. But is this true? What does it mean, exactly, to literalize a metaphor? The metaphor designates something (A) *as* something (B)—something in the quality of something not itself. To say that someone is a verminous bug is to designate a moral sensibility as something unlike itself, as a material sensation—complicated, of course, by the atmosphere of loathing that this sensation evokes. With I. A. Richards, I shall call the *tenor* of the metaphor (A), the thing designated, occulted, replaced, but otherwise established by the context of the figure; and the *vehicle*, the metaphor proper, (B), that thing *as* which the tenor is designated.[5] If the metaphor is taken out of context, however, if it is taken literally, it no longer functions as a vehicle but as a name, directing us to (B) as an abstraction or an object in the world. Moreover, it directs us to (B) in the totality of its qualities and not, as does the vehicle, only to those qualities of (B) that can be assigned to (A).

4. Maurice Blanchot, "The Diaries: The Exigency of the Work of Art," trans. Lyall H. Powers, in *Franz Kafka Today*, ed. Angel Flores and Homer Swander (Madison: University of Wisconsin Press, 1964), p. 207.
5. In other words, the tenor of a metaphor is the thing or person it means; the vehicle is its immediate, literal content. See I. A. Richards, *The Philosophy of Rhetoric* (New York: Oxford University Press, 1936), p. 96.

This analysis will suggest the destructively paradoxical consequence of "taking the metaphor literally," supposing now that such a thing is possible. Reading the figure literally, we go to (B) as an object in the world in its totality; yet reading it metaphorically, we go to (B) only in its quality as a predicate of (A). As literalization proceeds, as we attempt to experience in (B) more and more qualities that can be accommodated by (A), we *metamorphose* (A). But if the metaphor is to be preserved and (A) and (B) are to remain unlike, we must stop before the metamorphosis is complete. If, now, the tenor—as in *The Metamorphosis*—is a human consciousness, the increasing literalization of the vehicle transforms the tenor into a monster.

This genesis of monsters occurs independently of the nature of the vehicle. The intent toward literalization of a metaphor linking a human consciousness and a material sensation produces a monster in every instance, no matter whether the vehicle is odious or not, whether we begin with the metaphor of a "louse" or of a man who is a "jewel" or a "rock." It now appears that Anders is not correct in suggesting that in *The Metamorphosis* literalization of the metaphor is actually accomplished; for then we should have not an indefinite monster but simply a bug. Indeed, the continual alteration of Gregor's body suggests ongoing metamorphosis, the *process* of literalization in various directions and not its end state. Nor would Sokel's earlier formulation appear to be tenable: the metaphor is not treated "like an actual fact." Only the alien cleaning woman gives Gregor Samsa the factual, entomological identity of a "dung beetle," but precisely "to forms of address like these Gregor would not respond" (M 45) [33]. The cleaning woman does not know that a metamorphosis has occurred, that within this insect shape there is a human consciousness—one superior at times to the ordinary consciousness of Gregor Samsa. It appears, then, that the metamorphosis in the Samsa household of man into vermin is unsettling not only because vermin are disturbing, or because the vivid representation of a human "louse" is disturbing, but because the indeterminate, fluid crossing of a human tenor and a material vehicle is in itself unsettling. Gregor is at one moment pure rapture and at another very nearly pure dung beetle, at times grossly human and at times airily buglike. In shifting incessantly the relation of Gregor's mind and body, Kafka shatters the suppositious unity of ideal tenor and bodily vehicle within the metaphor. This destruction must distress common sense, which defines itself by such "genuine" relations, such natural assertions of analogues between consciousness and matter, and in this way masks the knowledge of its own strangeness. The ontological legitimation for asserting analogues is missing in Kafka, who maintains the most ruthless division between the fire of the spirit and the "filth" of the world: "What we call the world of the senses is the Evil in the spiritual world" (DF 39).

The distortion of the metaphor in *The Metamorphosis* is inspired by a radical aesthetic intention, which proceeds by destruction and results in creation—of a monster, virtually nameless, existing as an opaque sign.[6] "The name alone, revealed through a natural death, not the living soul, vouches for that in man which is immortal."[7] But what is remarkable in *The Metamorphosis* is that "the immortal part" of the writer accomplishes itself odiously, in the quality of an indeterminacy sheerly negative. The exact sense of his intention is captured in the *Ungeziefer*, a word that cannot be expressed by the English words "bug" or "vermin." *Ungeziefer* derives (as Kafka probably knew) from the late Middle High German word originally meaning "the unclean animal not suited for sacrifice."[8] If for Kafka "writing . . . [is] a form of prayer" (DF 312), this act of writing reflects its own hopelessness. As a distortion of the "genuine" names of things, without significance as metaphor or as literal fact, the monster of *The Metamorphosis* is, like writing itself, a "fever" and a "despair."

Kafka's metamorphosis—through aberrant literalization—of the metaphor "this man is a vermin" appears to be an intricate and comprehensive act in which one can discern three orders of significance, all of which inform *The Metamorphosis*. These meanings emerge separately as one focuses critically on three facts: that the metaphor distorted is a familiar element of ordinary language; that, the distortion being incomplete, the body of the original metaphor maintains a shadow existence within the metamorphosis, and the body of *this* metaphor— a verminous bug—is negative and repulsive; and finally, that the source of the metamorphosis is, properly speaking, not the familiar metaphor but a radical aesthetic intention. Together these meanings interpenetrate in a dialectical way. For example, the aesthetic intention reflects itself in a monster but does so by distorting an initially monstrous metaphor; the outcome of its destroying a negative is itself a negative. These relations illuminate both Kafka's saying, "Doing the negative thing is imposed on us, an addition" (DF 36–37), and his remark to Milena Jesenská-Pollak, "But even the truth of longing is not so much its truth, rather is it an expression of the lie of everything else" (LM 200). For

---

6. Hasselblatt, *Zauber und Logik*, pp. 195, 200. This is consistent with the Expressionist desideratum par excellence: "For we are here to re-create every created thing: in language. To bring to life for the first time through ourselves: in language. *Sine verecundia* [without shame (Latin)]. Many have tried out the criticism of language. . . . More urgent than criticism is the creation of language" (Alfred Kerr, "Sexueller Ursprung der Sprache," *Pan* 3, nos. 16–17 [1913–1914]: 280).
7. Theodor Adorno, *Prisms*, trans. Samuel and Shierry Weber (London: Spearman, 1967), p. 271.
8. Kafka studied medieval German literature at the University of Prague in 1902. Cf. Klaus Wagenbach, *Franz Kafka: Eine Biographie seiner Jugend (1883–1912)* (Bern: Francke, 1958), p. 100. He assiduously consulted Grimm's etymological dictionary. Cf. Max Brod, *Über Franz Kafka* (Frankfurt am Main: Fischer, 1966), pp. 110, 213. The citation from Grimm is discussed in depth by Kurt Weinberg, *Kafkas Dichtungen: Die Travestien des Mythos* (Bern: Francke, 1963), pp. 316–17.

the sake of analysis, each of the three intents can be separated and discussed independently.

Kafka metamorphoses a figure of speech embedded in ordinary language. The intent is to make strange the familiar, not to invent the new; Kafka's diaries for the period around 1912 show that his created metaphors are more complex than "salesmen are vermin." To stress the estrangement of the monster from his familiar setting in the metaphor—the dirty bug—is to stress Gregor Samsa's estrangement from his identity in the family. Gregor harks back to, yet defiantly resists, integration into the "ordinary language" of the family. The condition of the distorted metaphor, estranged from familiar speech, shapes the family drama of *The Metamorphosis*; the *Ungeziefer* is in the fullest sense of the word *ungeheuer* (monstrous)—a being that cannot be accommodated in a family.[9]

Is it too odd an idea to see this family drama as the conflict between ordinary language and a being having the character of an indecipherable word? It will seem less odd, at any rate, to grasp the family life of the Samsas as a characteristic language. The family defines itself by the ease with which it enters into collusion on the question of Gregor. Divisions of opinion do arise—touching, say, on the severity of the treatment due Gregor—but issue at once into new decisions. The family's projects develop within the universe of their concerns, through transparent words and gestures that communicate without effort. At the end, images of family unity survive the story: the mother and father in complete union; mother, father, and daughter emerging arm in arm from the parents' bedroom to confront the boarders; mother and father "growing quieter and communicating almost unconsciously through glances" at the sight of their good-looking, shapely daughter (M 58) [42].

Family language in *The Metamorphosis* has a precise symbolic correlative, Kimberly Sparks suggests, in the newspaper. The person in power at any moment reads or manipulates the newspaper.[1] Gregor has clipped the love object that hangs on his wall from an illustrated newspaper; his evening custom as head of the family had been to sit at the table and read the newspaper. It is a sorry comment on his loss of power and identity within the family that it is on newspaper that his first meal of garbage is served; the father, meanwhile, downcast for a while, fails to read the newspaper aloud to the family. When the boarders come to dominate the family, it is they who ostentatiously read the newspaper at the dinner table. The newspaper represents an order of efficient language from which Gregor is excluded.

The task of interpreting the monstrous noun that Gregor has become

9. Weinberg, *Kafkas Dichtungen*, p. 317.
1. Kimberly Sparks, "Drei schwarze Kaninchen: Zu einer Deutung der Zimmerherren in Kafkas 'Die Verwandlung,'" *Zeitschrift für deutsche Philologie* 84 (1965): 78–79.

is more difficult; his transformation is essentially obscure and can be understood only through approximations. One such approximation is the *intelligible* transformation that also results in Gregor's becoming an opaque sign.

If Gregor had lost the ability to make himself understood by the others but had preserved his human shape, the family would have been inclined to interpret the change as temporary, would have encouraged Gregor to speak; the mere loss of language would not result in isolation and insignificance. But if Kafka wished to suggest the solitude resulting from the absolute loss of all significance, he had to present this condition as a consequence of the loss of the human form. The sense of Gregor's opaque body is thus to maintain him in a solitude without speech or intelligible gesture, in the solitude of an indecipherable sign. To put it another way: his body is the speech in which the impossibility of ordinary language expresses its own despair.

The conception of Gregor as a mutilated metaphor, uprooted from familiar language, brings another element of this family drama to light. The transformed metaphor preserves a trace of its original state. The consciousness of Gregor, like the uprooted metaphor, is defined by its reference to its former state: though Gregor cannot communicate, he continues to remember. This point underscores a feature of Kafka's metamorphosis which distinguishes it from the classical metamorphosis in Ovid,[2] where a human consciousness is converted into a natural object. *The Metamorphosis* converts a word having a quasi-natural identity, the rooted and familiar identity of ordinary speech, into a word having the character of a unique consciousness. The distorted word, without presence or future, suggests a mind dominated by nostalgia for its former life—a life of obscure habit and occupation rewarded by secure family ties.

Gregor's future is mainly obstructed by a particular form of the tyranny of nostalgia, by the "consideration" he shows his family (M 23, 48 [17, 35]). Kafka's word *Rücksicht*, with its connotations of hindsight, of looking backward, is exactly right for Gregor: his consideration arises from his clinging to a mythic past—one that is, in fact, hopelessly lost (E 96, 129). The play of Gregor's "consideration" reveals his family feeling as necessarily ambivalent, moving between extremes of solicitude and indifference.

The key passage has been pointed out by William Empson, though his interpretation of it is actually misleading. According to Empson, Kafka can only have been nodding when he wrote, in the scene of the sister's violin playing: "It hardly surprised [Gregor] that lately he was showing so little consideration for the others; once such consideration had been his greatest pride. . . . Now . . . his indifference to everything

---

2. See above, p. 2.

was much too deep for him to have gotten on his back and scrubbed himself clean against the carpet, as once he had done several times a day" (M 48) [35]. "After the apple incident," Empson points out, "there could surely be no question of . . . this," for the apple fired at Gregor by his father has lodged in his back and caused a festering wound.[3] But Kafka's chiding Gregor for his indifference precisely at this point is not an "inconsistency." The moment teaches us to regard Gregor's consideration for the others as an aberration, an impulse opposite to his own most genuine concern, such as it is. It is in forgetting a useless consideration and pursuing the sound of the music that Gregor is able to discover his own condition, to perceive his irreducible strangeness. The abandonment of a *Rücksicht* that is bent on reintegration into ordinary life enables him for one moment (he did not formerly "understand" music) to imagine the music of the world in a finer tone. In our perspective this moment emerges as a restitution of language to Gregor, yet of a language fundamentally unlike the language he has lost. The character of the lost language is approximated by the abrupt fantasy of violence and incest following the violin music, into which Gregor's experience of music collapses. The language of music is degraded when it is made the means for the restitution of a family relationship.

Gregor's ambivalent relation to his family, inspired partly by the relationship between literary and conventional figurative language, suggests Kafka's own ambivalent feeling about intimacy. His ambivalence, centering as it does on an idea of renunciation, is spelled out in an early account of his love for the Yiddish actress Mrs. Tschissik. "A young man . . . declares to this woman his love to which he has completely fallen victim and . . . immediately renounces the woman. . . . Should I be grateful or should I curse the fact that despite all misfortune I can still feel love, an unearthly love but still for earthly objects?" (DI 139). We know that Kafka at times thought the utmost a man might achieve was to found a family; he liked to quote the words attributed to Flaubert describing a family full of children: "*Ils sont dans le vrai* [they are living the truthful life]."[4] But he also wrote to Felice Bauer, "Rather put on blinkers and go my way to the limit than have the familiar pack [*das heimatliche Rudel*] mill around me and distract my gaze" (DII 167, Ta 514). The precarious existence that Kafka maintained outside "the house of life" required vigilant curbing of his nostalgia.

3. William Empson, "A Family Monster" (review of *The Metamorphosis*), *Nation* 138 (December 7, 1946): 653. Empson's surmise—"Maybe [Kafka] could never bear to read over the manuscript"—is incorrect; Kafka speaks of proofreading *The Metamorphosis* (DII 13). For the scrupulousness with which he edited his stories, see Ludwig Dietz, "Franz Kafka, Drucke zu seinen Lebzeiten: Eine textkritisch-bibliographische Studie," *Jahrbuch der deutschen Schillergesellschaft* 7 (1963) 416–57.
4. Brod, *Über Franz Kafka*, p. 89.

The separateness and nostalgia that inform Gregor's relation to his family (and reflect Kafka's ambivalent feelings about intimate relations) dramatize still more sharply Kafka's relation to the familiar language on which he drew. In "Description of a Struggle," Kafka alluded to that fevered soul who could not be contented with the genuine names of things but had to scatter arbitrary names over familiar things. But later in the same text the same fictional persona declares, "When as a child I opened my eyes after a brief afternoon nap, still not quite sure I was alive, I heard my mother up on the balcony asking in a natural tone of voice: 'What are you doing, my dear? Goodness, isn't it hot?' From the garden a woman answered: 'Me, I'm having my tea on the lawn [*Ich jause so im Grünen*].' They spoke casually and not very distinctly, as though this woman had expected the question, my mother the answer' " (DS 62; B 44). In the model of a dialogue in ordinary language, Kafka communicates his early, intense longing for and insistence on wholeness and clarity—in Klaus Wagenbach's phrase, Kafka's "plain marveling at the magic of the simple." This is the simplicity of common speech in which names and things fit effortlessly together. Kafka's "idolatrous admiration of the truth, which grows more and more marked," Wagenbach continues, "is at the root of his decision to confine himself to the linguistic material offered him by his environment."[5] But Hermann Pongs foresees in this decision a dangerous end: the result of Kafka's confining himself to the juiceless, stilted language of Prague is Gregor Samsa's ongoing metamorphosis. "The fate of the animal voice, into which human sound is changed, becomes a terrible symptom of Kafka's being cut off from the substrata of the inner form of language. Kafka scholarship has brought to light the fact that the Prague German available to Kafka, homeless between Germans, Jews and Czechs in the region of Prague, was an already etiolated literary German, obliged to do without any forces of rejuvenation through dialect."[6]

There is some truth in this statement, to which Kafka's frequent animadversions on the German of Prague testify (but then, of course, the fate of the animal voice is not a "symptom" but a conscious reflection of Kafka's alienation). "Yesterday," writes Kafka, "it occurred to me that I did not always love my mother as she deserved and as I could, only because the German language prevented it. The Jewish mother is no 'Mutter' " (DI 111). In a letter to Max Brod composed in June 1921, Kafka discusses the predicament of the Jewish writer writing in German. The literary language of such a Jew he calls *mauscheln*, which ordinarily means "to speak German with a Yiddish accent": "This is not to

5. Klaus Wagenbach, *Franz Kafka in Selbstzeugnissen und Bilddokumenten* (Hamburg: Rowohlt, 1964), pp. 41–56.
6. Hermann Pongs, "Franz Kafka—'Die Verwandlung': Zwischen West und Ost," in *Dichtung im gespaltenen Deutschland* (Stuttgart: Union, 1966), p. 276.

say anything against *mauscheln*—in itself it is fine. It is an organic compound of bookish German [*Papierdeutsch*] and pantomime . . . and the product of a sensitive feeling for language which has recognized that in German only the dialects are really alive, and except for them, only the most individual High German, while all the rest, the linguistic middle ground, is nothing but embers which can be brought to a semblance of life only when excessively lively Jewish hands rummage through them" (L 288; Br 336–37). The middle ground of the German that Kafka heard around him was frequently not the object of his nostalgia but "clamor" (DI 220) or inanity—"in the next room . . . they are talking about vermin" (DI 258).

Now it is precisely through this act of "rummaging" about that Kafka names, elliptically and ironically, the kind of creative distortion to which he submitted the figures of the conventional idiom. That the metamorphic character of Kafka's relation to ordinary language is frequently misunderstood, however, is particularly clear from critics' speculations about the source of this act. Wagenbach suggests that Kafka's distortions are in fact the work of Prague German, which "of its own accord" provoked the counter-metamorphosis of metaphors. Kafka's native German, Wagenbach writes, "always possessed a vestige of unfamiliarity; distance, too, vis-à-vis the individual word set in of its own accord. Removed from the leveling effect of everyday usage, words, metaphors, and verbal constructions recovered their original variety of meaning, became richer in images, richer in associative possibilities. As a result, in Kafka's work too on almost every page such chains of association are found arising from taking words with strict literalness."[7]

But it is as questionable to maintain that *of its own accord* Prague German proffered its metaphors literally as it is to maintain, as Martin Greenberg does, that Kafka's sociological situation determined his use of metaphor, that "thanks to his distance as a Prague Jew from the German language, he [was] able to see it in an 'analytic' way."[8] In the seven hundred closely printed pages of Kafka's letters to Felice Bauer —letters written, of course, in Prague German—Kafka is not tempted to rummage about in the metaphors of the conventional idiom, to take them literally, or to see them in an analytic way. In these letters Kafka achieves the most palpable intimacy, the native coldness of Prague German notwithstanding; indeed, so intimate is the world he conjures up and creates through language that it becomes for him as much of the married state as he can bear. It is not Prague German that imposes on Kafka his sense of the untruthfulness of the metaphor and hence the fundamental form of his writing; the source lies prior to his reflections on a particular kind and state of language.

7. Wagenbach, *Franz Kafka in Selbstzeugnissen*, p. 56.
8. Martin Greenberg, *The Terror of Art: Kafka and Modern Literature* (New York: Basic Books, 1968), pp. 26–27.

Kafka, writes Martin Walser, "accomplished the metamorphosis of reality prior to the work, by reducing—indeed, destroying—his bourgeois-biographical personality for the sake of a development that has for its goal the personality of the poet; this poetic personality, the *poetica personalità*, establishes the form."[9] It is Kafka's literary consciousness, reflecting itself in the destruction of all intimacy even with itself, which from the beginning puts distance between Kafka and the world of Prague German. Tzvetan Todorov, too, stresses "the difference in the hierarchy of the two ideas [of figurative language and poetic language]: figurative language is a sort of potential stock inside language, while poetic language is already a construction, a utilization of this raw material. . . . Figurative language opposes transparent language in order to impose the presence of words; literary language opposes ordinary language in order to impose the presence of things"[1]—things unheard before, new realities, reflections of the poetic self.

Kafka's attachment to the everyday language of Prague is only one impetus in the thrust of his poetic consciousness toward its own truth. His language probes the depths of the imaginary—a depth that lies concealed within ordinary language but can be brought to light through the willful distortion of the figurative underlayer of ordinary language. The primitiveness of the vermin reflects Kafka's radical thrust toward origins. His destruction of his native personality for the sake of a poetic development destroys the privilege of inherited language.

Conceiving, then, the opening of *The Metamorphosis* as the metamorphosis of a familiar metaphor, we can identify minor and major movements of Kafka's spirit: the retrospective attachment to the familiar, and the movement of the spirit toward its own reality. As opposite movements, they cannot be accommodated within the metaphor that asserts an analogy between the spirit and the common life it negates. Only the metamorphosis destroying the metaphor establishes their distinction.

Our second approach to *Metamorphosis* stresses the presence in the fiction of Gregor Samsa of the residue of a real meaning, the real vermin in the conventional metaphor "the man is a vermin." This method opens a path to that whole range of criticism aiming to relate *The Metamorphosis* to empirical experiences and, by extension, to Kafka's personal life. Kafka, the approach stresses, has distorted but preserved through distortion the sense of a man debased in the way that vermin are debased. As Kafka incorporates in the story the empirical sense of a biting

9. Martin Walser, *Beschreibung einer Form* (Munich: Hanser, 1961), p. 11.
1. Tzvetan Todorov, *Littérature et signification* (Paris: Larousse, 1967), pp. 115–17.

and sucking insect—so this argument proceeds—he incorporates as well his sense of his empirical self.[2] An essentially realistic tale of humiliation and neurosis reflects Kafka's tortured personality.

Innumerable attempts have been made to explain Gregor's debasement in terms of the ways in which a man can be humiliated. The Marxist critic Helmut Richter, for example, alludes to the deformed products of a mechanical work process, to Gregor the alienated salesman; Sokel, as a psychologist, stresses Gregor's intent to punish by means of his repulsiveness the family that had enslaved him. Hellmuth Kaiser views the metamorphosis as retribution for an Oedipal rebellion; the pathologist Wilfredo Dalmau Castañón sees it as the symptomatology of tuberculosis.[3] In most of these readings the evidence of Kafka's empirical personality is brought directly into court; the ne plus ultra[4] of this sort of criticism is an essay by Giuliano Baioni, which sees the metamorphosis as repeating Kafka's feeling of guilt and absolving him of it. Kafka is guilty and must be punished simply for being himself, for being his father's son, for hating his father, for getting engaged, for not loving enough, for being incapable of loving, for being a writer who is thinking about his father, for being a factory manager and not writing, and finally, for being an imperfect creature whose body is a foreign body and stands condemned by a Hasidic ideal of unity.[5] A critical bibliography of The Metamorphosis compiled in 1973 describes more than one hundred published critiques of an empirical or programmatic kind.[6] Though all are plausible, they are privative; Kafka, this most highly conscious of artists, implacable skeptic of psychoanalysis, never conceived of writing as enactment of or compensation for his troubled personality.

For Kafka, personal happiness is not the goal but a stake and as such alienable—a means, functioning essentially through its renunciation, to an altogether different elation (and anxiety), which is at the heart of literature, his "real life" (DI 211). In a passage in Amerika written shortly before the composition of The Metamorphosis, Karl Rossman, as he plays the piano, feels "rising within him a sorrow which reached past the end of the song, seeking another end which it could not find"

2. Autobiographical critics frequently attempt to force the identification of Kafka and Gregor Samsa by citing the passage (DF 195) in which Kafka has his father compare him to a stinging, bloodsucking vermin. This is done despite Kafka's explicit warning that "Samsa is not altogether Kafka" (J 55) [75].
3. Helmut Richter, Franz Kafka: Werk und Entwurf (Berlin: Ruetten & Loening) pp. 112–19; Sokel, "Kafka's 'Metamorphosis,'" 213; Hellmuth Kaiser, "Franz Kafkas Inferno: Eine psychologische Deutung seiner Strafphantasie," Imago 17, no. 1 (1931): 41–104; Wilfredo Dalmau Castañón, "El caso clinico de Kafka en 'La Metamorfosis,'" Cuadernos Hispano-americanos (Madrid) 27 (March 1952): 385–88.
4. "The highest degree" (Latin).
5. Giuliano Baioni, Kafka: Romanzo e parabola (Milan: Feltrinelli, 1962), pp. 81–100.
6. In Stanley Corngold, The Commentators' Despair: The Interpretation of Kafka's "Metamorphosis" (Port Washington, N.Y.: Kennikat Press, 1973).

(A 88).[7] "Art for the artist," said Kafka, "is only suffering, through which he releases himself for further suffering" (J 28). In a letter to Max Brod of July 5, 1922, Kafka links his writing to the amelioration of his life in a merely concessive way: "I don't mean, of course, that my life is better when I don't write. Rather it is much worse then and wholly unbearable and has to end in madness" (L 333) [72–73]. But this relation between not writing and madness obtains only because he is fundamentally a writer, and a writer who does not write is an absurdity (*Unding*) that would call down madness. The only madness that writing cures is the madness of not writing.

The attempt to interpret *The Metamorphosis* through Kafka's empirical personality suffers, by implication, from the difficulty of interpreting the vermin through the residual empirical sense of the metaphor of the vermin. The author of a monograph on the story, Jürg Schubiger, notes a concrete disparity between the form of the vermin and any bug that can be visualized:

> [The head] ends in "nostrils" and in strong jaws, which take the place of human jaws. Compared with what we are accustomed to in bugs, the head is unusually mobile. Not only can the creature lower and raise it, draw it in and stretch it out; he can even turn it so far to the side that he sees just what is going on behind him. . . . Statements about the weight of the creature . . . "two strong persons" would have been necessary to lift him out of bed (M 8) [7] . . . are incompatible with Gregor's later ability to wander over the walls and ceiling; even with glue, a bug weighing at least seventy pounds cannot hang on the ceiling.

"And so," Schubiger concludes, "the bodily 'data' must not be understood as facts . . . they are bodily imaged questions and answers in the bug's dialogue with the world."[8] Kafka himself confirmed this conclusion when he specifically forbade his publisher to illustrate the first edition of *The Metamorphosis* with a drawing of the creature: "The insect itself cannot be depicted" (L 115).

The importance within *The Metamorphosis* of the original metaphor "this man is a vermin" is not for Kafka the empirical identity of a bug. What is paramount is the form of the metaphor as such, which is then deformed; hence, any metaphor would do, with this provision (as formulated by Jacques Lacan): "Any conjunction of two signifiers would be equally sufficient to constitute a metaphor, except for the additional requirement of the greatest possible disparity of the images signified, needed for the production of the poetic spark, or in other words for

---

7. This text mistakenly reads the word *Leid* ("sorrow") as *Lied* ("song"); I have made the correction.
8. Jürg Schubiger, *Franz Kafka: Die Verwandlung, Eine Interpretation* (Zurich: Atlantis, 1969), pp. 55–57.

there to be metaphoric creation."[9] In the most powerful metaphor, vehicle and tenor are poles apart; this power is appropriated by the act of aesthetic distortion. Kafka's metaphor is only impoverished when the tenor, a traveling salesman, is equated with Kafka's empirical personality as factory manager.

Lacan's insight helps, moreover, to clarify another crux. Anders originally saw the metaphor underlying *The Metamorphosis* as "This man, who wants to live as an artist, is a nasty bug." Dieter Hasselblatt has argued against this formulation, asserting, "Nowhere in the text is there any mention of the problem of the artist and society."[1] Of course it is true that Gregor Samsa is not an artist *manqué*.[2] But as the occasion of a metamorphosis, he becomes an aesthetic object—the unique correlative of a poetic intention. Indeed, Hasselblatt's own view of *The Metamorphosis* as the response of the everyday world to the inconceivable gives the work an essential bearing on the theme of poetic language. The empirical identity of the tenor, be it artist or any other man, is inconsequential because *Metamorphosis* is dominated by an aesthetic intent. The intent to literalize a metaphor produces a being wholly divorced from empirical reality.

The third approach focuses upon this aesthetic intent, which aims, through metamorphosis of the metaphor, to assert its own autonomy. We can no longer take our bearings from the empirical sense of the vermin. Yet neither are we obliged to abandon every attempt at interpreting the signifier. For Kafka has already established a link between the bug and the activity of writing itself. In his 1907 "Wedding Preparations in the Country" (DF 2–31), of which only a fragment survives, Kafka conjures a hero, Eduard Raban, reluctant to take action in the world (he is supposed to go to the country to arrange his wedding). Raban dreams instead of autonomy, self-sufficiency, and omnipotence. For this transparent reflection of his early literary consciousness, Kafka finds the emblem of a beetle, about which there hovers an odd indeterminacy:

> And besides, can't I do it the way I always did as a child when dangerous matters were involved. I don't even have to go to the country myself, it isn't necessary. I'll send [only] my clothed body. [So I shall send this clothed body.] If it staggers to the door on the way out of my room, the staggering will indicate not fear but its nullity. It is also not a sign of excitement if it stumbles on the stairs, if it goes to the country sobbing, and eats its dinner there in tears. For I, I am meanwhile lying in my bed, all covered up with a yellow-brown blanket, exposed to the breeze that blows in

9. Jacques Lacan, "The Insistence of the Letter in the Unconscious," *Yale French Studies* 36/37 (October 1966): 125.
1. Anders, *Kafka—Pro und Contra*, p. 40; Hasselblatt, *Zauber und Logik*, p. 203.
2. Failed artist (French).

through the barely opened window. The carriages and people in the street move and walk hesitantly on shining ground, for I am still dreaming. Coachmen and pedestrians are shy, and every step they want to advance they ask as a favor from me, by looking at me. I encourage them, and they encounter no obstacle.

*   *   *

As I lie in bed I assume the shape of a big beetle, a stag beetle or a June beetle, I think.

* * * The form of a big beetle, yes. Then I would pretend it were a matter of hibernating, and I would press my little legs against my bulging body. And I whisper a few words. These are instructions to my sad body, which stands close beside me, bent over. Soon I have finished, it bows, it goes swiftly, and it will do everything the best way possible while I rest. (61)

The figure of the omnipotent bug is positive throughout this passage and suggests the inwardness of the act of writing rendered in its power and freedom, in its mystic exaltation, evidence of which abounds in Kafka's early diary entries:

The special nature of my inspiration . . . is such that I can do everything, and not only what is directed to a definite piece of work. When I arbitrarily write a single sentence, for instance, "He looked out of the window," it already has perfection. (DI 45)

My happiness, my abilities, and every possibility of being useful in any way have always been in the literary field. And here I have, to be sure, experienced states . . . in which I completely dwelt in every idea, but also filled every idea, and in which I not only felt myself at my boundary, but at the boundary of the human in general. (DI 58)

Again it was the power of my dreams, shining forth into wakefulness even before I fall asleep, which did not let me sleep. In the evening and the morning my consciousness of the creative abilities in me is more than I can encompass. I feel shaken to the core of my being and can get out of myself whatever I desire. . . . It is a matter of . . . mysterious powers which are of an ultimate significance to me. (DI 76)

How everything can be said, how for everything, for the strangest fancies, there waits a great fire in which they perish and rise up again. (DI 276)

But this is only one side of Kafka's poetic consciousness. The other is expressed through the narrator's hesitation in defining his trance by means of an objective correlative ("a stag-beetle . . . I think"), which suggests beyond his particular distress the general impossibility of the metaphor's naming, by means of a material image, the being of an inward state and hence a doubt that will go to the root of writing itself. After 1912 there are few such positive emblems for the inwardness and solitude of the act of writing; this "beautiful" bug[3] is projected in ignorance; the truer emblem of the alien poetic consciousness which "has no basis, no substance" (L 334) [73], which must suffer "the eternal torments of dying" (DII 77) [70], becomes the vermin Gregor. The movement from the beautiful bug Raban to the monstrous bug Gregor marks an accession of self-knowledge—an increasing awareness of the poverty and shortcomings of writing.[4]

The direction of Kafka's reflection on literature is fundamentally defined, however, by "The Judgment," the story written immediately before *The Metamorphosis*. "The Judgment" struck Kafka as a breakthrough into his own style and produced an ecstatic notation in his diary. But later in his interpretation Kafka described the story in a somewhat more sinister tonality, as having "come out of me like a real birth, covered with filth and slime" (DI 278). The image has the violence and inevitability of a natural process, but its filth and slime cannot fail to remind the reader of the strange birth that is the subject of Kafka's next story—the incubus trailing filth and slime through the household of its family.

Two major aspects of "The Judgment," I think, inspire in Kafka a sense of the authenticity of the story important enough for it to be commemorated in the figure of the vermin. First, the figure of the friend in Russia represents with the greatest clarity to date the negativity of the "business" of writing: the friend is said by the father to be "yellow enough to be thrown away" (S 87). Second, "The Judgment," like *The Metamorphosis*, develops as the implications of a distorted metaphor are enacted: "The Judgment" metamorphoses the father's "judgment" or "estimate" into a fatal "verdict," a death "sentence."[5]

Kafka's awareness that "The Judgment" originates from the distortion of the metaphor dictates the conclusion of his "interpretation." The highly formal tonality of this structural analysis surprises the reader, following as it does on the organic simile of the sudden birth: "The friend is the link between father and son, he is their strongest common bond. Sitting alone at his window, Georg rummages voluptuously in this consciousness of what they have in common, believes he has his father within him, and would be at peace with everything if it were not for a fleeting, sad thoughtfulness. In the course of the story the father . . . uses the common bond of the friend to set himself up as Georg's

3. Sokel, "Kafka's 'Metamorphosis,' " 81.
4. "For writing to be possible, it must be born out of the death of what it speaks about; but this death makes writing itself impossible, for there is no longer anything to write" (Tzvetan Todorov, discussing Blanchot's Kafka, in *The Fantastic: A Structural Approach to a Literary Genre*, trans. Richard Howard [Cleveland, Ohio: Press of Case Western Reserve University, 1973], p. 175).
5. Greenberg, *The Terror of Art*, p. 48.

antagonist" (DI 278). This analysis employs the structural model of the metamorphosed metaphor. At first Georg considers the father *as* the friend, and his friend *as* the metaphor of the father. But Georg's doom is to take the metaphor literally, to suppose that by sharing the quality of the friend, he possesses the father in fact. In a violent countermovement the father distorts the initial metaphor, drawing the friend's existence into himself; and Georg, who now feels "what they have in common . . . only as something foreign, something that has become independent, that he has never given enough protection" (DI 279), accepts his sentence.

It is this new art, generated from the distortion of relations modeled on the metaphor, that came to Kafka as an elation, a gross new birth, and a sentence. The aesthetic intention comes to light negatively when it must express itself through so tormented and elliptical a strategem as the metamorphosis of the metaphor. The restriction and misery of this art is the explicit subject of *The Metamorphosis*; the invention that henceforth shapes Kafka's existence as a writer is original, arbitrary, and fundamentally strange. In a later autobiographical note he writes: "All that he does seems to him, it is true, extraordinarily new, but also, because of the incredible spate of new things, extraordinarily amateurish, indeed scarcely tolerable, incapable of becoming history, breaking short the chain of the generations, cutting off for the first time at its most profound source the music of the world, which before him could at least be divined. Sometimes in his arrogance he has more anxiety for the world than for himself" (GW 263–64). Kafka's pride in his separateness equals his nostalgia for "the music of the world." His tension defines the violently distorted metaphor Gregor Samsa, who, in responding to his sister's violin playing, causes this music to be broken off. That being who lives as a distortion of nature—and without a history and without a future still maintains a certain sovereignty—conjures up through the extremity of his separation the clearest possible idea of the music he cannot possess.

In the light of the beautiful beetle of "Wedding Preparations" and the trail of filth and mucus that "The Judgment" leaves behind, the vermin in *The Metamorphosis* is revealed as expressing a hermeneutical relation, as reflecting Kafka's sense of his literary destiny. But the negative character of this vermin, this judgment, still has to be clarified.[6] It is a seductive hypothesis to suppose that *The Metamorphosis* describes

---

6. *The Metamorphosis* distorts a metaphor alluding to an earlier act of writing; as such it prefigures Kafka's next published work, "In the Penal Colony." The main action of this story, the operation of a terrible machine that kills a criminal by inscribing immediately into his flesh the commandment he had disobeyed, follows from the distortion of a metaphor about writing or engraving, of the experience that engraves itself on a person's memory. The vehicle here, an act of writing, is without even a residual sense of Kafka's empirical personality. Kafka himself noted: "But for me, who believe that I shall be able to lie contentedly on my deathbed, such scenes are secretly a game" (DII 102). The more comprehensive meaning of this vehicle is supplied by Kafka's sense that in writing he was engraving his own tombstone.

the fate of the writer who does not write, whose "business," like that of the Russian friend in "The Judgment," is not flourishing.

For this assumption there is a good deal of evidence in Kafka's letters. On November 1, 1912, two weeks before conceiving *The Metamorphosis*, Kafka wrote to Felice, with uncanny relevance to the story: "My life consists, and basically always has consisted, of attempts at writing, mostly unsuccessful. But when I didn't write, I was at once flat on the floor, fit for the dustbin" (LF 20).[7] It is as a wholly literary being, albeit one who is foundering, that Kafka identifies himself with the corpse that will be swept out of the bedroom. On November 18, *The Metamorphosis* becomes a "cautionary tale" for the writer at a standstill: "I was just sitting down to yesterday's story with an infinite longing to pour myself into it, obviously stimulated by my despair. Harassed by so much, uncertain of you, completely incapable of coping with the office, in view of the novel's [*Amerika's*] being at a standstill for a day with a wild desire to continue the new, equally cautionary [*mahnend*] story" (LF 49; BF 105) [64–65]. Several days after completing *The Metamorphosis*, Kafka wrote to Felice, "And don't talk about the greatness hidden in me, or do you think there is something great about spending a two-day interruption of my writing in permanent fear of never being able to write again, a fear, by the way, that this evening has proved to be not altogether unfounded?" (LF 97).

This matter is given definite formulation in 1922, when Kafka finds an image for the danger of not writing that is powerfully reminiscent of the vermin's attempt to cling to his human past: "Since the existence of the writer is truly dependent upon his desk and if he wants to keep madness at bay he must never go far from his desk, he must hold on to it with his teeth" (L 335). Here, then, as Erich Heller writes (in his edition of the letters to Felice), is Kafka's "curse: he is nothing when he cannot write." But he is also "in a different kind of nothingness, if, rarely enough, he believes he has written well [writing does 'accept' him, *ihn 'aufnimmt'*]" (LF xvi; BF 24).

What is this "different kind of nothingness" to which a vermin image for the act of writing bears witness? Can it be grasped, as many critics believe, through Kafka's impulse to view the writer in the perspective of the nonwriter, the normal *Bürger*? In Kafka's earliest works—for ex-

---

7. An episode from the life of Kierkegaard parallels remarkably this sentiment and the incident from *Metamorphosis*: "Well," the cleaning woman answered, "you don't have to worry about getting rid of the stuff next door. It's already been taken care of" (M 57) [42]. Walter Lowrie, writing in his *Short Life of Kierkegaard* (Princeton, N.J.: Princeton University Press, 1971), p. 41, of the spinal trouble that eventually caused Kierkegaard's death, reports: "We have several accounts of similar attacks which were not permanent. For example, at a social gathering he once fell from the sofa and lay impotent upon the floor—beseeching his friends not to pick 'it' up but to 'leave it there till the maid comes in the morning to sweep.'" Theodore Ziolkowski noted this parallel with the Danish philosopher and religious thinker (1813–55). For a study of the relation between Kafka and Kierkegaard, see Fritz Billeter, *Das Dichterische bei Kafka und Kierkegaard* (Winterthur: Keller, 1965).

ample, in the developed but unfinished story beginning, " 'You,' I said"—the writer appears in the eyes of others as the dim figure of the bachelor, the nonentity who must drag out his days in feeble solitude, without children or possessions (DI 22–29). "The Judgment," too, presents the writer in an alien and insulting perspective; the essential character of this relation is stressed through the alliance said to exist between the vindictive father and the friend, a transparent persona of the writer. The clearest formulation of this theme occurs in 1919, in Kafka's "Letter to His Father": "My writing was all about you," Kafka declared to his father. "All I did there, after all, was to bemoan what I could not bemoan upon your breast. It was an intentionally long-drawn-out leave-taking from you, yet, although it was brought about by force on your part, it did take its course in the direction determined by me" (DF 177).[8] In these passages, the origin of the writer appears to be fundamentally shaped by the perspective of the father; Gregor Samsa, too, needs to have his metamorphosis confirmed by the judgment of his family.

But in fact this idea is neither predominant nor even highly significant in *The Metamorphosis*. The work frequently stresses the son's defiance of the father: Gregor comes out in the open to hear the language of music despite his father's prohibition. What is more, the truth and pathos of the story stem from the reader's occupying throughout—with the exception of the "unsatisfactory" conclusion—a consciousness very nearly identical with Gregor's own [69]. The center of gravity of the work is Gregor's sense of the world: he sees himself as a vermin, we do not see him as a vermin through the eyes of the others. Significantly, the omniscient narrator of the close of the story confirms Gregor's body to be actually verminous.

The negativity of the vermin has to be seen as rooted, in an absolute sense, in the literary enterprise itself, as coming to light in the perspective that the act of writing offers of itself. Here the activity of writing appears only autonomous enough to demand the loss of happiness and the renunciation of life. But of its own accord it has no power to restitute these sacrifices in a finer key. Over Kafka's writing stands a constant sign of negativity and incompleteness:

> When it became clear in my organism that writing was the most productive direction for my being to take, everything rushed in that direction and left empty all those abilities which were directed toward the joys of sex, eating, drinking, philosophical reflection and above all music. I atrophied in all these directions. . . . My

8. I have modified this translation. The German text concludes, of Kafka's writing as a leave-taking, "daß er zwar von Dir erzwungen war, aber in der von mir bestimmten Richtung verlief" (H 203) Kaiser and Wilkins translate these clauses, "although it was brought about by force on your part, it did not [*sic*] take its course in the direction determined by me" (DF 177).

development is now complete and, so far as I can see, there is nothing left to sacrifice; I need only throw my work in the office out of this complex in order to begin my real life. (DI 211)

The path to Kafka's "real life" is strewn with sacrifices; and the fact that he was never able to throw off his professional work until he had become fatally ill reflects the inherent inaccessibility of his ideal.

In a letter of July 5, 1922, to Max Brod, Kafka envisions the writer as inhabiting a place outside the house of life—as a dead man, one of those "departed," of the "Reflections," who long to be flooded back to us (DF 34). It cannot be otherwise; the writer "has no basis, has no substance [*ist etwas nicht Bestehendes*]"; what he produces is devilish, "the reward for service to the devil. This descent to the dark powers, this unbinding of spirits by nature bound, dubious embraces and whatever else may go on below, of which one no longer knows anything above ground, when in the sunlight one writes stories. Perhaps there is another kind of writing, I only know this one" (Br 385) [73].[9] "Yet," as Erich Heller remarks, "it remains dubious who this 'one' is who 'writes stories in the sunshine.' Kafka himself? 'The Judgment'—and sunshine? *Metamorphosis* . . . and sunshine? . . . How must it have been 'in the nether parts' if 'in the higher parts' blossoms like these burst forth?" (BF 22).

Kafka's art, which Kafka elsewhere calls a conjuration of spirits, brings into the light of language the experience of descent and doubt. And even this experience has to be repeated perpetually. "And so I waver, fly incessantly to the summit of the mountain, but can keep myself on top for hardly a moment. . . . [I]t is not death, alas, but the eternal torments of dying" (DII 77) [70]. There is no true duration in this desperate flight; conjuring up his own death, Kafka writes: "The writer in me of course will die at once, for such a figure has no basis, has no substance, isn't even of dust; it is only a little bit possible in the maddest earthly life, it is only a construction of the craving for enjoyment [*Genußsucht*]. This is the writer" (Br 385) [73]. The self-indulgence that defines the writer is that of the being who perpetually reflects on himself and others. The word "figure" in the passage above can be taken literally: the writer is defined by his verbal figures, conceived at a distance from life, inspired by a devilish aesthetic detachment with a craving to indulge itself; but he suffers as well the meaninglessness of the figure uprooted from the language of life—the dead figure. Kafka's spirit, then, does spend itself "zur Illuminierung meines Leichnams," in lighting up—but also in furnishing figural decorations for—his corpse (Br 385; L 334).

It is this dwelling outside the house of life, *Schriftstellersein*,[1] the

9. I have modified the Winstons' translation.
1. The state of being a writer (German).

negative condition of writing as such, that is named in *The Metamorphosis*; but it cannot name itself directly, in a language that designates things that exist or in the figures that suggest the relations between things constituting the common imagination of life. Instead, in *The Metamorphosis* Kafka utters a word for a being unacceptable to man (*ungeheuer*) and unacceptable to God (*Ungeziefer*), a word unsuited either to intimate speech or to prayer (E 71). This word evokes a distortion without visual identity or self-awareness—engenders, for a hero, a pure sign. The creature of *The Metamorphosis* is not a self speaking or keeping silent but language itself (*parole*)—a word broken loose from the context of language (*langue*), fallen into a void the meaning of which it cannot signify, near others who cannot understand it.

As the story of a metamorphosed metaphor, *The Metamorphosis* is not just one among Kafka's stories but an exemplary Kafkan story; the title reflects the generative principle of Kafka's fiction—a metamorphosis of the function of language. In organizing itself around a distortion of ordinary language, *The Metamorphosis* projects into its center a sign that absorbs its own significance (as Gregor's opaque body occludes his awareness of self) and thus aims in a direction opposite to the art of the symbol; for there, in the words of Maurice Merleau-Ponty, the sign is "devoured" by its signification.[2] The outcome of this tendency of *The Metamorphosis* is its ugliness. Symbolic art, modeled on the metaphor that occults the signifier to the level of signification, strikes us as beautiful: our notion of the beautiful harmony of sign and significance is one dominated by the human signification, by the form of the person which in Schiller's classical conception of art "extirpates the material reference."[3] These expectations are disappointed by the opaque and impoverished sign in Kafka. His art devours the human meaning of itself and, indeed, must soon raise the question of a suitable nourishment. It is thus internally coherent that the vermin—the word without significance—should divine fresh nourishment and affinity in music, the language of signs without significance.[4]

But the song Gregor hears does not transform his suffering: the music breaks off; the monster finds nourishment in a cruder fantasy of anger and possession. This scene communicates the total discrepancy between the vermin's body and the cravings appropriate to it and the other sort of nourishment for which he yearns; the moment produces not symbolic harmony but the intolerable tension of irreconcilables. In Kaf-

---

2. Maurice Merleau-Ponty, *Phénoménologie de la perception* (Paris: Gallimard, 1945), p. 213.

3. "Darin also besteht das eigentliche Kunstgeheimnis des Meisters, daß er den Stoff durch die Form vertilgt" ("The real artistic secret of the master consists in his erasing the substance [or matter] by means of form") (Friedrich Schiller, "Zweiundzwanzigster Brief," in *Über die ästhetische Erziehung des Menschen in einer Reihe von Briefen, Sämtliche Werke* [Munich: Carl Hanser, 1967], 5:639).

4. "[Music] speaks by means of mere sensations without concepts and so does not, like poetry, leave behind it any food for reflection" (Immanuel Kant, *The Critique of Judgement*, trans. James Creed Meredith [Oxford: Clarendon, 1928], p. 193).

ka's unfathomable sentence, "Was he an animal, that music could move him so?" (M 49) [36], paradox echoes jarringly without end.

At the close of *The Metamorphosis* Gregor is issued a death sentence by his family which he promptly adopts as his own; he then passes into a vacant trance.

> He had pains, of course, throughout his whole body, but it seemed to him that they were gradually getting fainter and fainter and would finally go away altogether. The rotten apple in his back and the inflamed area around it, which were completely covered with fluffy dust, already hardly bothered him. He thought back on his family with deep emotion and love. His conviction that he would have to disappear was, if possible, even firmer than his sister's. He remained in this state of empty and peaceful reflection until the tower clock struck three in the morning. (M 53–54) [39]

He is empty of all practical concerns; his body has dwindled to a mere dry husk, substantial enough to have become sonorous, too substantial not to have been betrayed by the promise of harmony in music. He suggests the Christ of John (19:30)—but not the Christ of Matthew (27:50) or Mark (15:37)—for Gregor's last moment is silent and painless. "He still saw that outside the window everything was beginning to grow light. Then, without his consent, his head sank down to the floor, and from his nostrils streamed his last weak breath" (M 54) [39]. For a moment the dim desert of Gregor's world grows luminous; his opaque body, progressively impoverished, achieves a faint translucency. Through the destruction of the specious harmony of the metaphor and the aesthetic claims of the symbol, Kafka engenders another sort of beauty and, with this, closes a circle of reflection on his own work. For in 1910, just before his mature art originated as the distortion of the metaphor, Kafka wrote in the story fragment, " 'You,' I said . . .": "Already, what protected me seemed to dissolve here in the city. I was beautiful in the early days, for this dissolution takes place as an apotheosis, in which everything that holds us to life flies away, but even in flying away illumines us for the last time with its human light" (DI 28).

At the close of *The Metamorphosis*, the ongoing metamorphosis of the metaphor accomplishes itself through a consciousness empty of all practical attention and a body that preserves its opacity, but in so dwindled a form that it achieves the condition of a painless translucency, a kind of beauty. In creating in the vermin a figure for the distortion of the metaphor, the generative principle of his art, Kafka underscores the negativity of writing but at the same time enters the music of the historical world at a crucial juncture. His art reveals at its root a powerful Romantic aesthetic tradition associated with the names of Rousseau, Hölderlin, Wordsworth, and Schlegel, which criticizes symbolic form and metaphorical diction in the name of a kind of allegorical language.[5] The figures of this secular allegory do not refer doctrinally to scripture; rather, they relate to the source of the decision to constitute them. They replace the dogmatic unity of sign and significance with the temporal relation of the sign to its luminous source. This relation comes to light through the temporal difference between the allegorical sign and the sign prefiguring it; the exact meaning of the signs is less important than the temporal character of their relation. The vermin that alludes to vermin figures in Kafka's early work, and whose death amid increasing luminosity alludes casually to Christ's, is just such a figure. But to stress the temporal character of the metamorphosed metaphor of *The Metamorphosis* is to distinguish it importantly from the "extended metaphor" of Anders's and Sokel's discussion, for in this organistic conception of the figure, sign and significance coincide as forms of extension. And if Expressionism is to be defined by its further extension of metaphor, then *The Metamorphosis* cannot be accommodated in an Expressionist tradition. The matter should be put differently and more strongly: if Expressionism is the literary movement that takes a continual impetus from metamorphosis of the metaphor—from the allegory, critique, and deconstruction of metaphor—then Kafka is primordially Expressionist.

The Metamorphosis alludes to a certain tradition of Romantic allegory but does so only for a moment before abruptly departing from it. The light in which Gregor dies is said explicitly to emanate from outside the window and not from a source within the subject. The creature turned away from life, facing death—and, as such, a pure sign of the poetic consciousness—keeps for Kafka its opaque and tellurian character. It is as a distorted body that Gregor is struck by the light; and it is in this light, principally unlike the source of poetic creation, that the work of art barely comes to recognize its own truth. For, wrote Kafka, "our art is a way of being dazzled by truth; the light on the grotesquely grimacing retreating face is true, and nothing else" (DF 41). Because the language of Kafka's fiction originates so knowingly from a reflection on ordinary speech, it cannot show the truth except as a solid body reflecting the light, a blank fragment of "what we call the world of the senses, [which] is the Evil in the spiritual world" (DF 39).

And so the figure of the nameless vermin remains principally opaque. More fundamental than the moment of translucency, reflected in the fact that this moment is obtained only at death and without a witness,

5. This observation and those in the three sentences that follow it are taken from Paul de Man's "The Rhetoric of Temporality," in *Blindness and Insight: Essays in the Rhetoric of Contemporary Criticism*, rev. 2d ed. (Minneapolis: University of Minnesota Press, 1983), p. 207. [Jean-Jacques Rousseau (1712–1778), French philosopher, novelist, and social thinker; Friedrich Hölderlin (1770–1843), German poet; William Wordsworth (1770–1850), English poet; Friedrich von Schlegel (1772–1829), German critic, philosopher, and poet.]

is the horror that writing can never amount to anything more than the twisted grimace on which glances a light not its own. Here Kafka's essentially linguistic imagination joins him to a disruptive modern tradition, described by Michel Foucault:

> The literature in our day, fascinated by the being of language, . . . gives prominence, in all their empirical vivacity, to the fundamental forms of finitude. From within language experienced and traversed as language, in the play of its possibilities extended to their furthest point, what emerges is that man has "come to an end," and that, by reaching the summit of all possible speech, he arrives not at the very heart of himself but at the brink of that which limits him; in that region where death prowls, where thought is extinguished, where the promise of the origin interminably recedes. . . . And as if this experiencing of the forms of finitude in language were insupportable . . . it is within madness that it manifested itself—the figure of finitude thus positing itself in language (as that which unveils itself within it), but also before it, preceding it, as that formless, mute, unsignifying region where language can find its freedom. And it is indeed in this space thus revealed that literature . . . more and more purely, with Kafka, Bataille, and Blanchot, posited itself . . . as experience of finitude.[6]

ABBREVIATIONS

The following abbreviations are used throughout Corngold's text and notes, followed by the appropriate page numbers.

A   *Amerika: A Novel*, trans. Edwin and Willa Muir. New York: Schocken, 1962. See R.
B   *Beschreibung eines Kampfes*, ed. Max Brod. Frankfurt am Main: Fischer, 1954. See DS and GW.
BF   *Briefe an Felice*, ed. Erich Heller and Jürgen Born. Frankfurt am Main: Fischer, 1967. See LF.
Br   *Briefe, 1902–1924*, ed. Max Brod. Frankfurt am Main: Fischer, 1958. See L.
C   *The Castle*, trans. Willa and Edwin Muir. Harmondsworth, Middlesex: Penguin, 1966.
DI   *The Diaries of Franz Kafka, 1910–1913*, trans. Joseph Kresh. New York: Schocken, 1948. See Ta.
DII   *The Diaries of Franz Kafka, 1914–1923*, trans. Martin Greenberg. New York: Schocken, 1949. See Ta.
DF   *Dearest Father*, trans. Ernst Kaiser and Eithne Wilkins. New York: Schocken, 1954. See H.
DS   *Description of a Struggle*, trans. Tania and James Stern. New York: Schocken, 1958. See B.
E   *Erzählungen*, ed. Max Brod. Frankfurt am Main: Fischer, 1946. See S.
GW   *The Great Wall of China*, trans. Willa and Edwin Muir. New York: Schocken, 1960.
H   *Hochzeitsvorbereitungen auf dem Lande und andere Prosa aus dem Nachlaß*, ed. Max Brod. Frankfurt am Main: Fischer, 1953. See DF.
J   Gustav Janouch, *Conversations with Kafka*, trans. Goronwy Rees. New York: New Directions, 1971.
L   *Letters to Friends, Family, and Editors*, trans. Richard and Clara Winston. New York: Schocken, 1977. See Br.
LF   *Letters to Felice*, trans. James Stern and Elizabeth Duckworth. New York: Schocken, 1973. See BF.

6. Michel Foucault, *The Order of Things: An Archaeology of the Human Sciences* (a translation of *Les mots et les choses*) (New York: Pantheon, 1970), pp. 383–84.

M   *Letters to Milena*, ed. Willi Haas, trans. Tania and James Stern. New York: Schocken, 1953.
M   *The Metamorphosis*, ed. and trans. Stanley Corngold. New York: Bantam Books, 1972. See E.
S   *The Complete Stories*, ed. Nahum Glatzer. New York: Schocken, 1971. See E.
Ta   *Tagebücher*, ed. Max Brod. Frankfurt am Main: Fischer, 1951. See DI, DII.

IRIS BRUCE

Elements of Jewish Folklore in Kafka's *Metamorphosis*†

Most readers have quite rightly seen Gregor Samsa's metamorphosis as a metaphor of alienation; yet they have also tended to downplay the significance of the transformation itself as a thematic and structural narrative device.[1] To ignore Gregor's metamorphosis, however, along with the various senses of metamorphosis with which Kafka was acquainted, is to ignore an important level of textual reference in the story. Aside from Ovid's *Metamorphoses*, which Kafka read in school, and fairy-tale metamorphoses, which he must have known, Kafka was familiar with the metamorphosis motif from Jewish literature. In the following discussion of *The Metamorphosis*, I will highlight intertexts from the Jewish narrative tradition. True, the Samsa family is not specifically Jewish, but Christian, yet as such they represent the dominant German culture with which the majority of Prague Jews identified. This fact should not therefore lead scholars to ignore the many Jewish elements that Kafka employs in his story. A knowledge of the popular and mystic dimensions of this tradition is essential for an understanding of the text.

A look at Kafka's actual knowledge of Judaism before he wrote *The Metamorphosis* (November/December 1912) testifies to Kafka's interest in the history of Judaism, as well as in texts of the religious tradition. Kafka's provable interest in Judaism began in 1911 when he was introduced to a Yiddish theater group which visited Prague from October 24, 1911, to January 21, 1912.[2] Despite his awareness of the poor quality

---

† Originally "Kafka's *Metamorphosis*: Folklore, Hasidism and the Jewish Tradition," *Journal of the Kafka Society of America* 11.1/2 (June/December 1987) 9–27. Revised 1994. Reprinted by permission of the Journal of the Kafka Society of America. Copyright © Kafka Society of America. Unless otherwise indicated, all translations are mine. Many thanks to Stanley Corngold for his generous and invaluable criticism.

1. Marthe Robert, for example, in her psychological biography on Kafka, believes that even Gregor's metamorphosis can be ignored: "If we disregard the metamorphosis itself," she writes, "which is quite possible without disrupting the logic of the events, we observe that the story describes the characteristic development of a schizophrenic state with remarkable accuracy" (Marthe Robert, *As Lonely as Franz Kafka*, trans. Ralph Manheim [*Seul, comme Franz Kafka* (1979)] [New York: Schocken, 1986] 240 n. 32).

2. Hugo Bergmann rightly sees the encounter with the Yiddish theater group from Oct. 1911 to Feb. 1912 as a "turning point in Franz's life" ("Erinnerungen an Franz Kafka," *Universitas: Zeitschrift für Wissenschaft, Kunst und Literatur* 27.7 [1972]: 746). For a description of the Yiddish theatre and the kind of group Kafka encountered, see, further, Evelyn Torton Beck, *Kafka and the Yiddish Theater: Its Impact on His Work* (Madison: U of Wisconsin P, 1971).

of some of the performances, Kafka attended one play after the other and even saw some of them several times.[3] His interest in Yiddish culture became a catalyst for learning more about Judaism in general.[4] In January 1912 he read Meyer I. Pinès' Yiddish literary history: ". . . read, and indeed greedily, Pinès' *L'histoire de la littérature judéo-allemande* [The History of German-Jewish Literature], 500 pages, with such thoroughness, haste and joy as I have never yet shown in the case of similar books; . . ."[5] Pinès' study is a doctoral dissertation aimed at a European audience unfamiliar with Yiddish culture and literature and without access to any of its literary productions, since these texts were written in Hebrew characters. For this reason Pinès strives to give the reader as complete an overview as possible, providing the necessary cultural background as well as numerous plot summaries and quotations from representative works of major Yiddish writers up to the turn of the nineteenth century. Pinès devotes much space to folk and hasidic[6] tales, which are infused with kabbalistic thought and symbolism, including metamorphoses. Moreover, by the time *The Metamorphosis* was written, Kafka was also already familiar with the writings of Martin Buber, who had started collecting hasidic tales in the first decade of the twentieth century.[7]

The concept of metamorphosis is a very common motif in Jewish folklore, so common, in fact, that the eminent scholar Gershom Scholem calls it an "integral part of Jewish popular belief and Jewish folklore."[8] A more specific term for metamorphosis is *gilgul*, the Hebrew word for "metempsychosis," i.e., the belief in transmigration of the soul.[9] The origin of this belief is not specifically Jewish: the concept of metamorphosis was widespread in antiquity, as evidenced by Ovid's

---

3. After attending his first play, Kafka wrote, "Would like to see a large Yiddish theater as the production may after all suffer because of the small cast and inadequate rehearsal" (*The Diaries of Franz Kafka, 1910–1913*, ed. Max Brod, trans. Joseph Kresh [New York: Schocken, 1948] 87).

4. In November 1911, for example, Kafka began reading Heinrich Graetz's *Geschichte des Judentums* [History of Jewry], a standard work on Jewish history, and in January 1912 Jakob Fromer's *Organismus des Judentums* [The Organism of Jewry] (*Diaries, 1910–1913*, 125, 223).

5. Ibid. 223.

6. "Hasidic" tales are legends and anecdotes about miracles performed by Israel Baal Schem Tov (1699–1761) and his followers. Baal Schem is the founder of hasidism, a revivalist religious and social movement in Eastern Europe in the eighteenth and nineteenth centuries. "Kabbalistic" refers to *Kabbalah*, lit. "tradition," a Hebrew term for (1) the texts of medieval Jewish mysticism, in which (for example) every letter, word, or number contains mysteries to be interpreted; or (2) the complex structure of Kabbalah symbolism.

7. Martin Buber (1878–1965), German-Jewish man of letters, philosopher, and theologian, translated and commented on legends and tales from the religious culture of Eastern European Jewry [*Editor*]. In his correspondence with Felice Bauer, Kafka refers to Buber's "books of legends" (i.e., *The Tales of Rabbi Nachman* and *The Legend of the Baal Shem*) (Franz Kafka, *Letters to Felice*, ed. Erich Heller and Jürgen Born, trans. James Stern and Elisabeth Duckworth [1963; New York: Schocken, 1973] 164).

8. Gershom G. Scholem, *Major Trends in Jewish Mysticism* (New York: Schocken, 1961) 283.

9. For an overview of the history of *gilgul*, see Scholem, "Gilgul," *Kabbalah* (Jerusalem: Keter Publishing House, 1974) 344–50, and *Major Trends* 280–84.

Metamorphoses (ca. A.D. 8).[1] Yet this does not contradict the fact that the notion later on came to assume a variety of forms and functions in Jewish writing. Many such narratives can be seen, according to one authority, as "Judaized versions of myths or folk-motifs that must have circulated throughout the ancient world."[2] In the Jewish narrative tradition, the concept can be traced back to the late twelfth century, where it found its "first literary expression in the *Sefer ha-Behir* [book Bahir]"—"the earliest work of kabbalistic literature" (Scholem, *Kabbalah* 345, 312). A common point of origin with metamorphosis in antiquity—in Ovid, for instance—is its connection with punishment for sexual transgressions. The same view was held by the early kabbalists: They, too, believed metempsychosis was "connected essentially with offenses against procreation and sexual transgressions" (Scholem, *Kabbalah* 346).

As the concept evolved, its function became increasingly religious: in sixteenth-century Lurianic Kabbala, for example, it involved a complex set of symbolisms and became a whole philosophy of life.[3] Its particular significance was to help provide religious consolation. The belief in the existence of a continual metamorphosis after death was reassuring to the sinful, for reincarnation gave individuals "a chance of fulfilling the commandments which it was not given to the soul to fulfil before . . ." (Scholem, *Major Trends* 282). It became part of an entire philosophy of life by offering a rational explanation for the existence of injustice and "an answer to the problem of the suffering of the righteous and the prospering of the wicked: the righteous man, for example, is punished for his sins in a previous *gilgul*" (Scholem, *Kabbalah* 345). Furthermore, within the framework of Jewish history, the experience of displacement and repeated "punishment" in the absence of a clearly identifiable crime demanded a rational or religious explanation. Hence, the concept of metamorphosis came to be increasingly charged with biblical notions of transgression, punishment, exile, and redemption, offering a specifically Jewish philosophy of life.

This world view is prominent in the hasidic tales of Rabbi Nachman of Bratslav (1772–1810). His religious folk parables present the cycle of transgression, punishment, exile, numerous trials, and the longing for redemption in various allegorical disguises which call for an interpretation within a narrowly confined cultural and religious field of refer-

---

1. See introductory note to *The Metamorphosis*, opposite p. 3, above.
2. David Stern, "Aggadah," *Contemporary Jewish Religious Thought*, ed. A. A. Cohen and P. Mendes-Flohr (New York: Charles Scribner's, 1987) 8.
3. "The Kabbalah of Isaac Luria (1534–1572) may be described as a mystical interpretation of Exile and Redemption. . . . This new doctrine of God and the universe corresponds to the new moral idea of humanity which it propagates: the ideal of the ascetic whose aim is . . . the extinction of the world's blemish, the restitution of all things in God . . ." (Scholem, *Major Trends* 286).

ences.[4] In his tales, metamorphosis is a major structural and thematic device. The particular form of animal metamorphosis is only one of its many possible manifestations. Generally the protagonists are shown to undergo several metamorphoses in their lives as they move through the kabbalistic cycle of transgression, punishment, exile, and trials in hope of deliverance and redemption.

Rabbi Nachman's treatment of metamorphosis can be illustrated through his parable "The Prince Who Thought He Was a Rooster." Here a prince believes he is a rooster, takes off all his clothes, sits under the table, and refuses to eat anything but cornseed. No one can cure him, until a wise man comes; he pretends to be a rooster himself, and so the two of them sit under the table. Step by step, the wise man convinces the prince that a rooster can wear clothes if he wants to, that he can also eat human food and still be a good rooster, and that there is no reason why a rooster should not walk about. The "moral" is: "After he began dressing like a person, eating like a person, and walking like a person, he gradually recovered his senses and began to live like a person" (Gates 458).

Here, the metamorphosis into a rooster does not actually take place, but the metaphor is used to allude to a state of existence that can best be characterized as "dehumanization of the humane," a phrase which well describes the function of metamorphosis in Kafka.[5] The prince's imagined metamorphosis indicates his reduction to a less than human level, and Nachman presents the reader/listener with an idealistic moral solution to the problem. In a hasidic sense, by "descending" to the level of the victim's own delusion, the wise man is able to "raise" that person and cure him. Critics have pointed out similarities between Kafka and Nachman,[6] and Laurent Cohen cites Elie Wiesel's insightful comment that the above story "brings us close to *The Metamorphosis*,"[7] though this story was not actually included in Buber's retelling of Nachman's legends in *The Tales of Rabbi Nachman*.

In the middle and late nineteenth century, with the rise and growing popularity of the Jewish Enlightenment—the Haskalah—the originally religious function of metamorphosis changed radically. Although, in representations of metamorphoses, religious and biblical references were still employed, they lost their religious function for the most part

4. See Arnold Band for a discussion of the allegorical nature of the Bratslav Tales: "Introduction," *Nahman of Bratslav. The Tales*, ed./trans. A. Band (New York: Paulist Press, 1978) 37–38. For further animal motifs in Nachman which bear religious allegorical meaning, see "The Spider and the Fly," *Gates to the New City: A Treasury of Modern Jewish Tales*, ed. H. Schwartz (New York: Avon, 1983) 199–203.
5. Karl-Heinz Fingerhut, *Die Funktion der Tierfiguren im Werke Franz Kafkas* (Bonn: H. Bouvier & Co. Verlag, 1969) 97.
6. Jack Riemer, "Franz Kafka and Rabbi Nachman," *Jewish Frontier* (April 1961): 16–20. Howard Schwartz, "Introduction," *Gates* 43–44.
7. Laurent Cohen, *Variations autour de K. Pour une lecture juive de Franz Kafka* (Paris: Intertextes, 1991) 68.

and took on a secular meaning which was often humorous or satiric. Metamorphosis is treated in a humorously ironic fashion, for example, in the tales of the Yiddish writer I. L. Peretz (1852–1915), particularly in "Thou Shalt Not Covet."[8] At the outset, the narrator announces the religious function of reincarnation in a preaching tone that foreshadows the following ironic treatment:

> As you all know, every Jew must fulfill all the commandments of the Torah. And whatever one fails to perform in one incarnation,[9] must be made up in another. The faults of one incarnation have to be made good in another because the soul must return to the throne of glory perfect and without fault, pure and without blemish (*Selected Stories* 29).

A life of metamorphosis is identified here with the condition of exile in this world—and again, it is associated with religious notions of transgression, punishment, exile and (possibly) redemption, a state in which the soul will be allowed to return "to the throne of glory." Peretz develops the concept clearly for humorous ends when he suggests that, quite conceivably, this cycle could be endless, particularly if we are dealing with ordinary sinful mortals: "Great saints undergo but one incarnation, or at most two, while ordinary mortals—may you be spared such a fate!—undergo a hundred or more incarnations" (*Selected Stories* 29). In fact, Peretz shows through the trials of a great rabbi that even "saints" are only "ordinary mortals" (*Selected Stories* 29). Having lived a virtuous and strict life according to the Commandments, the rabbi has never really "lived" and enjoyed life. Now his time has come when he is to be rewarded in heaven, but the Angel of Death has to struggle to make the soul leave the body. All the individual members of the rabbi's body revolt, and his agony is so great that the rabbi wishes for an easy death. But a Jew is not allowed to "covet" anything, not even an easy death (*Selected Stories* 30). Thus a new cycle of metamorphosis begins. In his new life, the rabbi is once again very virtuous—but . . . just before he has completed his cycle, the evil spirit tempts him again. As he is standing in the cold, his attention is caught by an inn across from him. He enters and sees peasants sitting by a warm stove, "drinking liquor, wiping it down with herring and pickles, and talking obscenities" (*Selected Stories* 33). Only for a split second he "envies" them and wishes he could do the same. But this is his downfall. His trials are never-ending as a new cycle begins. Peretz humorously satirizes the

8. I. L. Peretz, "Thou Shalt Not Covet," *Selected Stories*, ed. Irving Howe and Eliezer Greenberg (New York: Schocken, 1975). This text is included in Peretz's *Volkstümliche Erzählungen* (Berlin: Jüdischer Verlag, 1913), a book which Kafka sent to his fiancée Felice Bauer in 1916 as suitable reading material for the refugee children in the Jewish *Volksheim* in Berlin.

9. *Torah* refers to (1) the Five Books of Moses—i.e., to written law) or (2) to both written and oral dimensions of the law (i.e., the Bible and the sum total of everything that has been said by scholars and sages in explanation of this written corpus).

strict religious laws by underlining the all too human nature of the rabbi's transgressions, which are "some trivial matter, a mere nothing" (*Selected Stories* 29) and out of proportion with the punishment he receives.

In such Haskalah representations of metamorphosis, four perspectives can be distinguished that present the notion of transformation from different though interrelated angles. The first perspective is to treat it humorously, the second to see it in terms of transgression and punishment, the third to emphasize the experience of exile, and the last to address the possibility of liberation or atonement. The interconnection of these perspectives is vivid in a passage from a nineteenth-century Yiddish story by A. B. Gotlober (1811–1899), in which a man undergoes transformations from horse to fish, donkey, leech, and dog until he is finally turned into a pig:

> When I was a horse, a fish, a donkey, a leech, even a dog, I always ended up with Jews, . . . until my soul ascended and I was reincarnated as a human being, a Jew, an awful Jew, yet still and all a Jew! But now that I had become a swine, how dreadful was my life! What suffering! No Jew would lay eyes upon me! I could only associate with Gentiles, I was miserable, . . . —how was my soul to be elevated? I did everything I possibly could to get into a Jewish home, . . . —but all my trouble was for nothing. The moment the Jew caught sight of my unkosher snout, he was thunderstruck.[1]

It is striking that the transformations are treated humorously; all are inflicted as punishment for transgressions against the Commandments; the result of each transformation is the individual's banishment from his family or community, so that his transgressions make an outcast of him and condemn him to a life in both inner and outer exile; and, finally, his existence as a pig in Exile is tainted and impure. There is, furthermore, a religious reason behind his desperate efforts to return to the Jewish community, a longing for redemption, for he asks: "How was my soul to be elevated?"

The central aspect of Kafka's relation to Judaism emerges from Kafka's belief, in the words of one observer, that "all archetypical patterns of Fall, Expulsion or Redemption happen now and forever."[2] In *The Metamorphosis* Kafka's preoccupation with notions of transgression, punishment, and redemption is apparent, and Kafka's use of the folk motif of metamorphosis further places the story within a Jewish con-

---

1. A. B. Gotlober, "The Gilgul or The Transmigration," *Yenne Velt: The Great Works of Jewish Fantasy and Occult*, ed./trans. Joachim Neugroschel (New York: Pocket Books, 1976) 432.
2. Leslie A. Fiedler, "Kafka and the Myth of the Jew" (*No! In Thunder: Essays on Myth and Literature* [Boston: Beacon Press, 1960] 99–100).

text.[3] In terms of the religious associations of uncleanness, Gregor's metamorphosis is just as degrading as the transformation into a pig described in Gottlober's text; nonetheless, Gregor's transformation is also treated humorously. It, too, is associated with punishment for transgression; Gregor is banished from his community and condemned to lead an impure existence in both inner and outer exile; and, finally, Gregor, too, makes several attempts to return to his family. There is, moreover, a religious significance in the trials he undergoes.

In the tradition of modern Jewish literature, metamorphoses tend to be treated humorously; in Kafka studies, however, the question of humor tends to be avoided.[4] After World War II, it is understandable that scholars would not readily regard the transformation of a human being into vermin as funny. The scholar and playwright George Steiner argues that Kafka was

> possessed of a fearful premonition: he saw, to the point of exact detail, the horror gathering. . . . Gregor Samsa's metamorphosis . . . was to be the literal fate of millions of human beings. The very word for vermin, *Ungeziefer*, is a stroke of tragic clairvoyance; so the Nazis were to designate the gassed.[5]

By implication, however, a great deal of the humor in Yiddish literature would be lost if seen from only a post-Holocaust perspective. In Gotlober's story, for example, the protagonist is at one time transformed into a hasidic singer who, at the moment of highest religious ecstasy, is so saturated with alcohol that he provokes a spontaneous combustion: "The alcohol, which filled me like a barrel, had grown so hot that it kindled and began to burn quite cheerily . . . and I was charred to a

3. The first scholar, to my knowledge, to have pointed out the relationship of Gregor's metamorphosis to the Jewish folk and mystic tradition is Maurice Blanchot, who writes: "That the theme of 'The Metamorphosis' (as well as the obsessing fictions of animality) is a reminiscence, an allusion to the cabalistic metempsychosis, can well be imagined . . ." ("The Diaries: The Exigency of the Work of Art," trans. Lyall H. Powers, in *Franz Kafka Today*, ed. Angel Flores and Homer Swander [Madison: U of Wisconsin P, 1964] 218, n. 5]. Blanchot also refers to the concept of metamorphosis as having developed out of the experience of the Jewish exile.

4. In 1939 Walter Benjamin pointed out the importance of humor in Kafka: "It seems to me more and more that the most essential point about Kafka is his humor. . . . I believe someone who tried to see *the humorous side of Jewish theology* would have the key to Kafka" (*Benjamin über Kafka. Texte, Briefzeugnisse, Aufzeichnungen*, ed. Hermann Schweppenhäuser [Frankfurt: Suhrkamp, 1981] 90–91). Benjamin's argument has never really been critically pursued. However, a serious attempt to study the humorous dimension in Kafka has been made by Michel Dentan in his *Humour et création littéraire dans l'oeuvre de Kafka* (Geneva and Paris: Droz and Minard, 1961); see pp. 11–16 on *The Metamorphosis*. This is as it should be. Malcolm Pasley rightly takes issue with the general reluctance among Kafka scholars to acknowledge the presence of humor in Kafka's texts: "Kafka's covert jokes and puns are as much disputed as his riddling devices to which they are related. It is often thought derogatory and impudent even to suggest their presence in such 'serious writing.' And yet if we ignore the playful spirit which informs many of his stories, we miss their special flavor. . . . This playfulness is not only compatible with the highest seriousness, but it is actually inseparable from it" ("Semi-Private Games," *The Kafka Debate*, ed. Angel Flores [New York: Gordian Press, 1977] 189).

5. George Steiner, *Language and Silence* (New York: Atheneum, 1970) 121.

crisp" (*Yenne Velt* 393). Asked by the Angel of the Dead about his name, he cannot remember it and replies:

> Dead drunk, burnt to a crisp—how was I supposed to remember? I didn't answer. He even wanted to get to work and whip me a bit, which is what he normally does to a corpse that can't tell him its name. But what can you whip if everything's burnt up? How could he whip a heap of cinders? The hell with it! He didn't fool around with me for long, he promptly told me my judgment . . . and—*poof*! I was a horse!! (*Yenne Velt* 394)

For anyone who has seen Claude Lanzmann's film *Shoah*, it might be very difficult to find this funny, and Gregor's metamorphosis admittedly creates a similar problem. Yet while stressing that "[i]t is unlikely that many of Kafka's readers since the war have been able to detect the playful element in any of his death scenes," Stanley Corngold, for one, detects an "element of play" in the recurring motifs of "deaths and survivals" in Kafka's work."[6] Certainly death and humor can be inter-related if the link is seen as an attempt to face the unimaginable and not succumb to despair or be driven into madness.

In *The Metamorphosis*, the mood at the outset is not one of terror, nor does Gregor view himself as a horrible monster. As long as he sees the metamorphosis as a trick played on him by his imagination,[7] he is willing momentarily to accept his new verminous shape and to play with it. When he tries to rock himself out of bed, for example, he considers ". . . the new method . . . more of a game than a struggle" (8)[7]. Having accepted the "reality" of his metamorphosis, Gregor's associative thinking can take other leaps as well. He tries to picture an encounter between himself and his family and finds the situation amus-ing: "In spite of all his miseries, he could not repress a smile at this thought" (8–9) [7]. As a result of his own experience he begins to see everything around him in a different light, and he can imagine a world in which supernatural events are ordinary daily occurrences. Thus he starts speculating as to whether such transformations might not happen to other people as well, wishing one on his adversary, his superior—a kind of revenge which is accompanied by *Schadenfreude* [malicious joy]: "Gregor tried to imagine whether something like what had hap-pened to him today could one day happen even to the manager; you really had to grant the possibility" (9–10) [8].

The sort of humor that accompanies Gregor's transformation, as well

---

6. Stanley Corngold, "Introduction," *The Metamorphosis by Franz Kafka*, trans./ed. S. Corngold (New York: Bantam, 1972) xxi. All subsequent quotations from *Metamorphosis* are cited par-enthetically in the text. Norton Critical Edition page numbers appear in brackets.
7. His rational self tells him that his imagination is playing a trick on him because he is over-worked: ". . . he was eager to see how today's fantasy would gradually fade away" (6)[6]. He also talks about "a dizzy spell" [*Schwindelanfall*] (12) [10], the double meaning of *Schwindel* in German—fainting and trick—again suggesting that he sees it as a kind of bad joke.

as the state of mind of a person who can momentarily accept the "reality" of transformations, is part of the Jewish literary tradition. It is particularly well-described, for example, in the following parody from *The Mare* (1876), a nineteenth-century Yiddish novel by Mendele Moicher-Sforim (c. 1836–1917), which Kafka was familiar with through Pinès:

> The Hindus, who believe that human souls pass into all sorts of creatures, and the Kabbalists (if you'll excuse my mentioning them in the same breath) are right, so it seems. The entire world is nothing but transmigrations. . . . And if such is the case, the world seems altogether different, you have to look at it with different eyes and regard everything in a completely different way. That may really be a man in the dog-house, and a dog in the man's house. A pound of fresh fish may really be a pound of palpitating souls, a fine carp may contain a chatterbox, an orator, with pepper and onions, on the platter right in front of me.[8]

Of course there is an element of tragi-comedy in the uncertainty displayed by Gregor Samsa vis-à-vis himself and with regard to others. In Mendele's *The Mare*, the protagonist similarly experiences a severe identity crisis, which is, however, described in an engaging way: he becomes

> skeptical of everything, not only of other people, being perplexed as to who and what they are—but skeptical even of yours truly, my own true self. Perhaps I was not truly I. Perhaps I was in the hand of another power living within me and I was not the master of my body, doing everything according to my will and mind. Perhaps that other force controlled me and compelled me to do what he wants, to do his business and live his life as he once lived it. Perhaps I am the substance and he the spirit; I, the matter, and he, the mind. Perhaps I am merely the mule who doesn't matter and who has to mind the master, whereas he, the master, is all that matters, and it is he who does the minding. But no matter. And never mind. (*Yenne Velt* 565)

Gregor the vermin could indeed be seen as a *dybbuk,* an evil spirit from Jewish folklore, which enters and possesses people. The metamorphosis into vermin would then suggest a kind of alter-ego that assumes control and makes Gregor give in to his self-destructive desires, rendering him ultimately helpless and passive. In Peretz's story "The Mad Talmudist" (which Kafka also knew through Pinès), we see the effect such a *dybbuk* has on people; the following passage shows the merging of humor and despair which we also see in Gregor:

---

8. Mendele Moicher-Sforim, *The Mare* (1876) (*Yenne Velt* 565). Pinès, in his Yiddish literary history, devotes seventy pages to a discussion of Mendele's work; twenty pages are on *The Mare* alone.

> . . . who the devil am I? A *dybbuk* must have entered me, someone
> else, an Other who thinks for me—while I go around thinking it's
> I who do the thinking. . . . How is it possible for a man in this
> world to understand himself? What does it mean to want to un-
> derstand yourself? I want to tear myself out of my body, I want to
> stand apart from myself, or have the Other stand apart from me.
> Then "he" can look at me or I-he can look at him-I. (*Gates* 235)

In *The Metamorphosis*, the humor, too, in part derives from the fact
that Gregor has split in two.[9] Gregor's rational self regards the transformation as a trick played on him by his imagination; thus, he still believes that he will eventually be able to catch the train and go to work.
This confusion between reality and imagination has a humorous effect.
Gregor's split personality is again in play when Gregor the human being, who has kept his reason, observes but is unable to control Gregor
the vermin, who reacts instinctively. Gregor's attempt to hold back the
manager starts up a chain of comic reactions that begins to suggest a
Chaplinesque tragi-comedy:[1] it is both tragic and comic that he feels
so sorry for his mother, and yet he cannot control his instinctive reactions. The sight of Gregor suddenly in front of her "rocking with repressed motion" (17) [14] makes the mother first jump up into the air
and then sit on the table and knock over the coffee. This in turn leads
Gregor to "snap[] his jaws several times in the air" (18) [14], which
makes his mother faint. The climax is reached when the manager
jumps down the stairs. The importance of gesture and sound in this
situation comedy has a strong theatrical effect and quite possibly goes
back to Kafka's experience of the Yiddish theater, since Chaplin's films
came to Europe only in 1920.

But a transformation can be humorous only as long as it is seen as
a product of the imagination. The experience of turning into vermin
becomes increasingly "real" when Gregor is rejected and particularly
when, at the end of Part I, he is physically attacked by his father. At
this point, the humor stops altogether: ". . . now this was really no joke
any more" (19) [15]. From now on, the metamorphosis must be seen
as a symbol of degradation and humiliation.

Transformations in Jewish folklore are generally inflicted as punishment for transgressions. Gregor's metamorphosis, too, is related to
man's first transgression, which represents the root of all evil: Original
Sin. The connection with the "Fall" is clearly established at the end
of Part II, when the "father" (in the paternal and the religious sense)
"punishes" Gregor by bombarding him with apples.

9. For a detailed analysis of narrative distance in this respect, which would allow for humor, see
    Stanley Corngold, "The Author Survives on the Margin of His Breaks: Kafka's Narrative
    Perspective," *The Fate of the Self* (Durham, N.C.: Duke UP, 1994) 161–79.
1. See Evelyn T. Beck, who also points out the presence of humor in this scene, *Kafka and the
    Yiddish Theater* 141, as well as Meno Spann, *Franz Kafka* (Boston: Twayne, 1976) 73.

The interpretation of Original Sin in the story accords with the Jewish tradition, which has been distinguished from the Christian as follows:

> Christian tradition reads [the Garden] story as evidence of "original sin," the irreparable flaw in human nature that can be redeemed only by God's sacrifice of his only son. In the context of the Torah, however, the man and woman leave the mythical garden to live a mundane existence in the real world. They do not "fall" from grace.[2]

At the end of *The Metamorphosis* life begins anew for the Samsa family. They literally leave the apartment, i.e., the place associated with Original Sin, and go out into the world. "New life" becomes a concrete possibility through Grete, and the parents are suddenly aware "that it would soon be time, too, to find her a good husband" (58) [42]. Thus Gregor's metamorphosis can be seen as a metaphor for the internal process of transgression and punishment that everyone in his family undergoes, the result of which is a longing for redemption. When this cycle is about to be completed, Gregor, as metaphor, ceases to be.

In an important sense Gregor and Grete exemplify together the interpretation of the Garden Story in the context of the Jewish tradition. The fact that they represent opposite poles is no argument to the contrary because there is an inherent paradox in the Garden Story itself that leads to seemingly contradictory interpretations. The dialectical ambiguity in the original text consists in the following: on the one hand, Original Sin is represented as a curse in that it puts an end to eternal life; on the other hand, however, this curse can be interpreted positively, in that it leads to procreation, "without which generational continuity and history as such are impossible."[3] One could say that Gregor as vermin metaphorically represents one side of the dialectic, i.e., the curse, while Grete personifies the positive side of Original Sin: she is capable of initiating new life and of establishing "a new link in the chain of generations" (Rosenberg 55)—a kind of modified version of the original "eternal life," though in the temporal world. Furthermore, a dialectical ambiguity is already embodied in the vermin metaphor itself: the negative attributes associated with Gregor seem to justify his expulsion from the community, and yet the equally clear process of victimization that he undergoes puts the inhuman treatment of Gregor into question. Such inherent incongruities partly account for the many contradictory interpretations of *The Metamorphosis*.

The transgression implied in Original Sin can also be interpreted as an assertion of the self towards independence: "In the Garden of Eden

---

2. Edward L. Greenstein, "Biblical Law," *Back to the Sources: Reading the Classic Jewish Texts*, ed. Barry W. Holtz (New York: Summit Books, 1984) 88.
3. Joel Rosenberg, "Biblical Narrative," *Back to the Sources* 55.

. . . the humans assert their difference, the independence of their will from God's by disobeying him . . ." (Greenstein 91). In this wider sense we can discern a pattern in *The Metamorphosis*, a cycle of transgression and punishment in which everyone gets caught up and which runs full circle in the "fall" and "rise" of the Samsa family.

Before the story begins, Gregor has displaced the "father" by becoming the sole provider for the family, choosing their abode, feeling responsible for the sister's education, and so forth. He is punished for his self-assertion by the "father." The manager asserts himself by humiliating Gregor and is inadvertently humiliated and driven out of the apartment by Gregor in return. The mother asserts herself twice: the first time to plead for Gregor's life—significantly she is not punished for this. But then she, too, becomes caught up in the cycle. When she takes the initiative the second time and cleans Gregor's room, she is promptly "punished" by Grete and the "father": ". . . his mother's punishment was not long in coming" (44) [32].

Grete gradually makes Gregor as well as her parents dependent on herself: the more individuality she gains, the more Gregor and his parents lose. In Part II, Grete tries to gain absolute power when she deprives Gregor of his furniture: "Into a room in which Gregor ruled the bare walls all alone, no human being beside Grete was ever likely to set foot" (34) [25]. In this scene and shortly thereafter, Grete is called by her first name twelve times, whereas she is referred to as the "sister" only four times. Her ascent to power is further underlined by her language and gestures: when Gregor tries to rebel in Part II, she threatens him and turns against him "with raised fist" (36) [26]. Her father had used a similar gesture in Part I on seeing Gregor for the first time (he "clenched his fist"—15 [12])—an attempt to demonstrate his power and superiority before he breaks down. Grete has thus achieved equal status with the "father" at this moment. But she is "punished," too. Like the rest of the family she is displaced by the roomers: she has to give up her room and sleep in the living room (55). Notably, in Part III she is addressed as "Grete" only once by the mother (42) [31]—as in Part I (13) [10]—and otherwise simply referred to as the "sister" until Gregor's death (54) [39]. With Gregor's death, though, the "wheel of transgression and punishment" finally comes full circle. The Samsa family asserts itself again and regains its earlier identity: the parents are seen as united ("The couple Mr. and Mrs. Samsa"—54 [40]) and referred to respectfully as "Mr. and Mrs. Samsa," while the sister is called "Grete" again. Now it is the roomers' and the cleaning woman's turn to be humbled and dismissed.

The interpretation of Original Sin as initiating a whole cycle of transgressions and punishments goes beyond the religious notion of punishment for a particular transgression that is associated with metamorphosis. The vermin metaphor can represent a more nearly universal state of sinfulness which is characterized as a whole cycle of transgressions and punishments that no one seems able to escape.

Thus Gregor's metamorphosis also comes to exemplify the victimized state of all the individuals who are caught up in the wheel of transgression and punishment. The mother, for example, who earlier pleaded for Gregor, cannot stand up for him any more once she is caught in the cycle. The sister passes judgment on him when the family finds itself at the lowest point on the wheel, being displaced by and dependent on the roomers who have just threatened to move out. Like everyone else in the story, Grete, at this point, has fallen victim to the particular circumstances and plays her part in the vicious circle. The "father" himself is portrayed as being implicated in the "original" transgression: not only is he the one who throws the apples, but he is also associated with the snake, "hissing like a wild man" (19) [15]. In this context the vermin metaphor does indeed represent a "curse" that does not end with Gregor's death but will continue in the chain of generations.

The concept of metamorphosis also expresses "the reality of Exile" (Scholem, *Major Trends* 281). In Mendele's novel *The Mare* a Wandering Mare states that she has been in this peculiar shape "[a]s long as the Jewish Exile!"[4] The result of the specific historical exile is a more general, personal "inner" exile, and thus transformations are also "a symbol for the exile of the soul" (Scholem, *Major Trends* 281). Furthermore, there are different *degrees* of "inner" exile, because "banishment into the prison of strange forms of existence, into wild beasts, into plants and stones, is regarded as a particularly dreadful form of exile" (Scholem, *Major Trends* 282). This description allows us to see many of the animals in Kafka's stories—ranging from vermin to apes, jackals, the martenlike creature in the synagogue, dogs and mice—as signifying different degrees of exile.

Gregor, then, represents another such "dreadful form of exile," particularly since life in Exile is connected with uncleanliness. He certainly surpasses all of the other animals in this regard and reaches the height of impurity in Part III: ". . . he too was completely covered with dust; he dragged around with him on his back and along his sides fluff and hairs and scraps of food" (48) [35]. When we see him at this moment, he is drawn to the living room by his sister playing the violin. The music is associated with the higher religious realm, with Christmas, in that it reminds Gregor of the violin lessons he had planned for his sister as a Christmas present. The contrast with the "divine" realm shows how low Gregor has sunk.

However, it is not just Gregor who becomes increasingly impure, but his room and his family as well. Again we can discern a pattern: ev-

---

4. *Yenne Velt* 557. *The Mare* is discussed in Pinès' Yiddish literary history, especially in its relation to the experience of exile.

eryone becomes associated with uncleanliness after the apple scene at the end of Part II, i.e., after the connection with the Fall is established. The father's uniform becomes and remains "dirty" (the German *fleckig* carries associations of *befleckt* [tainted]) "in spite of all the mother's and sister's care" (41) [30]. When Grete plays the violin—for the first time since Gregor's transformation—the whole family has reached its nadir, too, to the extent of needing the roomers' permission to play music in their own living room.

In this framework, then, Gregor's desire to be tolerated as "a member of the family, . . . who could not be treated as an enemy; [it being . . .] the commandment of family duty to swallow their disgust and endure him, endure him and nothing more" (40) [29] assumes a greater significance. The fact that both Gregor *and* his family lead an impure existence after the Fall stresses the need for a "humane" treatment of Gregor. In Judaism, with the experience of the Diaspora,[5] religious laws were reformulated towards humanitarian ends; and one famous midrashic[6] passage reads: "The Temple and its sacrifices do not alone expiate our sins, rather we have an equivalent way of making atonement and that is through deeds of human kindness."[7]

Finally, Jewish Exile in general is regarded "either as a punishment for Israel's sins or as a test of Israel's faith" (Scholem, *Major Trends* 284). Thus, Gregor's "exile" can also be seen as a further infliction of punishment; as for exile's serving to test faith, however, the Samsas' increasingly inhuman treatment of Gregor suggests that exile here will not prove successful. Kafka increasingly transforms the particular historical and biblical associations of metamorphosis to convey his own philosophical position.

Biblical law prescribes that "one must undergo a metamorphosis of ritual stages" in order "to reinstate oneself in the divine presence" (Greenstein 95). But the humorous treatment of metamorphosis, the secular wheel of transgression and punishment, as well as the characters' growing impurity culminating in Gregor's death without redemption, all seem to support a modernist position which is summed up by Walter Benjamin as follows: "The achievement of the Thora, to be sure, has been thwarted if we abide by Kafka's representation" (*Benjamin über Kafka* 78). From a modernist perspective, *The Metamorphosis* on the whole suggests a reversal of "[t]he sequence creation-revelation-redemption [that] forms the essential theological drama of Judaism,"[8] in that Part I depicts the creation of something impure, Part II the

---

5. The dispersion of the Jews outside Palestine following the Babylonian exile. [*Editor*].
6. From the word *Midrash*, meaning "to search out." It is not a single book but the act and process of interpreting the Jewish Bible. *Midrash* fills in the gaps and details that the Bible leaves out in the realms of biblical law (*Halakha*) and biblical legends (*Aggadah*).
7. Cited in Barry W. Holtz, "Midrash," *Back to the Sources* 181.
8. Alan Mintz, "Prayer and the Prayerbook," *Back to the Sources* 410.

revelation not of the Torah but of Original Sin, and Part III profound skepticism about the possibility of redemption.

Kafka's reversal of formal religion can be shown, however, to be characteristic of the mystic position, as Scholem argues. What Benjamin sees as "breakdown of tradition," i.e., the break with the religious realm and the loss of truth, "lies in the very nature of the mystic tradition itself," according to Scholem (*Benjamin über Kafka* 87, 89–90), and is indeed the starting point in mysticism. The loss of Truth begins with Original Sin: "Only the Fall has caused God to become 'transcendent'" (Scholem, *Major Trends* 224). Consequently, mysticism is based on the notion of a gap between "the lower world, or the world of separation" and the religious realm, "the upper world, or the world of unity."[9]

In *The Metamorphosis*, the Samsas' break with the religious tradition is obvious when Gregor asks himself the question, "Certainly Christmas had come and gone?" (49) [36]. This implies not only that Gregor has lost all sense of time but that the whole family has missed Christmas, the birth of the Savior, and thus signals an increasing indifference to religion as a consequence of their impure existence after the Fall. But there are other elements in the story that can be linked with the mystic tradition more clearly. First of all, there is the complexity of the question of evil in *The Metamorphosis*, where everyone including the "father" is seen as "implicated": in the mystic tradition, evil is seen as having "its root somewhere in the mystery of God" (Scholem, *Major Trends* 238), i.e., in the "father."

Again, in Jewish mysticism any transformation is regarded as "part of the process of restoration" (Scholem, *Major Trends* 283). In fact, the sole purpose of metamorphosis is "the purification of the soul and the opportunity, in a new trial, to improve its deeds."[1] The use of the word "trial" is significant here, in that it characterizes the process (cf. Kafka's novel *Der Proceß [The Trial]*!) of striving for redemption that is initiated by the metamorphosis. In Peretz's story "Thou Shalt Not Covet," the narrator similarly calls the rabbi's transformation "the saint's trial" (*Selected Stories* 30). This indicates a likely connection between Gregor's trial and that of Josef K. in *The Trial*, whose transgression is also related to Original Sin. To extend the notion of trial even further, in mysticism "every individual provides, by his behavior, countless occasions for ever renewed exile" (Scholem, *Major Trends* 282), and "[t]he task of all human beings is to *restore* the original harmony through ritual and moral activity" (Fine 328). For this reason there are numerous occasions for ever-renewed trials of penitents. This concept also constitutes a very common motif in hasidic folklore.

9. Lawrence Fine, "Kabbalistic Texts," *Back to the Sources* 325.
1. In *Encyclopaedia Judaica*, vol. 7 (Jerusalem: Keter Publishing House, 1971) 575.

A crucial motif in hasidic tales is the mystic longing for redemption. Atonement can here be reached only by going through the ritual stages of punishment, including exile—in other words according to the principle "[d]escent for the sake of ascent."[2] In another of Peretz's stories, "Devotion Without End" (also discussed by Pinès), a youth is cursed for his transgressions: his punishment is that he forgets the Torah, and "it was further decreed that he wander in exile, clad in sackcloth" (*Selected Stories* 125). The way to redemption is through punishment and humiliation: " 'But I must suffer, Rabbi, I should suffer, and the more I am shamed the sooner will my curse be lifted' " (*Selected Stories* 122). In this context, then, the two patterns we discerned in *The Metamorphosis* (transgression and punishment, and increasing impurity) can be seen as necessary stages that have to be passed through in the quest for atonement.

The concept of "turning" is crucial for redemption. Benjamin comments on its importance for Kafka: "Kafka's messianic category is that of the 'turning' [*Umkehr*] or of 'study' " (*Benjamin über Kafka* 78). In Part I we see Gregor *dancing* around the lock in order to "turn" the key (14) [11]. Then, at the height of impurity in Part III and confronted with the "divine" music, Gregor is ready for the crucial process of "turning": "Now maybe they'll let me turn around, Gregor thought, and began his labors again" (53) [38]. And a little later we hear, "When he had completed the turn, he immediately began to crawl back in a straight line" (53) [39]. However, as in the earlier attempt where Gregor succeeds in "turning" the "key" but defiles it with brown liquid at the same time (14) [11], here, too, he successfully completes the process of "turning"—except that he is turning in the wrong direction, away from the music and back to his room. What we have here resembles the many examples of "false" turning in Buber's hasidic tales, where the very concept of "true" and "false" turning is a topos.

Furthermore, the music of the violin that Gregor and his family are drawn to is a key tragic motif associated with the longing for redemption. Both Gregor and his family have reached the height of impurity, humiliation, and displacement at this point, and, significantly, they can respond to the music while the roomers cannot: like Gregor, the family is said to be "completely absorbed by the violin-playing; the roomers, on the other hand . . . soon withdrew to the window, talking to each other in an undertone, their heads lowered . . ." (48) [35]. There is a similar relationship between personal debasement and increasing readiness for attaining the realm of the divine in Peretz's "Cabalists" (also discussed by Pinès): a Yeshivah[3] student imposes a penitence fast on

2. Arthur Green, "Teachings of the Hasidic Masters," *Back to the Sources* 392.
3. A Talmudic academy or rabbinical seminary [*Editor*].

himself and achieves different degrees of revelation until he finally hears "a kind of music . . . as if I had a violin within me. . . ."[4]

In both stories the clear sound of the violin symbolizes the purity of the divine in contrast to the impure environment. And Gregor, too, has been fasting. When he hears the music of the violin, he feels "as if the way to the unknown nourishment he longed for were coming to light" (49) [36]. Fasting thus becomes a means for gaining spiritual nourishment through the divine.

Gregor fails to reach redemption. But such "failure" is inherent in most trials. In Rabbi Nachman's stories redemption is out of reach but always striven for: in "The King's Son and the Maidservant's Son Who Were Switched" (1809), the protagonists are told by a wise forest man that the melody they hear is nothing compared to what he remembers: "Is *this* a marvel in your opinion? Even greater is the instrument I received from my parents who had inherited it from their forefathers . . ." (Band, *Nahman of Bratslav* 203). Even the Yeshivah student in Peretz's "Cabalists" does not find ultimate redemption. He is admitted as a singer in the heavenly host, but "the master of the yeshivah was not satisfied. 'Only a few fasts more,' he said, sighing, 'and he would have died with the Divine Kiss!'"[5] As a matter of fact, the rabbi in "Cabalists" is helpless himself: all he can do is hand on tradition with the hope that some day a student might once more gain intimate knowledge of the realm of the divine. He himself no longer knows more than "the fasts and 'combinations' required for this purpose" (*Treasury* 221); everything else is only a memory to him:

> ". . . there are numerous degrees," the master said. "One man knows a part, another knows a half, a third knows the entire melody. The rabbi, of blessed memory, knew the melody in its wholeness, with musical accompaniment, but I," he added mournfully, "I barely merit a little bit, no larger than this"—and he measured the small degree of his knowledge on his bony finger. (*Treasury* 220)

In Peretz's story "The Golem"[6] (discussed as well by Pinès) we have a similarly hopeless predicament. Here the golem is seen as a "savior" who, in the past, could be called upon in times of need. Now, however, he is no longer accessible to man, even though he has not quite dis-

4. *A Treasury of Yiddish Stories*, ed. Irving Howe and Eliezer Greenberg (New York: Schocken, 1973) 222.
5. Kafka noted down the reference to the Divine Kiss from Pinès' discussion of "Cabalists": "Mitat neshika, death by a kiss: reserved only for the most pious" (*Diaries, 1910–1913* 226). Kafka takes up the image of the kiss at the end of "A Hunger Artist." Cf. also Jean Jofen, *The Jewish Mystic in Kafka* (New York: Peter Lang, 1987) 94.
6. Lit. "shapeless mass," a creature in human form created by magical means and endowed with life in order to help and protect the Jews. The best-known legends are associated with the golem created by Rabbi Judah Loew of Prague: the remains of the golem are supposedly still in the Old-New Synagogue in Prague.

appeared, either, lying "hidden in the attic of the Prague synagogue, covered with cobwebs. . . ." In this story, too, memory remains the only tie to the past:

> The *golem*, you see, has not been forgotten. It is still here! But the Name by which it could be called to life in a day of need, the Name has disappeared. And the cobwebs grow and grow, and no one may touch them.
> What are we to do? (*Treasury* 246)

For Gregor, too, there is no new life and no redemption. But if his metamorphosis is indeed a metaphor for the cycle of transgression and punishment, including exile and the longing for redemption, he has not failed. Rather, he has completed his metaphorical purpose now and is no longer needed. Thus his death is not tragic but calm; Gregor has quite accepted his fate and agrees with it: "His conviction that he would have to disappear was, if possible, even firmer than his sister's" (54) [39]. In fact, even though he is all alone in the dark and cannot move any more, he feels "relatively comfortable" (53) [39] and ends his days "in this state of empty and peaceful reflection" (54) [39]. Moreover, just before he dies he is granted a shimmer of hope in the form of the breaking day: "He still saw that outside the window everything was beginning to grow light" (54) [39]. In Peretz's "Cabalists" the Yeshivah student suddenly sees "a great light" during his penitence fast, even though his eyes are closed (*Treasury* 222). With Gregor, the light of the breaking day is still dim; nonetheless, it intimates a possible future redemption not for him but for others. This is what allows Gregor to die in peace.

Whereas the vermin metaphor "succeeds" in that it fulfils its function in the structure of the text and can be discarded at the end, Gregor as vermin on the literal level of meaning most certainly "fails" to reach atonement. But even if we grant this, we might recall the ever-renewed trials in the hasidic tales despite the seemingly hopeless situation, and thus there is always a slight possibility of hope. In *The Metamorphosis*, too, even though the Samsas' break with the religious tradition is obvious, there is yet a very slight possibility of redemption with regard to future generations. The family experiences relief for the first time not at Gregor's death, but when a butcher's boy walks *up* the stairs, passing the roomers who are on their way *down*. The butcher is an important image in Kafka's work, being associated with ritual slaughter, sacrifice, and purification. In *The Metamorphosis* it is not the butcher himself who appears but his apprentice—a messenger who might represent a touch of hope, like the children in "A Hunger Artist," who show through "the brightness of their intent eyes that new and better times might be coming,"[7] when the message might once more be understood.

However, at the same time, the prospect for future generations looks chiefly bleak. Kurt Weinberg rightly points out "Kafka's rather dark irony,"[8] which emerges from the ironic contrast between Gregor's death and the dawn of a beautiful spring day that brings about feelings of hope and liberation for the family. In fact, this seemingly positive ending contains yet another ironic twist because the parents' final rise to power manifests itself in their sudden realization "that it would soon be time, too, to find [Grete] a good husband" (58) [42]. This resolution makes the ending appear highly ironic, since the parents are planning to re-establish the traditional patriarchal power relationship, in which yet another head of a family will be able to embark anew on the wheel of transgression and punishment.

In the context of the Jewish narrative tradition, then, *The Metamorphosis* emerges as a story about transgression and punishment, exile, and redemption. The concept of metamorphosis itself has its roots in the folk and mystic tradition, and Gregor's repeated attempts at restoration and his constant rebuffs can be said to resemble the numerous trials of the hasidic tales. The cycle of transgression, punishment, and the longing for redemption characterizes the trial that Gregor and his family undergo. The vermin metaphor makes this trial visible and thus exteriorizes the internal trial of Gregor and his family.

Obviously the use of motifs from the folk and mystic tradition should not suggest that Kafka was a mystic himself. As much as he was attracted by hasidic tales, Kafka made it very clear that he did not believe in hasidic piety: "I think that the deeper meaning is that there is none and in my opinion this is quite enough."[9] Scholars have long ago recognized Kafka's non-religious stance: Gershom Scholem, for one, regards Kafka's work as "a secular statement of the Kabbalistic world-feeling in a modern spirit. . . ."[1] There is no contradiction, then, in acknowledging the largely secular nature of Kafka's texts and arguing at the same time that Kafka, nonetheless, makes extensive use of motifs and narrative devices drawn from the sacred, folk, and mystic Jewish tradition.

7. Franz Kafka, *The Complete Stories*, ed. N. Glatzer (1946; New York: Schocken, 1983) 275.
8. Kurt Weinberg, *Kafkas Dichtungen: Die Travestien eines Mythos* (Bern/München: Francke Verlag, 1963) 241.
9. *Letters to Friends, Family, and Editors*, ed. B. Colman, N. Glatzer, C. Kuppig, W. Sauerlander, trans. Richard Winston and Clara Winston (New York: Schocken, 1977) 122.
1. David Biale, *Gershom Scholem: Kabbalah and Counter-History* (Cambridge: Harvard UP, 1982) 31. George Steiner also sees Kafka as a "modern Kabbalist" (*After Babel* [Oxford: Oxford UP, 1975] 67); and for Ernst Pawel, too, Kafka is "the worldly talmudist, the rational cabbalist" ("Franz Kafkas Judentum," in *Kafka und das Judentum*, ed. Karl Erich Grözinger, Stéphane Mosès, Hans Dieter Zimmermann [Frankfurt a. M.: Athenäum, 1987] 257).

NINA PELIKAN STRAUS

Transforming Franz Kafka's *Metamorphosis*†

In 1977 there were already ten thousand works on Franz Kafka in print,[1] nearly all of them written by men. The reasons for scholars' interest in Kafka, particularly his short masterpiece *Metamorphosis*, reflect a recognition on the part of students of religion, philosophy, psychoanalysis, political and social criticism, Marxism, and literature that Kafka's work is inexhaustible. No single interpretation invalidates or finally delivers the story's significance. Its quality of multivalence (*Vieldeutigkeit*) keeps us talking to each other, against each other, and to ourselves. For fifty years Kafka's work has been seeding thought and precluding that closure of discourse that would imprison us in our old histories. Yet until 1980, gender-based theories and feminist criticisms were rarely articulated in discussions of Kafka's stories.[2] *Metamorphosis* is an important source, therefore, for the recent addition to the traditional list of disciplines: feminist studies.

Kafka's story of a family whose son, Gregor Samsa, wakes one morning to find himself transformed into a "monstrous vermin" is what Christian Goodden calls "a literary Rorschach test. . . . Kafka critics have hitherto been looking into the mirror of his works to find reflected there the images of their own interpretive attitudes," when they should be looking at the "more significant . . . phenomenon of the mirror."[3] If the mirror of *Metamorphosis* reflects a different image for a feminist, it is because the ambiguities of Kafka's language effect a tension between culturally sanctioned attitudes toward women and his own exploration of those attitudes. Throughout the narration of his characters' experiences, Kafka holds in suspension European, urban, and early-twentieth-century masculine attitudes toward women and transforms these attitudes by presenting Grete and mother Samsa in the roles of Gregor's caretakers and feeders and then revealing their rebellion against these roles. Kafka's refusal (or inability) to provide his readers with a clear message about his work or his attitudes toward women is

---

† This is a slightly modified version of "Transforming Franz Kafka's *Metamorphosis*," *Signs: Journal of Women in Culture and Society* 14.3 (1989): 651–67. Revised 1994. Reprinted by permission of the publisher, the University of Chicago Press.

1. Christian Goodden, "Points of Departure," in *The Kafka Debate*, ed. Angel Flores (New York: Gordian Press, 1977) 2–9, esp. 2.

2. In 1980 and 1981 three articles discussing gender in the *Metamorphosis* appeared in English: Sammy McClean's "Doubling and Sexual Identity in Stories by Franz Kafka," *University of Hartford Studies in Literature* 12.1 (1980): 1–17; Larysa Mykyta's "Woman as the Obstacle and the Way," *Modern Language Notes* 95.3 (April 1980): 627–40; and Evelyn Torton Beck's "Kafka's Traffic in Women: Gender, Power and Sexuality," *Newsletter of the Kafka Society* 1 (June 1981): 3–14.

3. Goodden 8.

not only characteristic but also useful. By reserving judgment on his characters, Kafka puts traditional attitudes regarding gender on trial and deconstructs the reader's expectations as well. His story thus provides correctives to feminist as well as traditional readings that exacerbate through ideological fixations what they seek to remedy. *Metamorphosis* is about invalidation, our self-invalidations and our invalidations of others; and it does nothing—offers us nothing morally—but this vision of how we do it. The narration focuses on how Gregor invalidates his family, how his family invalidates and destroys Gregor, how his sister, Grete, learns to invalidate her brother. It also compels us, as readers of this fictive mirror, to seek out the perpetrator or the victim of this invalidation and in pointing at him, her, or it, establish our own validation at others' expense.

Traditionally, critics of *Metamorphosis* have underplayed the fact that the story is about not only Gregor's but also his family's and, especially, Grete's metamorphosis. Yet it is mainly Grete, woman, daughter, sister, on whom the social and psychoanalytic resonances of the text depend. It is she who will ironically "blossom" as her brother deteriorates; it is she whose mirror reflects women's present situations as we attempt to critique patriarchal dominance in order to create new lives that avoid the replication of invalidation. We cannot read *Metamorphosis* with the sense that we "emerge unscathed"[4] or without the sense that we are writing about "On Not Understanding Kafka."[5] Just as *Metamorphosis* is written in the kind of language that reflects upon what it is reflecting (what Stanley Corngold calls Kafka's "metamorphosis of the function of language"),[6] so the story of Gregor is a parabolic reflection of Kafka's own self-exposure and self-entombment in masculine roles. Kafka's distrust of figuration, his obsession with the duplicity of rhetoric and role-playing, may carry a specifically gendered connotation for a feminist reader.[7] *Metamorphosis* explores both male and female power-compulsions, but if this exploration is liberating in one sense, because writing releases the repressed, it is also dehumanizing because language can describe the human as nonhuman. The pattern of simultaneous liberation and dehumanization resonates with horror when Grete is pried loose from her social role only to be liberated at the end of the story so that, like Gregor, she must pay a dehumanizing price for her liberation. Thus *Metamorphosis* implicitly poses the question feminist psychologist Juliet

4. Réda Bensmaia, "Foreword: The Kafka Effect," trans. Terry Cochran, in *Kafka: Toward a Minor Literature*, Gilles Deleuze and Félix Guattari, trans. Dana Polan (Minneapolis: U of Minnesota P, 1986) ix–xxi, esp. ix.
5. Erich Heller, "On Not Understanding Kafka" in Flores, ed., 24–41.
6. Stanley Corngold, *Franz Kafka: The Necessity of Form* (Ithaca, N.Y.: Cornell UP, 1988) 76 [see above, p. 103—Editor].
7. In Hélène Cixous's *Readings: The Poetics of Blanchot, Kafka, Lispector, and Tsvetaeva*, ed. and trans. Verena Andirmatt Conley (Minneapolis: U of Minnesota P, 1991), Kafka is described as wishing "to break the law" suppressing femininity; the "time of feminine writing" has arrived in Kafka (27).

Mitchell put years later: "If the psychological power-compulsion of men originated [male dominance], what originated that—and what can replace it, other than the psychological power-compulsion of women?"[8]

If Grete is a symbol of anything, it is the irony of self-liberation in relation to the indeterminacy of gender roles. Grete's role as a woman unfolds as Gregor's life as a man collapses. It is no accident that this gender scrolling takes place in the literature of a writer who had curious experiences in his life with women—experiences of his own weakness and of women's strengths.[9] Traditionally, the text has been read not as revealing brother-sister or gender-based relationships, however, but as revealing a father-son conflict or Oedipus complex. Hellmuth Kaiser, for example, describes it as the merciless attack of the elder Samsa upon his insect son, through three chapters which climax consecutively in Gregor's maiming, starvation, and death. *Metamorphosis* has also been read by Marxist critics as a fable of alienation from capitalist culture, with its tyrannical bureaucracy, its class warfare, its conversion of workers (like the salesman Gregor Samsa) into dehumanized things whose labor is exploited. Feminist approaches, such as Evelyn Torton Beck's, make use of the Marxist-Engelian approach to stress Kafka's patriarchal treatment of women, pointing out that he refers to Gregor as "Samsa" but to Grete as "Grete," and implying that what Kafka describes, he sanctions. Only recently have critics expressed interest in the idea that Grete's experience is crucial to the meaning of the tale and that Kafka's attitude toward women needs further interpretation.[1]

Although it is clear that Grete's labor, like her brother's, is exploited and that she rises, as it were, from the ashes of Gregor's grave, few readers have been struck with surprise or horror at this transposition. Because the mirror of *Metamorphosis* has usually reflected masculinist attitudes and orientations, Grete's plight and role have been subsumed by the paradigm of male alienation. The Marxist focus on Gregor suggests that long before his metamorphosis into a gigantic insect, he discovered that "human power may be exchanged and utilized by converting man into a slave. Men had barely started to engage in exchange when they themselves were exchanged. The active became a passive,

8. Juliet Mitchell, *Woman's Estate* (New York: Random House, 1979) 176–79.
9. These experiences and their impact on Kafka's writing remained unexplored until the publication of Kafka's *Tagebücher* (Journals), his letters to Milena Jesenská (see Hartmut Böhme, "Mother Milena: On Kafka's Narcissism" [1962], in Flores, ed., 87) and, especially, his letters to Felice Bauer (see *Letters to Felice*, ed. Erich Heller and Jürgen Born, trans. James Stern and Elizabeth Duckworth [New York: Schocken, 1973]).
1. Hellmuth Kaiser, "Kafka's Fantasy of Punishment," in *"The Metamorphosis" by Franz Kafka*, trans. and ed. Stanley Corngold (New York: Bantam, 1972) 147–56; for Marxist critiques, see, e.g., *Franz Kafka: An Anthology of Marxist Criticism*, ed. Kenneth Hughes (Hanover, N.H.: UP of New England for Clark University, 1981). For works that address Kafka's attitudes toward women, see Nahum Norbert Glatzer, *The Loves of Franz Kafka* (New York: Schocken, 1986), and Rudolph Binion, *Soundings: Psychohistorical and Psycholiterary* (New York: Psychohistory Press, 1981).

whether man wanted it or not."[2] Engels' language of exchange, conversion, and passivity seems pertinent to Kafka's metamorphic trope because *Metamorphosis* transforms the subject into an object and addresses the father's power to barter with his children's bodies. "The sale of his children by the father," writes Engels, "such was the first fruit of father right and monogamy."[3] Gregor is so conditioned to an identity in which he must be sold and must sell that despite the discovery of his new insect body, he continues to agonize about missing a day of work, being "fired on the spot," and about the debt he owes his boss. "If I didn't hold back for my parents' sake, I would have quit long ago, I would have marched up to the boss and spoken my piece from the bottom of my heart."[4]

The Marxist focus brings with it an unfailing sympathy for Gregor as the symbol of all men who work, of the burden men carry in relation to their families and their women. This interpretation, however, fails to recognize that the women of the Samsa household also work and that Grete's work in particular has to do with cleaning Gregor's mess. Undeniably the story suggests a grotesque escape from Gregor's burdensome patriarchal obligations (vermin cannot be expected to pay off debts), but it is also about Gregor's exchange of roles within his family. In his subhuman form, Gregor exchanges responsibility for dependency, while Grete exchanges dependency for the burdensome efficiency and independence that Gregor formerly displayed. Once transformed, Gregor is consigned to inactivity and submission associated with the female role. As Bernard Bödeker has noted, the relations between those who are transformed suggest not only oedipal but family conflict.[5] The struggle is between the sexes, and the primary exchange occurs not between Gregor and his demoralized sloven of a father but between Gregor and Grete. The brother's and sister's interchange of male and female roles and powers, the hourglass-shaped progression of the plot as they switch positions, suggests the idea that *Metamorphosis* is Kafka's fantasy of a gender role change. The transformation of Gregor's body is a "trying out [of] some unreal fable or meaning life *might* have,"[6] but Grete's change also foreshadows our present reality. The text's deepest resonances involve the relations of men and women, of the man's wish to be a woman and the woman's wish to be a man.

2. Friedrich Engels, *The Origin of the Family, Private Property, and the State*, trans. Evelyn Reed (New York: Pathfinder, 1972) 163.
3. Ibid. 111.
4. *"The Metamorphosis" by Franz Kafka*, trans. and ed. Corngold, 4 [4]; all subsequent quotations from *Metamorphosis* are cited parenthetically in the text. Norton Critical Edition page numbers appear in brackets.
5. Bernard Bödeker, *Frau und Familie im erzählerischen Werk Franz Kafkas* (Bern and Frankfurt: Peter Lang, 1974).
6. Günther Anders, *Franz Kafka*, trans. A. Steer and A. K. Thorlby (London: Bowes & Bowes, 1960) 81–82.

Yet the emphasis on the exchange of daughter for son, like the financial exchanges that dominate the Samsas' world and Gregor's bodily changes, suggests for the feminist reader neither political prophesy nor transcendent resolution. A feminist reading enlists no parallel of recovery or resurrection at the story's end in the service of its interpretation, but it shares with Jungian analyses of *Metamorphosis*, such as Peter Dow Webster's, the idea of "the substitution of the reanimated and completely changed Grete (as *anima*) for the ego of the hero."[7] The ambiguities of Kafka's language do not suggest that Gregor becomes more spiritual or that Grete *gets anywhere* once she replaces her brother. As Günther Anders notes, Kafka's language allows "two or more possibilities to stand side by side without being able to say himself which he really means."[8] In the labyrinth of exchanges that dominates the text, exchange of powers may replicate exchange of identity and exchange of gender but not imply, in the exchange of sister for brother, the spiritual transformation of either.

The multivalence of Kafka's language, discussed by the most notable of Kafka critics,[9] situates Kafka's attitude toward women in an interpretable space that eludes easy feminist formulation. Although Sandra Gilbert and Susan Gubar argue that texts written by men about women symbolize Woman either as angel in the house or madwoman/bitch,[1] Kafka's language undermines such fixedly sexist habits of thought. Kafka's use of imagery in place of concepts, so that "rhetorical figures . . . enable him to verbalize his mental operations without ever freezing fluid processes into solid conclusions,"[2] serves not only to deconstruct political and philosophical certitudes but also to question the origin of such certitudes in sexual difference. Kafka's language "breaks forms, encourages ruptures and new sproutings"[3] as it explores the barriers imposed on language by notions of gender and biological destiny. Descriptions of Grete's intentions toward Gregor as she takes care of him and his room, for example, are deliberately rendered in a labyrinth of double-entendres that suggests the blurring and exchanging of masculine and feminine "essences." "[I]f the furniture prevented him from carrying on this senseless crawling around, then that was no loss but rather a great advantage. But his sister unfortunately had a different opinion; she had become accustomed, certainly not entirely without

7. Peter Dow Webster, "Franz Kafka's 'Metamorphosis' as Death and Resurrection Fantasy," *American Imago* 16 (1959): 349–65, esp. 365; reprinted in Corngold, trans. and ed., 157–68, esp. 167. [Carl Gustav Jung (1875–1961) was the founder of a system of psychoanalysis according to which the unconscious is informed by a male principle (*animus*) and a female principle (*anima*)—Editor.]
8. Anders 53.
9. This group includes Günther Anders, Walter Benjamin, Hartmut Binder, Elias Canetti, Stanley Corngold, Gilles Deleuze, Ronald Gray, Félix Guattari, Eric Heller, Kenneth Hughes, George Lukács, Karel Kosík, Walter Sokel, and Joseph Peter Stern.
1. Sandra Gilbert and Susan Gubar, *The Madwoman in the Attic* (New Haven: Yale UP, 1979).
2. Hartmut Binder, "The Letters, Form and Content," in Flores, ed., 223–41, esp. 229.
3. Deleuze and Guattari, 28–42, esp. 28.

justification, to adopt with her parents the role of the particularly well-qualified expert whenever Gregor's affairs were being discussed. . . . Of course it was not only childish defiance and the self-confidence she had recently acquired so unexpectedly and at such a cost that led her to make this demand; she had in fact noticed that Gregor needed plenty of room to crawl around in" (34) [25].

In this paragraph of Kafka's text, the phrase, "not entirely without justification" (sympathetic to Grete as a rational person) contradicts the initial "unfortunately" (critical of Grete's female fussiness), just as the words "defiance" and "self-confidence" (suggesting male qualities) contradict the words "childish" and "romantic enthusiasm of girls her age" (ascribed to femininity). The narrator serves as the advocate for Grete's new sense of self while simultaneously suggesting that her confidence is the result of a will to power achieved only "at such a cost" and over which neither gender holds the monopoly. In this sense, the principle of indeterminacy claimed by Alice Jardine and others as fundamental to female writing[4] is also fundamental to Kafka's writing—so fundamental that *Metamorphosis* can be read as disclosing the plight and tragic solution of one who is caught between the shameful desire to identify himself with women and the consciousness that he cannot identify himself with men. The rupture inscribed by Kafka's text parallels the fissure between a male identity (historically determined) which is obsessively concerned with Woman as its opposite and a male desire to *become woman*, not to possess her.

The word "shame" is central to both Grete and Gregor's experiences. It is a shame that Gregor cannot get out of bed, that he cannot get up to go to work, that his voice fails him, that he cannot open the door of his room with his insect pincers, that he must be fed, that he stinks and must hide his body that is a shame to others. Shame comes from seeing oneself through another's eyes, from Gregor's seeing himself through Grete's eyes, and from the reader's seeing Grete through the narrator's eyes. The text graphically mirrors how we see each other in various shameful (and comic) conditions. Through Gregor's condition, ultimately shameful because he is reduced to the dependency of an ugly baby, Kafka imagines what it is like to be dependent on the care of women. And Kafka is impressed with women's efforts to keep their households and bodies clean and alive. This impression is enlarged with every detail that humiliates and weakens Gregor while simultaneously empowering Grete, who cares for Gregor, ironically, at his own—and perhaps at Kafka's—expense.

The change or metamorphosis is in this sense a literary experiment that plays with problems the story's title barely suggests. For Kafka there can be no change without an exchange, no flourishing of Grete without

---

4. Alice Jardine, *Gynesis* (Ithaca, N.Y.: Cornell UP, 1985).

Gregor's withering; nor can the meaning of transformation entail a final closure that prevents further transformations. The metamorphosis occurs both in the first sentence of the text—"When Gregor Samsa awoke one morning from unsettling dreams, he found himself changed in his bed into a monstrous vermin" (3) [3]—and in the last paragraph of the story, which describes Grete's transformation into a woman "blossoming" and "stretching" toward the family's "new dreams" once Gregor has been transformed into garbage (58) [42]. Grete's final transformation, rendered in concrete bodily terms, is foreshadowed in Gregor's initial transformation from human into vermin. This deliberately reflective textual pattern implies that only when the distorting mirrors of the sexist fun house are dismantled can the sons of the patriarchs recognize themselves as dehumanized and dehumanizing. Only when Grete blooms into an eligible young woman, ripe for the job and marriage markets, can we recognize that her empowerment is also an ironic reification.[5] She has been transformed at another's expense, and she will carry within her the marketplace value that has ultimately destroyed Gregor.

As many readers have noted, Kafka records the damage that patriarchal capitalist society inscribes in the psyches of men, but Kafka also records the damage that is done to women. Kafka's transformation of the male role into the female, of Gregor into Grete, mitigates the differences between them and the disrespect accorded to women in a culture concerned with men's upward mobility, a concern with which Kafka was well acquainted in his professional and private life. Kafka's fantasies about the women in his world are revealed in the experiment of *Metamorphosis*, a text written with particular women in mind and suggesting that a relationship with a woman, as Elias Canetti notes, was necessary to Kafka's writing. The purpose of Kafka's correspondence with Felice Bauer, for example, was to forge "a channel between her efficiency and health and his indecisiveness and weakness." Kafka insisted that Felice Bauer provide him with the emotional security he needed to produce the work of "a great period in his life," which included *Metamorphosis*.[6] His fantasies about women's "fat" and strength are crucial to the understanding of a text in which descriptions of the male character's frailty, the drying up and flattening-out of Gregor's wounded vermin body, are chronicled with meticulous precision. Kafka's description of this process in fiction reflected his urge to resolve his own masculine identity, to decide whether he was fit as a husband and a man. As Canetti suggests, Kafka attempted this resolution by writing passionate letters to a strong and healthy woman and by describing his ailments to her in obsessive detail. The three most impor-

5. An instance of treating an abstraction or a conscious being as a real object or thing [*Editor*].
6. Elias Canetti, *Kafka's Other Trial: The Letters to Felice*, trans. Christopher Middleton (1969; rept., New York: Schocken, 1974) 12–13.

tant women in Kafka's life—Felice Bauer, Milena Jesenská, and Grete Block—were "securities somewhere far off, a source of strength, sufficiently distant to leave his sensitivity lucid . . . a woman who was there for him without expecting more than his words, a sort of *transformer* whose every technical fault he knew and mastered well enough to be able to rectify it at once by letter" (emphasis added).[7] By the time Kafka met Felice Bauer, he "had come to feel that his entire future hinged on the resolution of this terrifying dilemma."[8] Could he marry Felice and remain Kafka the writer? Kafka's marriage proposals to Felice took the form of letters that discussed marriage in general, and both Canetti and Ernst Pawel describe them as intimating a preordained failure, summarized by Kafka's statement, "I cannot live with her; and I cannot live without her."[9] The dilemma was ultimately resolved by his letter of April 1, 1913, in which he confessed to Felice Bauer, "My true fear—and surely nothing worse can ever be said or heard—is that I shall never be able to possess you, that at best I would be confined, like an insentient, faithful dog, to kissing your distractedly proffered hand, not as a sign of love, but merely as a token of despair on the part of an animal condemned to silence and eternal separation."[1]

By writing about Gregor's imprisonment in the armored insect body, a writing he pursued at the same time as he wrote his letters to Felice, Kafka seems to have found an image for his self-imposed distance from women as well as an image for the sickness that would make a particular woman, as a source of energy and transformation, necessary to him. Written in a period when his letters to Felice were most self-exposing and agonized, *Metamorphosis* engaged Kafka in deep self-scrutiny regarding his gender and sexual identity. It could be said that Kafka's writing sprang from his capacity for equivocal self-identifications: struggles with both male/father images and female/mother images that made him unable to live the role of dominating malehood (an incapacity represented by Gregor) but which also enabled him to invent a subversive language that undermined the traditional authority of his father tongue. The "permanent estrangement" resulting from his failure to form an "unequivocal" masculine identity, this arrival "at no solution at all," enabled him to imagine a world in which male and female desires, characteristics, and differences did not figure as essential properties of human nature.[2] The image of this gender neutrality emerges when Gregor is referred to as an "it." "It's croaked; it's lying there, dead as a doornail," the cleaning woman announces (54) [40]. The increas-

7. Ibid.
8. Ernst Pawel, *Franz Kafka: The Nightmare of Reason* (New York: Farrar Straus & Giroux, 1984) 265.
9. Quoted in ibid. 283.
1. Ibid. 286.
2. On the subject of equivocal masculine identities, see Sigmund Freud, *Introductory Lectures on Psychoanalysis*, trans. James Strachey (New York: Norton, 1966) 336.

ing reification or it-ness of Gregor's body is the ground for Grete's ultimate repudiation of him as a brother and for her own transformation. "But how can it be Gregor?" (52) [38] she asks, a question which echoes Kafka's own response in writing to Felice Bauer; "I just don't rest in myself . . . I am not always 'something,' and if I ever was 'something,' I pay for it by 'being nothing' for months on end."[3]

Such cryptic self-disclosures intimate that this "something" from which Kafka sought to escape by way of ambiguous writings, and from which Gregor escapes through his transformation, is Kafka's image of an unequivocal, completely virile body. In contrast, we must imagine Kafka's own body, a body with which he felt "nothing could be accomplished," and that body's imagistic parallel in the "pitifully thin legs" of the insect Gregor, waving "helplessly" around a "vaulted brown belly, sectioned by arch-shaped ribs" (3) [3]. The solution for this body, or the fantasy of its possible recovery, is linked to the fat and warmth that woman's body is imagined to provide. Writing to Felice Bauer, Kafka petitioned for warmth and life-giving blood that he felt his body lacked. "My body is too long for its weakness, it hasn't the least bit of fat to engender a blessed warmth, to preserve an inner fire, no fat on which the spirit could occasionally nourish itself beyond its daily need without damage to the whole. How shall the weak heart . . . be able to pound the blood through the entire lengths of these legs?"[4]

Woman's body, in contrast to Kafka's own, is fantasized as the carrier of a life force, just as Grete is the carrier of the nourishment (initially milk, then cheese) upon which Gregor greedily sucks. *Metamorphosis* unfolds by contrasting Gregor's maimed and dying body with the evolving, blossoming body of Grete, who takes Gregor's place as family provider and favorite. More than allegorical, the incident is the literal representation of the family's need. And since this need and the fantasy it engenders is situated in the text's images but also permeates the text's rhetoric as it eschews "solid conclusions," it signals Kafka's attempt to dismantle his own male presumptions by destroying Gregor's. Gregor's obsession with his father is transformed into an obsession with his mother and sister. To be closer to them, and because of them, he infantilizes his body, struggles with his sister, and, consequently, moves toward death. The source of the image of Gregor's gigantic, armorplated body is Kafka's fantasy about burying his own body and being born into another that can create (as he imagines woman's body does) a beneficial warmth, an inner fire.

While the first image in the story's first paragraph suggests a man buried in a vermin body, the desire for an exchange of bodies is even clearer in the second image of the paragraph, a picture Gregor keeps

3. Quoted in Canetti 33.
4. Franz Kafka, *The Diaries of Franz Kafka, 1910–1913*, ed. Max Brod, trans. Joseph Kresh (1948; rept., New York: Schocken, 1949) 160.

on his wall of the muff-laden "lady." This image extends the burial metaphor by indicating how one soft (symbolically female) image is followed swiftly by another "hard" (symbolically male) image, to conflate them in terms of gender. Sharply contrasted with Gregor's stiff, dome-like form, with its small openings that make it difficult for him to speak, the lady in furs has a large opening; she is vaginal and furry. The picture "showed a lady, done up in a fur hat and a fur boa, sitting upright and raising up against the viewer a heavy fur muff into which her whole forearm had disappeared" (3) [3]. In this ambiguous sentence, which suggests both Gregor's male erotic response to women, the desire to stick a phallic "forearm" into a fur muff, and Gregor's identification with a lady encased in fur the way he is encased in armor, a third possibility also arises: that this is a metaphor for a male-female compound. The lady is also engaged in a phallic or lesbian action on her own behalf, as if her body sported both penis and vagina, to which the male spectator can only respond: "!" Kafka's mocking of strict sexual symbolism, his conflation of male and female, parallels the duplication in the names "Gregor" and "Grete." The lady in the muff foreshadows the transformations that will occur in the Samsa siblings—the first a change of Gregor into a body that rocks to and fro (8) [7], that snaps its jaws but "has no real teeth" (14) [11], that "crawls" (29) [21], is "propped up on the chair" (29) [21], and sucks "greedily at the cheese" (24) [18]. Gregor's transformation is regression; his male sexuality is neutered and infantilized. He is suspended not only "between being and non-being" but also between opposing symbols in a world recreated to confound them. Gregor does not, as Kafka does not, "just . . . rest in [him]self," he wishes to rest somewhere else; namely, in another body, in a woman's body. Such a wish also indicates Gregor's wish to rest *in* Grete. She is an image of an alternative and possible self. "Only his sister had remained close to Gregor, and it was his secret plan that she who, unlike him, loved music and could play on the violin movingly, should be sent next year to the Conservatory, regardless of the great expense involved" (27) [20].

What Pawel, Kafka's biographer, calls Kafka's "crab-like approach to women" and "often most comically earnest eagerness . . . to foster women's intellectual growth," does not seem prompted, at least for Gregor, by what Pawel calls an "unconscious need to desexualize them."[5] Instead, it is Gregor who wishes to become unsexed or re-sexed, and Kafka who imagined, in his diaries, that a powerful woman could empower him as well: "With my sisters—and this was especially true in the early days—I was often an altogether different person than with other people. Fearless, vulnerable, powerful, surprising, moved as I otherwise only am when I am writing."[6] Kafka's sister Ottla would have

5. Pawel 84.
6. Quoted in ibid. 86.

served particularly well for the figure of Grete. "Throughout her rebellion and search for self, defying the father, working the land, breaking away from home, marrying a non-Jew—she in fact acted out her
brother's wildest and most impossible dreams."[7] If Ottla was the female
double who lived out Kafka's dreams, it can be argued that the
exchange motif in *Metamorphosis* is a radical autobiographical fantasy,
concerned not only with the relationships of fathers and sons, but also
with those of sisters and brothers, and suggesting what Kafka might have
been had he been more like Ottla. Inscribed within this wish, however,
is an ironic nightmare about masculinity that affects both brother and
sister: both Gregor and Grete.

Kafka's relation to Ottla, and Gregor's to Grete, cannot be subsumed
by the term "womb envy," but the notion of a masculine disorientation
so acute that the imagination en-tombs or en-wombs itself indicates the
degree to which the male world is a horror and a prison for both Kafka
and Gregor. Identification with the apelike father Samsa and the con-
temptuous, pseudo-urbane boarders (who demand that Grete play the
violin for their entertainment) becomes impossible for Kafkaesque men
whose introversion is the sign and style of their sensitivity to women,
as well as to masculinist brutality. Kafka's wish to feminize his being
appropriates the image of the "box" or "house" found frequently in
women's writings; Gregor's body is a kind of box or tomb in which his
maleness is both incarcerated and protected against masculine require-
ments and invasions.[8] In *Metamorphosis* Kafka imagines the stages by
which the repressed bachelor—whose only distraction is working with
his fretsaw as "he never goes out nights" (10) [8]—is replaced by the
potentially marriageable Grete with her lively "young body" and "prospects" (58) [42]. This replacement is envisioned as a transformation of
bodies. Descriptions of the vermin's body emphasize its passivity, its
being sealed off and shut in. Gregor's back is "as hard as armor plate"
(3) [3]; his words are "badly garbl[ed]" (5) [5]; his "lower part proved
too difficult to budge" (7) [6]; he "let himself fall against the back of
a nearby chair, clinging to its slats with his little legs" (13) [10]. Gregor
vacillates between the active, transcendent mode of the male and what
Simone de Beauvoir calls the "immanence" of the second-sex's condition,[9] first penetrating the world outside his room, from which he is
violently driven back by his father, then returning to rest passively
within his naked den to wait for his sister to minister to him.

Kafka's text is structured to represent systematically, in the most concrete terms possible, the process by which Gregor's male identity is

7. Ibid. 87.
8. Canetti writes in this connection that "Kafka's room is a shelter, it becomes an outer body,
   one can call it his 'forebody' " (27).
9. Simone de Beauvoir, *The Second Sex*, trans. H. M. Parshley (1953; rept., New York: Vintage
   Books, 1974) xxxii and passim. [De Beauvoir (1908–1986) was a French existentialist writer,
   social philosopher, and feminist thinker—*Editor*.]

demolished. Initially, he is preoccupied with male ideals: "I'll be at the office myself right away," he assures his family and the office manager (12) [10]. Even after he realizes what his body has become, he expects the attendance due an older brother; he expects Grete to "find out his likes and dislikes," to bring him "a wide assortment of things" to eat (24) [17]. Ironically, by making such demands, Gregor empowers Grete to make him her dependent, and when her attitude toward him becomes less sympathetic as he becomes more filthy and stinking ("hardly had she entered the room than she would . . . tear open the casements with eager hands"), he responds by becoming hostile: "but not only did she not come in, she even sprang back and locked the door; a stranger might easily have thought that Gregor had been lying in wait for her, wanting to bite her" (30) [22].

Using the subjunctive—"a stranger might easily have thought"—Gregor quickly distances himself from hostility and disassociates himself from the violent "stranger" he might become. With Grete's increasingly frequent gestures of disgust, Gregor passes through various stages of responsive male aggression, each of which is thwarted not only by his father's physical abuse but by his own awareness of Grete's growing "defiance" and "self-confidence" that tempts her to "make Gregor's situation even more terrifying in order that she might do even more for him" (34) [25]. She is no stranger to him once he begins to see himself through her eyes. He must submit his masculine prerogative to her. He must eat what she gives him (she becomes the family's cook), scuttle under the sofa, so that she is protected from the sight of him, even though he finds this difficult because he "had become a little bloated from the heavy meal" (25) [18], and he must remain there in deference to her. As Grete sweeps his room and feeds him—the only one who has not forgotten him—he realizes that he has relinquished his male status to her. The sentence, "This, then, was the way Gregor was fed each day" (25) [18], highlights, even grammatically, his passive, dependent relation to her and indicates the moment in the text when Gregor's degradation and gradual disappearance are exchanged for Grete's social upgrading and visibility. As Grete tires of functioning as Gregor's charwoman and nurse, he becomes dirtier, less human; without her ministrations he ceases to care for himself. As she withdraws her service from him, her female voice begins to rise independently in the text, alongside the conflated voice of narrator and male character. It is Grete, not the oedipal father or hysterical mother, who announces that Gregor "has to go. . . . That's the only answer, Father. You just have to try to get rid of the idea that it's Gregor. Believing it for so long, that is our real misfortune. But how can it be Gregor? If it were Gregor, he would have realized long ago that it isn't possible for human beings to live with such a creature, and he would have gone away of his own free will. Then we wouldn't have a brother . . ." (52) [38].

Speaking for her idea of Gregor and *as if she were* Gregor, Grete pronounces a death sentence whose symptomatic word choices ("answer," "it isn't possible," "then we wouldn't have a brother") mark the moment of her rite of passage into an independent, if harsh, sphere of womanhood that separates her from the world of her father(s). " 'We must try to get rid of it,' his sister now said. . . . 'People who already have to work as hard as we do can't put up with this constant torture at home, too. I can't stand it anymore either.' " (51) [38–39]. Having passed through stages of submission and sympathy, through the burden of symbolically mothering a being that resembles a sickly and degenerate child, and having replicated her brother's stages of maturation and professionalism (for she now has a job), Grete initiates her liberation. Like Gregor, who had wanted to "make the big break" (4) [4], Grete feels repressed and exploited at work. She becomes, in the words of Juliet Mitchell, "vulnerable to the return of (her) own repressed, oppressed characteristics." Her decision that Gregor "must go" involves her in a "tit-for-tat psycho-moral solution"[1] that dehumanizes her ethically as it ironically inspires the blossoming of her body and confidence.

The exchange of Grete for Gregor, of feminine for masculine prerogatives, is dramatized incrementally throughout the text but reaches a point of crisis when Grete is compelled to strip the picture of the lady in the muff from Gregor's walls. The image suggests Gregor's last physical contact with women, his need to be in-furred and enclosed, to objectify women as sex and "pussy," his wish to be taken care of by women who no longer want to take care of him. He "hurriedly crawled up on [the picture] and pressed himself against the glass. . . . At least no one would take away this picture, while Gregor completely covered it up" (35) [26]. Grete's decision to deprive him of the picture is perhaps motivated by her sense that it represents a pornographic image of women against which she has rebelled and to which Gregor still clings, yet her interpretation of the image oversimplifies the complex meaning it may have for him. " 'Well, what should we take now?' said Grete. . . . [Her] intent was clear to Gregor, she wanted to bring his mother into safety and then chase him down from the wall. Well, just let her try! He squatted on his picture and would not give it up. He would rather fly in Grete's face" (36) [26]. By yielding the picture to Grete finally, Gregor is made to abandon his male prerogative to exploit women's sexual image, and he is severed from the fixed libidinal habits of the patriarchal world. He not only gives in to Grete's will, but he also gives up his sexual image repertoire in exchange for her repertoire of new—and I will now say, feminist—desires. Grete's solution for Gregor thus becomes his solution for himself. "He thought back on his family

1. Mitchell 178–79.

with deep emotion and love. His conviction that he would have to disappear was, if possible, even firmer than his sister's" (54) [39]. With this emphasis, Kafka transfers power and responsibility from the traditional patriarchal inheritor, Gregor, to his sister Grete. The exchange is complicated by the fact that it occurs through the horrific metamorphosis and death of one whose doubles are both male and female: both father Samsa who beats his son and sister Grete whose "young body" emerges in spring from the "completely flat and dry" corpse (55) [40] of her brother. Kafka's final solution for Gregor involves both oedipal and female complexes; it represents the urge to kill the potential father figure who is himself, as well as the urge to become woman. Such a reading of *Metamorphosis*, through what might be called a biographical gender analysis, suggests that the tale is not merely an oedipal fantasy but more broadly a fantasy about a man who dies so that a woman may empower herself. Her self-empowering, the transference of a woman into a position where a man used to be, does not transform the social system, however, but merely perpetuates it. When women become as men are, Kafka seems to be saying, there is no progress—merely the exchange of one delusive solution for another.

In the finale of *Metamorphosis* a return to normal sex roles is parodically celebrated. Grete has "blossomed into a good-looking, shapely girl," and "it would soon be time, too, to find her a good husband" (58) [42]. The final irony of Kafka's text is that despite the bizarre experiences that the Samsas have endured, no tragic meaning has been attached to them. The exchange of Grete for Gregor represents the idea that persons, like utilities, can be replaced. Grete can serve as her family's breadwinner either as a woman married to a salaried husband or as a woman who has learned to exploit (and be exploited by) the system that has exploited her brother. The disappearance of Gregor simply means that the Samsas will move into a cheaper house, "but one better situated" (58) [42], and that they will take more journeys to improve the chances of procuring a husband for Grete (58) [42]. It is Grete who will now sell and be sold, who will perpetuate the system of exchanges and debts that was formerly Gregor's business. The significance of Gregor's death is referred to with the utter confidence of a blindness that all three Samsas now share equally: it is all a matter of not "brooding over the past" (57) [42]. Grete, not surprisingly, has become a little patriarch. The sale or sell-out of her brother Gregor is the "first fruit" of her new rights.

The reader who finds this interpretation of Kafka's mirror possible has probably already learned that some feminist projects are not metamorphoses but only changes into another kind of the same—which explains almost a century of interpretations that do not recognize Grete's centrality to the story or speak, particularly, to women. That Grete can be exchanged for Gregor in *Metamorphosis*, that her substi-

tution for him can be inscribed through male imagination, suggests
that we can distinguish between masculine writers and writers who are
male; we can acknowledge Kafka's discomfort with the male role and
with a language symbolically "owned" by a male literary establishment.
As a prophet of the complexities engendered by "the woman question,"
Kafka's text, fortunately, no longer delivers its message only to (alienated) men.

KEVIN W. SWEENEY

Competing Theories of Identity in Kafka's
The Metamorphosis†

Although *The Metamorphosis* begins with Gregor Samsa finding "himself changed in his bed into a monstrous vermin" [3], the transformation is at this stage psychologically incomplete, enabling Kafka to conduct a philosophical exploration of the nature of self, personhood, and
identity. Given the nature of the inquiry, it is significant that instead
of providing a monologic commentary with a consistent theoretical
framework, Kafka offers a dialogical, polyphonic work, an example of
what Mikhail Bakhtin has called a "heteroglossia" of opposed voices.[1]
Since Kafka does not privilege any one theoretical perspective, the
reader is encouraged to undertake what Giles Deleuze and Félix Guattari have called an "experimentation", a process which involves a recognition of the inadequacy of the respective opposed theories and an
acknowledgment of the unresolved nature of the debate.[2]

   Aiding the reader in this process of experimentation is the novella's
tripartite structure: in each section Gregor attempts to leave his bedroom only to be driven back into it. Repetitive in this way, however,
each section of the work also advances a different and opposing philosophical theory about the nature of the self and the maintenance of
personal identity. The first section presents a dualist conception of the
person: Gregor is a consciousness disembodied from his original body
and locked into an alien organism. In the second section, behaviorist
and materialist views challenge the earlier theory. Finally, in the third

---

† From *Mosaic* 23.4 (Fall 1990): 23–35. Reprinted by permission of the publisher.
1. Mikhail M. Bakhtin, *The Dialogic Imagination: Four Essays*, ed. Michael Holquist, trans.
   Caryl Emerson and Michael Holquist (Austin: U of Texas P, 1981) 262–64. [Bakhtin (1895–
   1975), a Soviet literary critic, is famous as a literary theorist and student of Rabelais and
   Dostoevsky—*Editor*.]
2. Gilles Deleuze and Félix Guattari, *Kafka: Towards a Minor Literature*, trans. Dana Polan
   (Minneapolis: U of Minneapolis P, 1986) 48–50.

section, both theories are countered by a social-constructionist theory of the self and personal identity.

In the history of Western, philosophical explorations of personal identity, John Locke's example of a prince's consciousness inhabiting the body of a cobbler is perhaps the most famous.[3] At the outset of *The Metamorphosis*, Gregor Samsa seems to be a cross-species variation of Locke's prince-in-the-cobbler, with Kafka exploring a Lockean-Cartesian[4] theory of self and personal identity. Like Descartes, Locke holds that a person (a self) is essentially a rational, unified consciousness. A person, says Locke, "is a thinking intelligent being, that has reason and reflection, and can consider itself, the same thinking thing, in different times and places. . . . For since consciousness always accompanies thinking, and it is that which makes every one to be what he calls *self* . . . as far as this consciousness can be extended backwards to any past action or thought, so far reaches the identity of that person. . . ."[5] Thus to Locke, an individual is *personally identical* with someone at an earlier time, if the later individual can remember as his or her own the experiences of the earlier. Although he does not share the Cartesian ontological view that consciousness is a separate substance distinct from the body, Locke, as Anthony Quinton persuasively argues,[6] agrees with Descartes's dualist view that the self could possibly exist independently of its original body.

According to Locke's memory test, the insect is certainly Gregor Samsa. Believing himself to be Gregor, he recognizes the bedroom, recalls Gregor's past experiences and worries about catching the morning train. A wide variety of mental phenomena (sensations, thoughts, intentions) are referred to, all seemingly connected to Gregor's psychological past. They support the conscious link to the past essential to the dualist theory of personal identity.

In keeping with the Lockean-Cartesian perspective, the first section of the novella highlights not only Gregor's consciousness but also his capacity for rational deliberation. For example, Gregor hesitates rocking his new body off the bed, thinking, "he had better not for the life of him lose consciousness . . . [yet] the most rational thing was to make any sacrifice for even the smallest hope of freeing himself from the bed."[7] Sharing access to much of Gregor's interior conscious life,

---

3. John Locke (1632–1704), English empirical philosopher and liberal political theorist [*Editor*].
4. Pertaining to the ideas of Locke and of René Descartes (1596–1650), French philosopher and mathematician, who rigorously pursued a skeptical "method of doubt" until reaching his famous principle *cogito ergo sum* [I think, therefore I am] [*Editor*].
5. John Locke, "Of Identity and Diversity," *An Essay Concerning Human Understanding*, vol. 1, ed. A. C. Fraser (New York: Dover, 1959) 448–49.
6. Anthony Quinton, "The Soul," *The Journal of Philosophy* 50 (1962): 396–97.
7. Stanley Corngold, trans., *The Metamorphosis by Franz Kafka* (New York: Bantam, 1972) 7. All subsequent quotations from *Metamorphosis* are cited parenthetically in the text. Norton Critical Edition page numbers appear in brackets.

the reader sympathizes with Gregor's plight and tries to understand the rationale behind his behavior. In this narratively privileged position, the reader initially accepts the Lockean-Cartesian explanation for this bizarre catastrophe.

From this perspective, the reader sees Gregor as more than just spatially separated from his family. Outside his room, imploring Gregor to open the locked door, the family are excluded from sharing his trauma and only indirectly sense that something must be wrong. The locked room—"a regular human room" (3) [3]—becomes a philosophical metonymy[8] for Gregor's private mentality. His predicament symbolizes the philosophical problem of other minds: inferring the existence of a mind from physical events and external behavior.

In his *Discourse on Method*, Descartes discusses two criteria for distinguishing "men from brutes", both of which play a role in the Samsa family's attempt to discover the truth about what is going on in Gregor's bedroom.[9] First, only human beings *qua*[1] persons have the linguistic ability to express thoughts. Secondly, while lower animals can do many things, some better than humans, they cannot act with rational deliberation but only react according to bodily predispositions. For Descartes, deliberate action and the rational use of language are the marks and test of a rational consciousness. Locke recognizes a similar test, although—citing the example of a talking parrot—he is not as confident that only human beings can speak.[2]

The Samsa family apply both of Descartes's criteria to interpret what is going on in the bedroom. On replying to his mother's questioning about not catching the early morning train, Gregor is "shocked to hear his own voice answering. . . . [It was] unmistakably his own voice, true, but . . . an insistent distressed chirping intruded, which left the clarity of his words intact only for a moment really, before so badly garbling them . . ." (5) [5]. These garbled sounds finally betray him when the office manager arrives, wanting an explanation for Gregor's missing the train. Startled by the manager's accusations, Gregor abandons caution and chirps out a long explanation. Family and manager are stunned at what they hear. "Did you understand a word? . . . That was the voice of an animal," says the manager (13) [10]. Realizing that his speech is now unintelligible to those outside his door, although it "had seemed clear enough to him," Gregor starts to lose confidence in his personal integrity. A metaphysical barrier now separates him from other people.

The family and office manager also doubt the rationality of Gregor's actions. Unable to understand why he continues to remain locked in

8. A figure of speech in which the name of one thing is used for something else associated with it, e.g., "the Pentagon" for "the military" [*Editor*].
9. René Descartes, *Discourse on Method, The Philosophical Works of Descartes*, vol. 1, trans. E. S. Haldane and G. R. T. Ross (Cambridge: Cambridge UP, 1911) 116–17.
1. In their capacity as (Latin) [*Editor*].
2. Locke, "Of Identity and Diversity," 446–47.

his room, the manager calls to him through the door, "I thought I knew you to be a quiet, reasonable person, and now you suddenly seem to want to start strutting about, flaunting strange whims" (11) [9]. Clearly both family and manager find his behavior irrational and out of character. When he hears them call for a doctor and a locksmith, Gregor anticipates being "integrated into human society once again and hoped for marvelous, amazing feats from both the doctor and the locksmith, without really distinguishing sharply between them" (13) [11]. Gregor hopes that the locksmith will remove not only a spatial barrier but will reintroduce him into the human and personal realm. Spatial access and medical attention are seen as reaffirming what has come into question: Gregor's status as a person.

When Gregor does unlock the door and reveal himself, however, the family and manager are even more convinced of his irrational behavior. They draw back in horror at his insect epiphany and consider his entrance into the living room to be outrageous behavior. Wielding the manager's cane, stamping his foot and hissing, the father drives the loathsome insect back into the bedroom. Rational persuasion is deemed inappropriate. "No plea of Gregor's helped," the narrator observes, "no plea was even understood; however humbly he might turn his head, his father merely stamped his feet more forcefully" (18) [14].

Faced with a being they believe to be incapable of linguistic comprehension and whom they see as acting irrationally, the family are in a moral and conceptual quandary. As the only being inside Gregor's locked bedroom who responds to their calls, the creature cannot be condemned simply as alien. Yet neither can it be accepted in its own right as a person. Their response is a compromise: they accept the creature as Gregor but take him to be suffering from a severe incapacitating illness. Adopting this attitude excuses his strange speech and behavior; they believe that he will be his *old self* again when he recovers. In the second section, both mother and father regularly ask their daughter whether Gregor has "perhaps shown a little improvement" (31) [23]. By believing Gregor to be ill, the family reconciles the opposing beliefs that Gregor still survives and that the monster in the bedroom is something less than a person.

The reader also comes to adopt a strategy of reconciliation, trying to bring together a dualist and a materialist theoretical context for the narrative. Although, as Harold Skulsky argues, it is implausible to interpret *The Metamorphosis* as a narrative of a "psychotic breakdown,"[3] Gregor's mental states are so at odds with his transformed body that the reader gives some credence to Gregor's thought that he might be dreaming or imagining the whole situation. Lying in bed, Gregor muses that "in the past he had often felt some kind of slight pain, possibly

---

3. Harold Skulsky, *Metamorphosis: The Mind in Exile* (Cambridge: Harvard UP, 1981) 171–73.

caused by lying in an uncomfortable position, which, when he got up, turned out to be purely imaginary, and he was eager to see how today's fantasy would gradually fade away" (6) [6]. The vividness of his experience coupled with the doubt about its veracity suggests Franz Brentano's theory about the relation of mind to the world.[4] From his attendance at lectures in philosophy at the university in Prague and his subsequent participation in a philosophical discussion group, Kafka, according to Ronald Hayman,[5] was thoroughly familiar with Brentano's views as presented by Brentano's pupil, Anton Marty.[6] For Brentano, mental phenomena exhibit *intentionality*: that is, all mental acts are aimed at objects which exist in the mind but for which no correlative object in the world might exist (i.e., one can think about or believe in the Fountain of Youth regardless of whether it actually exists).

The possibility that Gregor's predicament might be imaginary, even though the experience be vivid, challenges the reliability of his narrative point of view. By raising questions about the veracity of Gregor's self-conscious narration, the text makes room for an alternative conceptual explanation of Gregor's identity. Although the reader initially accepts the dualist perspective, Kafka gradually introduces an alternative to this original position, thereby raising doubts about whether the insect continues to be Gregor Samsa. As a result, the reader's attitude toward the underlying framework of the story begins to shift: while accepting the insect as Gregor, the reader comes to acknowledge evidence that undercuts this identity.

As Kafka initially presents it, the relation of Gregor's consciousness to his insect body is not a happy one. The carapace prevents him from acting as he chooses, not allowing him to get out of bed easily, unlock the door, or answer intelligibly his family's questions. He lacks that mental control over his new body that Descartes describes as being closer to one's body than a pilot to a ship. Gregor finds he has "numerous little legs, which were in every different kind of perpetual motion and which, besides, he could not control" (7) [6]. The new body also begins exhibiting a motivating character of its own, disrupting the integrity of Gregor's original character. A sign of this change occurs in the first section when Gregor enters the living room and involuntarily starts snapping his jaws at some coffee spilling from an overturned pot (18) [14]. The anxious reaction to his father's hissing is another example

4. Franz Brentano (1838–1916), German-Austrian philosopher concerned with empirical psychology, argued in his principal work *Psychology from an Empirical Standpoint* (1874) that "intentionality" distinguished mental from physical phenomena [*Editor*].
5. Ronald Hayman, *Kafka: A Biography* (New York: Oxford UP, 1982) 35–36.
6. Anton Marty (1847–1914), professor of philosophy at the Charles University in Prague, concentrated on the philosophy of language; his theory of meaning is based on Brentano's descriptive psychology. Cf. *The Foundations of General Linguistics* (1908) [*Editor*].

of insect behavior, one stressed later in the novella when Gregor himself hisses with rage (44) [32].

In the second section, more indications of an insectile nature emerge. He feels a greater sense of well-being when his new body is allowed to behave in its own natural way rather than being forced to stand upright in a human posture. He also discovers the usefulness of his antennae, an ability to crawl up the bedroom walls, and a penchant for hanging from the ceiling (19, 31–32) [15, 23]. Insect patterns of sleep and waking develop: sleepy trances alternate with wakeful periods punctuated with hunger pangs (23) [17]. His taste in food changes. Milk, which had formerly been his favorite drink, is now repugnant to him, as are fresh foods. He prefers leftovers and rotten vegetables, delighting in a "piece of cheese, which two days before Gregor had declared inedible" (24) [18]. The range of his vision decreases—"from day to day he saw things even a short distance away less and less distinctly"—as does his sense of connection with the outside world (29) [21]. He also begins not to notice the passage of time (49) [36].

His emotional reactions change, often in ways that he does not understand. He is anxious or frightened at things which formerly would not have affected him. He notices that "the empty high-ceilinged room in which he was forced to lie flat on the floor made him nervous without his being able to tell why . . ." (23) [17]. This same uneasiness and fear are provoked by his sister's cleaning his room (30) [22]. Of course, a change of tastes and habits *per se* need not show the replacement of one person by another (or a person by an insect). Yet, increasingly in the novella, these changes take place outside the scope and limits of Gregor's awareness: he either does not understand why the shifts in attitude and preference have occurred, or he is only dimly aware of the new motivation. In the beginning of the second section, he crawls to the bedroom door: "Only after he got to the door did he notice what had really attracted him—the smell of something to eat" (21) [16]. Increasingly, Gregor acts from animal instinct rather than from self-conscious awareness. This invasion of his private self by a new motivating agency suggests the gradual replacement of his former personality.

In one of his rare moments of reflection, when gobbling down the "inedible" cheese, he ponders: "Have I become less sensitive?" (24) [18]. However, unlike the reader who starts to question this creature's identity, he resists an answer. He continues to act in ignorance, on occasion even concocting spurious reasons for his behavior. For example, he worries about not being able to support his parents and sister. "In order not to get involved in such thoughts," the narrator adds, "Gregor decided to keep moving and he crawled up and down the room" (22) [16]. An air of false consciousness[7] pervades this "decision." Complicitously selective, the narrator withholds the full account of Gregor's motivations, providing only the rationale as Gregor perceives it. Instead of a conscious choice, a more likely motivation is that crawling up and down is an insect's instinctive response to a frightening situation. Gregor reacts in this same insect-like manner to other anxiety-producing incidents.

With the gradual encroachment of one character on another, the rational conscious self (on the Lockean-Cartesian model) loses its status as sole "pilot," and a new motivating agency exercises control. Gregor's individuality begins to unravel. When Grete (Gregor's sister) proposes to move some furniture out of Gregor's room in order to give him more crawling space, the mother protests: to her "the sight of the bare wall was heartbreaking; and why shouldn't Gregor have the same feeling." On hearing his mother's objection, Gregor realizes that in wanting the furniture removed he had been "on the verge of forgetting" his human past (33) [25]. If only for a moment, he perceives that his new attitudes and preferences are in conflict with his human past.

Gregor's awareness and understanding (mental activity identified with his humanity) clash with his new insectile character. In philosophical terms, the Lockean-Cartesian dualist account of Gregor-as-consciousness opposes a materialist-behaviorist account of his emerging instinctive character. From the latter perspective, the disposition to behave in insect-like ways is produced by the insect's physiology interacting with its environment. According to dualism, in contrast, Gregor's pre-transformational psyche or consciousness continues despite the physical changes that have taken place.

The clash between Gregor-as-insect and Gregor-as-consciousness can be seen in the following oppositions. First, the insect-states and behavior do not originate from Gregor's earlier human character: they are newly introduced and independent of Gregor's human past. Gregor's consciousness, however, is clearly related to his human past. Secondly, insect-character and human-character are unfused: no unified personality integrates both insect and human traits. Aside from a few acknowledgments of their existence, Gregor's new insectile attitudes and dispositions remain outside his consciousness. No sense of self-consciousness accompanies them. Although at times Gregor ponders their presence, he does not consciously claim them as his own. Thus, instead of a unified self, the transformed Gregor is fissured into two characters, clashing yet jointly existing in the same body.

Because of this unresolved theoretical clash, the novella does not provide an answer to the question of whether the insect is physiologically intact or composite. In their discussion of *The Metamorphosis*,

---

7. A term in Marxist thought designating an inability to see things, especially social relations, as they really are—namely, as produced by material factors [*Editor*].

both John Updike and Vladimir Nabokov see Gregor's physical inde-
terminateness as a necessary feature of the work.[8] This biological indeterminacy is revealed in numerous anthropomorphic descriptions of
the transformed Gregor (e.g., his "eyes streaming with tears of
contentment"—24 [18]). Leaving in doubt the exact nature of Gregor's
physiological transformation more forcefully pits dualism against ma-
terialism. To assume that the insect has at least part of a human brain,
allows the materialist/behaviorist a consistent explanation for both Gregor's human and insectile behavior.

Not only do dualist and materialist interpretations collide, but a third
account of personal identity intrudes. Dominating the novella's final
section, this third conception involves seeing a person as an individual
constituted by certain social relationships. Personal identity is maintained by preserving the constituting social relationships. Failure to preserve them, even though an individual maintains psychological or
material continuity, erodes personal identity.

Prefigured in Plato's *Republic*, social-constructionist theories of the
self have a long and eminent history.[9] Their most influential nineteenth-century advocates are Hegel ("Self-consciousness exists in itself
and for itself, in that, and by the fact that it exists for another self-
consciousness; that is to say, it *is* only by being acknowledged or 'recognized'") and Marx.[1] In this century, George Herbert Mead's theory
of the self as "social object" (136–44) and Louis Althusser's neo-Marxist
account are in that tradition.[2] Recently, Erving Goffman has promoted
a theory of the self as constituted by a nexus of social roles. Selves, he
claims, are produced by particular forms of social interaction and do
not exist independently of social contexts. For Goffman, the self "as a
performed character, is not an organic thing that has a specific location,
whose fundamental fate is to be born, to mature, and to die; it is a

8. John Updike, "Reflections: Kafka's Short Stories," *The New Yorker* (9 May 1983): 121–33.
   [Updike (b. 1932) is an important U.S. novelist and critic—*Editor*.] Vladimir Nabokov, *Lectures on Literature* (New York: Harcourt, 1980) 250–83. [Nabokov (1899–1977) was a Russian
   and thereafter U.S. author of novels of great wit and linguistic refinement—*Editor*.].
9. Plato (ca.429–347 B.C.) was a Greek philosopher and pupil of Socrates. In *The Republic*
   Plato compares justice in the soul and in the state and asserts that only those who can perceive
   the form of the good are fit to rule [*Editor*].
1. Georg Wilhelm Friedrich Hegel, *The Phenomenology of Mind*, trans. J. B. Baillie (New York:
   Harper, 1967) 229. [Hegel (1770–1831), a vastly influential German philosopher, traces the
   development of "Spirit" or "Mind" and its manifestations in the world, including the way
   that self-consciousness depends upon recognition by others, in his masterpiece *The Phenomenology of Mind* (1807)—*Editor*]. Karl Marx, "Theses on Feuerbach," *Writings of the Young
   Marx on Philosophy and Society*, ed. and trans. L. D. Easton and K. H. Guddat (Garden City,
   N.Y.: Doubleday, 1967) 400–402. [For Marx (1818–1883), German political economist and
   founder of revolutionary communism, historical development is an economically determined
   process driven by the class struggle—*Editor*.]
2. George Herbert Mead, *Mind, Self, and Society* (Chicago: U of Chicago P, 1934) 136–44.
   [Mead (1863–1931), influential U.S. pragmatist philosopher, asserted that "mind" emerged
   within the social processes of communication and self-reflection—*Editor*.] Louis Althusser,
   "Ideology and Ideological State Apparatuses," *Lenin and Philosophy*, trans. Ben Brewster (New
   York: Monthly Review, 1971) 127–86.

dramatic effect . . . [and] the means for producing and maintaining selves . . . are often bolted down in social establishments."[3]

Although most fully presented in the novella's final section, the social-constructionist theory of personal identity does appear in earlier sections. In the first section, the locked door, Gregor's chirping, and his peculiar behavior are not the only obstacles to social reintegration and self-validation. The family's reaction to Gregor's new body also plays a role. "If they were shocked," the narrator comments, "then Gregor had no further responsibility and could be calm. But if they took everything calmly, then he too, had no reason to get excited . . ." (12) [10]. If the family accepts him, then his self (defined as provider, son, brother, household member, etc.) is maintained. If they reject him, these same self-constituting ties are severed and Gregor's identity begins to unravel.

In the second section, after the calamitous rejection by his family, Gregor seeks to reestablish his relationship with them. Wondering how best to lead his new life, he concludes "that for the time being he would have to lie low and, by being patient and showing his family every possible consideration, help them bear the inconvenience which he simply had to cause them in his present condition" (23) [17]. His passive resignation in favor of patience and consideration, however, does not actively fulfill his role as family member. It is undertaken more for his own convenience than to mend a ruptured social tie. Being locked in his bedroom by his family is actually reassuring: he feels gratified that there will be no frightening intrusions.

Instead of reintegrating him, Gregor's self-deceived commitment to patient resignation widens the separation between him and his family. The widening gap between them is also a verbal one. After his chirping explanation to the office manager and his subsequent supplication to his mother, he never attempts to communicate verbally with anyone. In turn, his family abandons the notion that he is able to understand their speech: "since the others could not understand what he said, it did not occur to any of them, not even to his sister, that he could understand what they said . . ." (25) [19]. He receives news of them only indirectly.

Nevertheless, his sister Grete does try to establish a new relationship with Gregor. Unfortunately, their relationship lacks reciprocity and she ends up creating only a new family role and identity for herself. Up until Gregor's transformation, Grete has been a child with few family responsibilities. By assuming the duty of feeding Gregor and cleaning his room, she takes on the role of an adult and with it an adult self. Gregor hears the family say "how much they appreciated his sister's work, whereas until now they had frequently been annoyed with her

---

3. Erving Goffman, *The Presentation of the Self in Everyday Life* (Garden City, N.Y.: Doubleday, 1959) 252–53.

because she struck them as being a little useless" (31) [23]. Her childish indolence has given way to a more mature acceptance of responsibility. In her parents' eyes she has become an adult.

Although Grete maintains regular contact with Gregor, Grete and the family fail to reestablish a familial personal relationship with him. "If Gregor," the narrator says, "had only been able to speak to his sister and thank her for everything she had to do for him, he could have accepted her services more easily; as it was, they caused him pain" (29) [22]. Thus, for want of communication and a reciprocity of relations, Gregor's position in the family disintegrates and his sense of self erodes.

His insect-anxiety toward his sister increases until the watershed scene in which his sister and mother remove the furniture from his room. As the narrator notes, on hearing his mother's objections to moving the furniture, "Gregor realized that the monotony of family life, combined with the fact that not a soul had addressed a word directly to him, must have addled his brain in the course of the past two months, for he could not explain to himself in any other way how in all seriousness he could have been anxious to have his room cleared out." His decreasing contacts with his family have eroded his sense of being a person. Resolving to resist this gradual depersonalizing influence, he now wants "the beneficial influence of the furniture on his state of mind" (33) [25].

The furniture comes to represent Gregor's past self-preserving relationship with his family, awakening him to the intrusion of his animal instincts. When he frightens his mother in an effort to halt their removing the furniture, Grete starts to shout at Gregor. "These were the first words," the narrator interjects, that "she had addressed directly to him since his metamorphosis." They awaken the hope that a family relationship might be reestablished. In the confusion of Grete's ministering to their mother, Gregor runs out of the bedroom, leaving the depersonalizing isolation of his bedroom for the public interactive space of the living room. Hearing that "Gregor's broken out," the father once again drives him back into the confinement of the bedroom, this time wounding him with a thrown apple (37, 39) [27, 29]. Patriarchal intervention has dashed Gregor's hopes of reintegrating himself into the family circle.

The third section, the section in which the implications of the social-constructionist theory are most fully explored, begins with the family's seemingly begrudging acceptance of Gregor as a family member. His wound "seemed to have reminded even his father that Gregor was a member of the family, in spite of his present pathetic and repulsive shape . . . [and] it was the commandment of family duty to swallow their disgust and endure him, endure him and nothing else" (40) [29]. Yet this commitment to tolerance still allows Gregor no positive role in family matters. He eventually disregards both the open door, which the family leave ajar out of their awakened sense of duty, and his earlier resolution to be considerate of his family, especially in keeping himself clean (46) [34]. "It hardly surprised him," the reader learns, "that lately he was showing so little consideration for others; once such consideration had been his greatest pride" (48) [35]. Gregor is "hardly surprised" because much of his disregard for his family is motivated by his new instinctual character.

In keeping with this new character, Gregor now shows an interest in music. Unlike his sister who enjoys playing the violin, Gregor had earlier shown little interest in music. Nevertheless, in his role as provider and loving brother, he had planned to realize the "beautiful dream" of sending Grete to the conservatory to study her instrument (27) [20]. Hearing Grete playing her violin in the living room for three boarders whom the family have taken in to help meet expenses, Gregor once again leaves his bedroom, creeping through the inadvertently open doorway into the living room (48) [35]. Given his earlier complacency toward music, Gregor's attraction is likely produced by his insectile character. Although the Orphic myth[4] of music charming the beast is the underlying theme here, the ambiguity of Gregor's action (the narrator does not specify whether Gregor's attraction is due to animal magnetism or deliberate choice) is sustained by his asking, and failing to answer, another of his self-reflecting questions: "Was he an animal, that music could move him so?" (49) [36]. In the reverie of the moment, Gregor starts to fantasize about bringing Grete back to his room and revealing his plan to send her to the conservatory. In his fantasy he attempts to reconstitute his relationship with his sister and reclaim his sense of self. Yet so remote is the likelihood of the fantasy becoming fact (i.e., Gregor's *talking* to Grete, and her being kissed by something she considers repulsive) that it highlights the absurdity of their reestablishing any personal relationship. A boarder's shriek at Gregor's dust-covered carapace abruptly ends his reverie. This latest outrage by Gregor prompts the family to discuss getting rid of "the monster" (51) [37].

The social-constructionist theory of self underlies much of the family's discussion of what to do with the monster. "If he could understand us," the father bewails, "then maybe we could come to an agreement with him." To which Grete replies: "You just have to get rid of the idea that it's Gregor. Believing it for so long, that is our real misfortune. But how can it be Gregor? If it were Gregor, he would have realized long ago that it isn't possible for human beings to live with such a creature, and he would have gone away of his own free will. Then we wouldn't have a brother, but we'd be able to go on living and honor his memory" (52) [38]. Cut off from communicating with the creature,

---

4. According to Greek myth, Orpheus could sing and play the lyre so sweetly that wild beasts were charmed and tempests stilled [*Editor*].

the family can neither reforge the familial bond with Gregor nor establish a new one. The sister's argument against the monster's being her brother does not appeal to the physical impossibility of his continued existence. To a great extent the family have accepted Gregor's physical transformation. Instead the appeal is social: given the widening disparity between their two life forms, there is no basis for a personal relationship. Not only has Gregor changed, but the family has changed as well, becoming now more resourceful and self-sufficient. All three of them have jobs.

Since the creature cannot maintain the former relationship of being a son and brother, it must not be Gregor. The sister, however, does allow the creature one *limit-position* in which to be a brother: the monster could disappear and by so doing show its consideration for the family. Such an act would be a *brotherly* act, fulfilling a role while at the same time dissolving it.

In the hope of resolving the metaphysical impasse, the reader might be inclined to interpret Gregor's death early the next morning as such an act of brotherly consideration. The undercutting of one theory of self by another, however, extends also to his death. The nature of Gregor's death and its causes are equally open to question by the respective theories. No one theory convincingly explains his end.

According to the dualist perspective, Gregor could be seen as consciously committing suicide because he realizes the hopelessness of his situation. After all, the family take his gestures of concern to be either threatening or irrational. No longer wishing to live separated from those he loves, he starves himself to death. Corroborating this view is the narrator's observation: "[Gregor] thought back on his family with deep emotion and love. His conviction that he would have to disappear was, if possible, even firmer than his sister's" (54) [39]. According to this account, his earlier refusal to eat leads up to this "conviction."

The limited and shifting focus of the narration, however, also allows for a materialist reading: the change in eating habits and the death indicate not conscious choices but the course of the insect's life cycle, exacerbated by the infected wound from the apple thrown by the father. Since not all of Gregor's personal reflections are to be trusted (e.g., his conscious rationalizations for his instinctively motivated behavior), events leading up to his death should not be seen as excluding a materialist interpretation. In the description of Gregor's death, there occurs a curious phrase about his lack of volition: "Then, *without his consent*, his head sank down to the floor, and from his nostrils streamed his last breath" (54 [39]; emphasis mine). The denial of "consent" calls into question Gregor's agency: death might be the result of an enfeebled condition rather than an intended starvation.

The social-constructionist theory can also provide an account of Gregor's death. Just before being drawn into the living room by his sister's violin playing, Gregor listens to the boarders eating: "'I'm hungry enough,' Gregor said to himself, full of grief, 'but not for these things. Look how these roomers are gorging themselves, and I'm dying!'" (47) [34]. Hungry, "but not for these things," Gregor yearns for nourishment other than food, for an emotional sustenance derived from an active involvement with his family. With the dissolution of the family bond, he emotionally and socially starves to death.

Gregor's fantasy of announcing to Grete his intention to send her to the conservatory also supports a social-constructionist interpretation of his later demise. Even if his death is something he consciously contemplated, his passive and fantasized past behavior renders suspicious Gregor's "conviction that he would have to disappear . . ." (54) [39]. The narrator is unreliable about Gregor's passive "contributions" to his family: Gregor's patient hiding in his room is instinctively motivated rather than consciously intended. Thus, the reader should be suspicious of crediting Gregor with actively bringing about his own end. On the social-constructionist view, only within the bounds of the family relationship can Gregor act positively and have a sense of personal agency. Despite the sister's claim that Gregor would disappear if he were her brother, the family do not recognize his death as an act of consideration. In fact, they react to it as good fortune.

Thus, by maintaining an ambivalence among the dualist, materialist and social-constructionist explanations for Gregor's death, Kafka preserves the tension and opposition among all three of Gregor's "identities:" a self-consciousness, an instinctual organism, and a social persona—a "shadow being" trying fantastically to maintain itself in a disintegrating family relationship.

The sustained opposition and tension among the three positions cloud not only the nature of Gregor's death but the extent of the family's moral responsibility toward him. Each of the three theories undercuts the other two positions; this mutual undermining leaves unresolved questions about the limits of responsibility toward those whose personhood is in doubt, just as it leaves unresolved questions about the basis for moral relationships in the face of instinctual behavior and the extent to which social ties create moral responsibilities.

In contrast to the moral debate of the third section, the novella's epilogue introduces a false sense of closure. It drowns out the debate by depicting the family as reunified, smug in their togetherness, having weathered the catastrophe of Gregor's final appearance and death. The epilogue thus obscures an ethical issue that the reader must still confront: whether, prior to his death, Gregor stops being a person who deserves the moral support of his family. The epilogue, especially what Stanley Corngold has called "the falseness and banality of the tone of the ending," cuts off this moral questioning.[5] It closes the work by resolving its moral ambiguity, covering up its thematic antagonisms and destroying what Joseph Margolis sees as the philosophical tensions of the work.[6]

In his *Diaries*, Kafka himself expressed displeasure at the novella's "unreadable ending" [69].[7] For a writer who registered repeated disapproval of his writing, this castigation may be no more than the carping of a perpetually unsatisfied artist unwilling to acknowledge that the writing has ended. Yet, it may also register his adoption of the stance of the reader and a call for the type of "experimental" reading process I have described. Indeed, as Camus has noticed, "The whole art of Kafka consists in forcing the reader to reread. His endings, or his absence of endings, suggest explanations which, however, are not revealed in clear language but, before they seem justified, require that the story be reread from another point of view."[8] Rather than arriving at a "justified" closure, one is more apt on rereading the novella to sense the clash and mutual undercutting of philosophical theories. Perhaps Kafka's displeasure at the epilogue thus reveals not artistic dissatisfaction but rather a desire not to obscure the competing ethical and philosophical issues that the work raises.

In the twentieth century more than any other century, human beings have faced perplexing questions about the nature of their identities as persons. From our educational heritage, we have developed as rational consciousnesses, while at the same time we have increasingly come to understand the biological (i.e., material) determinants of our characters. The rapid social changes of the recent past have made us realize both the role that social organization plays in the constitution of who we are and our dependence on a stable social context for maintaining our identities. These ways of thinking about ourselves (as conscious, biological or social beings) are far from compatible conceptual schemas. Kafka's novella makes this incompatibility all too clear.

5. Stanley Corngold, *The Fate of the Self: German Writers and French Theory* (New York: Columbia UP, 1986) 174.
6. Joseph Margolis, "Kafka vs. Eudaimonia and Duty," *Philosophy and Phenomenological Research* 19 (1958): 27–42.
7. Franz Kafka, *The Diaries of Franz Kafka, 1914–1923*, trans. Martin Greenberg (New York: Schocken, 1949) 12.
8. Albert Camus, "Hope and the Absurd in the Works of Franz Kafka," *The Myth of Sisyphus*, trans. Justin O'Brien (New York: Vintage, 1955) 95–102. [Camus (1913–1960), charismatic French novelist and thinker, was born in Algeria; his work, existentialist, confronts the experience of absurdity—*Editor*.]

MARK M. ANDERSON

Sliding Down the Evolutionary Ladder?
Aesthetic Autonomy in *The Metamorphosis*†

Was he an animal that music moved him so?
(*The Metamorphosis* [36])

I

A few years ago an art gallery in New York created a mild sensation by dousing a number of human models, clothes and bodies, in green paint and hanging them on its bare white walls. Although the models adopted various poses, they made no attempt to deny their living status, and interacted freely with the bemused public. Somewhat at a loss to describe the artwork, which apparently was not for sale, the media spoke of "Dada," "performance," and "action" art.[1] Franz Kafka's literary masterpiece of 1912, *The Metamorphosis*, enacts essentially the same scenario when its human-sized bug hero climbs the wall of his bedroom and usurps the aesthetic space occupied by a gilt-framed photograph, hugging his flat body against the glass until it "completely covers" the picture [26]. When his mother, less blasé than a New York audience of the 1980s, enters the room, her senses are overwhelmed. She perceives only a huge brownish spot against the flowered wallpaper and, crying out "Oh God! Oh God!" [26], falls into a dead faint. No avant-garde artist of the modern period could ask for a more satisfying public response.

Since the story's initial publication in 1915, few if any readers of *The Metamorphosis* have wished to recognize Gregor Samsa's metamorphosed body as an aesthetic form. For Kafka's early public the bug was simply too repulsive, and was explained away with allegorical notions like "alienated labor" or "unconscious self-loathing."[2] Further, although

---

† Reprinted from *Kafka's Clothes: Ornament and Aestheticism in the Habsburg Fin de Siècle* (Oxford: Clarendon Press, 1992) 123–44, by permission of Oxford University Press. Copyright © Mark M. Anderson 1992.

1. Dada was an iconoclastic literary and artistic movement from ca. 1916–22 in Zurich, Berlin, and New York: it ridiculed bourgeois culture, which had been called into question by World War I. Performance art is an artistic event which can include elements of theater, music, and the visual arts. Action art—i.e., action painting—is a form of abstract expressionism in which paint is splashed on the canvas to emphasize the physicality of painting and record the process of creation [*Editor*]. Norton Critical Edition page numbers appear in brackets.

2. ["Alienated labor" is a Marxist term, designating labor whose products become something independent of their creator and dominate him or her—*Editor*.] For an overview of the secondary literature on *The Metamorphosis*, see S. Corngold's *The Commentators' Despair: The Interpretation of Kafka's "Metamorphosis"* (Port Washington: Kennikat Press, 1973) and P. Beicken's *Franz Kafka: Eine kritische Einführung in die Forschung* (Frankfurt: Fischer Taschenbuch, 1974), 261–72. One of the earliest interpretations of the story in psychoanalytic terms was by H. Kaiser, whose "Franz Kafkas Inferno: eine psychologische Deutung seiner Strafphantasie" appeared in the official psychoanalytic journal *Imago* in 1931. A large number

154

Günther Anders in an early and quite perceptive essay interpreted Gregor Samsa as a *Luftmensch* and "artist" figure,[3] and although subsequent critics have seen a parallel between Gregor's isolated condition and Franz Kafka's monk-like dedication to his writing,[4] readers have been hard put to reconcile this aesthetic dimension with the specificity of Gregor's outward form. In fact, close scrutiny of the story has led critics to deny that the bug has any reliable visual specificity at all: actual descriptive details are scant and contradictory, and since the story is narrated largely from Gregor's perspective, his own body tends to disappear from the reader's view. The opening designation of Gregor as an "ungeheure Ungeziefer" or "giant vermin" is notoriously ambiguous, for *Ungeziefer* refers to a broad range of animal parasites rather than a single type, *ungeheuer* ("monstrous") is by definition vague, and the "un-" prefixes in both words double the term's lack of specificity into a kind of negative infinity. Significantly, when the cleaning lady calls to Gregor with the precise term *Mistkäfer* (dung beetle), he refuses to respond. Thus abstractly or negatively defined, the bug would seem to have no discernible form, and to the reader at least it remains a visual cipher.

This critical tendency to de-emphasize the bug's status as a visual object of representation reached its most extreme and brilliant limit in Stanley Corngold's influential essay "The Metamorphosis of the Metaphor."[5] Drawing on Anders's insight that Kafka often literalizes metaphors as the basis for his central images and plot lines, Corngold interprets Gregor's form as primarily linguistic and rhetorical rather than visual. Because the text circumvents the dialectical relationship of metaphor, insisting that Gregor *is* a bug but without denying him specifically human traits, the monstrous vermin form functions as a "mutilated metaphor, uprooted from familiar language" (59) [89], an "opaque sign" (56) [87]. Anything disturbing about his appearance arises pri-

of critics have taken over Kaiser's notion of a "punishment fantasy," including H. Tauber, H. D. Luke, C. Neider, W. Sokel. [See Selected Bibliography, pp. 215–18.] For Marxist readings of the story, see K. Hughes (ed.), *Franz Kafka: An Anthology of Marxist Criticism* (Concord: University Press of New England, 1981).

3. "Because Gregor Samsa wishes to live as an artist (i.e. 'free as air' [*wie ein Luftmensch*]), he is considered in the eyes of the respectable, down-to-earth world, to be a 'bit of an insect'; thus, in *The Metamorphosis*, he wakes up as a beetle, whose idea of happiness is to be clinging to the ceiling." *Franz Kafka*, trans. A. Steer and A. K. Thorlby (London: Bowes & Bowes, 1960), 43 [81].

4. Corngold offers the suggestive hypothesis that Kafka's experience of writing "The Judgment" in September 1912, the story which "came out of [him] like a real birth, covered with filth and slime" (*DI* 278), is the implicit biographical meaning of *The Metamorphosis*. See the expanded version of his essay "The Metamorphosis of the Metaphor," in *Franz Kafka: The Necessity of Form* (Ithaca, NY: Cornell University Press, 1988). [See above, pp. 79–107—*Editor.*] P. Cersowsky notes interestingly the tradition of metamorphosis into an animal as "an extreme image of the melancholy disposition," thereby linking Gregor to the melancholy "decadent type." See "*Mein ganzes Wesen ist auf Literatur gerichtet*" (Würzburg: Königshausen & Neumann, 1983), p. 76.

5. First published in 1970, the essay was reprinted in an expanded version in *The Necessity of Form*, which is the edition quoted here. [See above, pp. 79–107—*Editor.*]

marily from a disturbing use of rhetorical structure, an "unclean" mixing of the metaphor's human tenor and its material vehicle:

> It appears, then, that the metamorphosis in the Samsa household of man into vermin is unsettling not only because vermin are disturbing, or because the vivid representation of a human "louse" is disturbing, but because the indeterminate, fluid crossing of a human tenor and a material vehicle is in itself unsettling. (56)[6]

Such interpretations have an indisputable hold on Kafka's story and, I suspect, are ultimately correct. Kafka knew that his story was a kind of literary tease, that it depended on the reader's imagination to visualize what is only suggested by the text. When confronted with his editor's plan to illustrate the bug for the cover of the first edition, his response was unambiguous: "The insect itself cannot be depicted" (letter of 25 October 1915). He proposed instead the image of a half-opened door with only darkness behind it—the bug itself remains unseen and the reader must perform the same act of imagination that is required by the text in the passage from linguistic sign to mental image. Kafka's suggestion was in fact taken up, and a black-and-white illustration by Ottomar Starke adorned the story's first edition in Kurt Wolff's series *Die weißen Blätter*.[7]

None the less, one cannot help feeling that such critical and authorial strictures have something of a magician's legerdemain—Now you see him, now you don't—and hide as much as they reveal. Although the text is a verbal artefact which expertly subverts the metaphorical function of language, it also requires the reader to make a sustained effort to visualize the bug within a minutely described environment. Moreover, such strictures obscure the fact that the text repeatedly displays Gregor's body as a visual object of unusual power—a scandalous, grotesque object difficult to behold, yes, but one that is attributed with an undeniable aesthetic function, as in the scene when Gregor hangs himself on the wall in front of his mother and sister. Indeed, the basic movement of all three sections of the novella consists in covering and uncovering Gregor's body, like a monster at a fair or a sacred icon.

Accordingly, this [essay] will attempt to describe Gregor's form in visual and aesthetic terms, even when the text itself leaves these terms vague or obscures their reference. Two avenues of interpretation will be followed: a historical, deliberately digressive approach that compares Kafka's use of the vermin image to contemporary developments in science and literature, and a textual reading in terms of the problematic

6. See above, p. 86.
7. Kurt Wolff (1887–1963) was until 1930 an important publisher of innovative works in Germany. See below, p. 172, n. 5. *Die weißen Blätter* means "the white pages" [*Editor*].

of *Verkehr*,[8] clothing, and corporeal gymnastics that I have delineated in the preceding chapters and on which *The Metamorphosis*, perhaps more crucially than any of Kafka's other writings, depends.

II

Kafka's most famous text has been with us so long that it is easy to forget the audacity of using a human-sized cockroach as the main figure in a literary text. Nothing in the classical literature of animal fables or even in the Romantic literature of the uncanny or the grotesque is quite like *The Metamorphosis*, with its mixing of the monstrous and the everyday, the repulsive and the beautiful.[9] And yet there is precedent for Kafka's modernist masterpiece in the scientific and aesthetic discourses of the *fin de siècle*.[1] His story is about a metamorphosis from human to animal form, and like all his animal narratives it arises from—and in reaction to—the ubiquitous presence of Darwin's theory of evolution.[2] The idea of "metamorphosis" was in the air. Goethe's *Metamorphosis of Plants* and the *Metamorphosis of Animals* were held in high regard in scientific circles as Romantic harbingers of Darwin's own writings. German scientists like Ernst Haeckel and Wilhelm Bölsche propagated Darwin's teachings in Germany, not only in their research but in popular lecture series and *Volksausgaben* for a broad audience;[3] Haeckel held an influential lecture on the evolutionary theories of Goethe, Lamarck, and Darwin in 1882,[4] a year before Kafka's birth. Largely because of Haeckel's efforts, Darwin's evolutionary monism gained increasing currency in German-speaking countries, as all life forms were understood to be united in a great chain of being stretching from single-celled plasma to the highest primates.

Such theorizations found their equivalent in art and literature of the

8. A word meaning "traffic, circulation (as of commodities), and also sexual intercourse" [*Editor*].
9. In his *Introduction à la littérature fantastique* (Paris: Éditions du Seuil, 1970), Todorov rejects an affiliation with the fantastic, noting that Kafka's text proceeds in an opposite movement: "Le récit fantastique partait d'une situation parfaitement naturelle pour aboutir au surnaturel, *la Métamorphose* part de l'événement surnaturel pour lui donner, en cours de récit, un air de plus en plus naturel; et la fin de l'histoire est la plus éloignée qui soit du surnaturel" (179). ["The fantastic starts from a perfectly natural situation, to reach its climax in the supernatural. *The Metamorphosis* starts from a supernatural event, and during the course of the narrative gives it an increasingly natural atmosphere—until at the end, the story has moved as far as possible from the supernatural" (*The Fantastic* [Cleveland: Press of Case Western University, 1973] 171)—*Editor*.]
1. End of the nineteenth century [*Editor*].
2. See Margot Norris's discussion of Darwin and Nietzsche in relation to Kafka in *Beasts of the Modern Imagination* (Baltimore: Johns Hopkins University Press, 1985).
3. Ernst Haeckel (1834–1919) was a German zoologist; Wilhelm Bölsche (1861–1939) was a German writer who communicated the findings of biology in an easy-to-understand style in cheap popular editions [*Editor*].
4. Johann Wolfgang von Goethe (1749–1832) was Germany's most famous author: a universal thinker, whose works include *The Sorrows of Young Werther* (1749), *Faust* (1770–1831), and a number of important scientific essays. Jean Baptiste Pierre de Monet Lamarck (1744–1829), a French scientist, was the first great theorist of evolution, asserting that the biological characteristics developed through specialization are inherited [*Editor*].

period. The *Jugendstil*,[5] with its proliferation of swirling plant, mineral, and animal forms, espoused a monistic philosophy of an all-permeating life force, of organic change and becoming. Not infrequently, *Jugendstil* artists drew inspiration from contemporary scientific representations, which increasingly emphasized unusual, unknown, exotic, or otherwise bizarre forms of the natural world. Haeckel's *Kunstformen der Natur* (*Art-forms of Nature*, 1899–1903), which included 100 color illustrations of protozoa, ocean sponges, medusas, coral, tropical birds, flowers, and exotic insects, served as a veritable handbook for the *Jugendstil* movement.[6] In his foreword he notes that the higher forms of plants and vertebrate animals that had dominated scholarly and artistic attention until the nineteenth century have given way to "strange and marvellous forms."[7] Addressing himself explicitly to contemporary artists, he promises that his book will bring these hidden treasures to light, thereby providing them with a "rich supply of new and beautiful motifs."[8]

Haeckel's work had a twofold importance for literary and visual artists at the turn of the century. First, it offered them spectacular new material—vivid colors, flowing lines, translucent textures, grotesque and fantastic creatures from another realm of experience—that could be used in representations of organic and inorganic forms. It thus helped to enlarge the canon of aesthetically valid subjects, treating what might have been dismissed as ugly, overly stylized, bizarre, or lowly organisms as beautiful aesthetic forms in their own right. On a theoretical level, Haeckel promoted the notion of an originary *Kunsttrieb* or artistic impulse that could be found in all of nature. Attempting to explain the remarkable sensuous beauty, symmetry, and variety of even the most primitive organisms, he posited a "soul" within each cell that constantly struggled for "plastic" definition and self-realization: "One can describe the artistic impulses of protists as 'plastic cellular instincts,' for they stand on the same rung of the soul's activity as the well-known instincts of higher, multiple-celled animals and plants" (12). The will to art not merely as a democratic possibility but as a biological necessity arising from the depths of every living organism—here was a philosophy for turn-of-the-century reformists and educators.

Kafka's first encounter with these ideas came in the *Gymnasium*.[9]

---

5. A school or style in the fine and applied arts, architecture, fashion, and design which flourished from the 1890s until World War I [*Editor*].
6. See Jörg Mathes, introduction to *Theorie des literarischen Jugendstils* (Stuttgart: Reclam, 1984), 32.
7. Foreword to 1st edn., *Kunstformen der Natur* (Leipzig: Bibliographisches Institut, 1899).
8. As it turned out, Haeckel was richly rewarded for his efforts. In his 1913 introduction to *Die Natur als Künstlerin* (*Nature as Artist*) (Berlin: Vita), he remarks that since the publication of his earlier work he has received numerous pieces of furniture, dishes, cups, and pillows, all "tastefully embellished with the charming forms of the above-mentioned protists" (12).
9. Elite secondary school offering humanistic education based on the study of Greek and Latin. Kafka's school was the Altstädter [Old Town] *Gymnasium* in Prague [*Editor*].

Under the influence of his science teacher Adolf Gottwald, a convinced Darwinist, he read the author of *On the Origin of Species* at age 16. And according to his classmate Hugo Bergmann, he read Haeckel's *Welträtsel* (*The Riddle of the Universe*, 1899) with "unusual enthusiasm" in the same period.[1] A few years later he would find similar ideas in the literary writings of Hugo von Hofmannsthal and his friend Max Brod. The ornamental exoticism that one finds in their early work, as indeed that of the entire *fin-de-siècle* and *Jugendstil* generation, is sustained and legitimized by their naturalist curiosity in contemporary evolutionary theories linking plant, animal, and human intelligence.[2] Brod's early novellas abound in vegetable and animal exotica whose *correspondance* with the human soul he attempts to convey by an abundance of synaesthetic tropes. The following description from his "Carina Island" (in which he portrays Kafka as a detached, melancholy aesthete) gives us a typical sampling:

> It was a forest full of passion through which we strode. In the deep tranquillity and solitude, magnificent magnolia trees put forth their blossoms like large, violet bowls of porcelain. Humming-birds flashed through fragrant symphonies of scarlet and snow-white oceans of flowers, through palagonitic bushes and lilies and begonias. Giant silk-like moths spread their shimmering wings, butterflies showed off their violet and emerald-blue shades of colour. Giant beetles, which looked like precious jewels or like foliage, crept their way through the oily, red soil.[3]

Hofmannsthal[4] also echoes Haeckel's monistic exoticism in his early *Jugendstil* story "Fairytale of the 672nd Night" (1895), when the main protagonist recognizes in the ornaments of his plush, *fin-de-siècle* furniture "a magic image of the intertwined wonders of the world." In these carved ornaments he sees "the forms of animals and the forms of flowers and the merging of flowers with animals; the dolphins, lions, tulips, pearls and acanthus . . . It was a great heritage, the divine work of all generations and species."[5] In his Lord Chandos "Letter" written seven years later, the emphasis on ornamental flora and fauna shifts to less exotic, indeed "insignificant" creatures; but Haeckel's influence is

1. As quoted by K. Wagenbach, *Franz Kafka: Eine Biographie seiner Jugend* (Berne: Francke, 1958), 60.
2. Maurice Maeterlinck, whose writings played a key role in Symbolist and *fin-de-siècle* literary movements, was an amateur zoologist and botanist who dedicated several works to minute descriptions of ants, bees, and the *intelligence des fleurs*; he felt that their activity revealed a sense of order and beauty, an innate "artistic instinct." Other writers, notably Jens Peter Jacobsen (a trained botanist who translated Darwin into Danish), Joris-Karl Huysmans, and Octave Mirbeau in France, developed similar ideas about natural evolution in their works.
3. "Die Insel Carina," in *Experimente* (Berlin: Axel Juncker, 1907), 46.
4. Hugo von Hofmannsthal (1874–1929) was a Viennese author of lyric and dramatic poems and of libretti for operas composed by Richard Strauss, e.g., *Elektra* (1909) and *The Rosenkavalier* (1911) [Editor].
5. "Das Märchen der 672. Nacht," in J. Mathes (ed.), *Prosa des Jugendstils* (Stuttgart: Reclam, 1982), 41–2.

still evident in the fluid, evanescent passage between them and the protagonist's human consciousness. The text, which Kafka knew and valued, is particularly relevant to *The Metamorphosis*:

> In these moments an insignificant creature—a dog, a rat, a beetle, a crippled appletree, a lane winding over the hill, a moss-covered stone—mean more to me than the most beautiful, abandoned mistress of the happiest night. . . . [Such creatures] can become the vehicle of a divine revelation . . . of my flowing over into those creatures, or my feeling that a fluid of life and death, dream and waking, flowed into them for an instant—but from where?[6]

Kafka's story is another matter, of course. His beetle does not crawl through the earth of Brod's exotic tropical island but through the drab, petty bourgeois apartment of a European city. And unlike Hofmannsthal, who keeps Chandos's mystical revelation within a human framework, Kafka reverses the camera angle, forcing us to see not so much the insect as the world of higher primates from the insect's perspective. Moreover, Gregor's metamorphosed body does not cater to contemporary aesthetic taste for stylized exotica. Like the cockroach that Kafka mentions in the "Letter to His Father,"[7] the vermin form in *The Metamorphosis* is meant to sting and bite its audience, to upset traditional aesthetic notions with a scandalous, "inhuman" otherness. Frau Samsa's reaction—her appeal to "God" as well as her fainting—is again exemplary.

As an assault on conventional bourgeois taste, the novella thus definitely belongs within the canon of Expressionist and avant-garde modernism, rather than in *fin-de-siècle* "decadence" or the *Jugendstil*.[8] Its closest visual counterpart is to be found in the early drawings of Kafka's Prague contemporary and acquaintance Alfred Kubin, whose allegorical symbolism often relies on a similar grotesque crossing of human and abstract insect-like figures. But like Kubin's zoological fantasies, Kafka's story draws on the visual forms promoted by *fin-de-siècle* scientific and literary discourse, on "strange and marvelous forms" from a radically other realm of experience. More crucially, it insists on what one might well call the animal's "humanness," which emerges most poignantly in his relation to art. Just as Haeckel recognized in single-celled protozoa a human "soul" and a primal *Kunsttrieb*, so does *The Metamorphosis* endow a lowly, potentially repulsive form with a human consciousness and a will toward art. However grotesque and "other" the *Ungeziefer*

---

6. "Ein Brief," as reprinted in U. Karthaus (ed.), *Impressionismus, Symbolismus und Jugendstil* (Stuttgart: Reclam, 1977), 148–50, my translation. The above quotations appear in three separate passages but all refer to the same mystical, unutterable experience.
7. See above, p. 71 [*Editor*].
8. Expressionist writers and artists aimed to express the impulses of unconscious life in distorted forms and shocking graphic effects. Writers and artists associated with "decadence" elaborated in a refined and subtle style themes held to be artificial and abnormal [*Editor*].

may appear to the Samsa family, the text's true subject (as in Kafka's other animal stories) is the condition of being caught between human and animal forms, caught in the fluid of an evolutionary life force. That Gregor slides down the evolutionary ladder in his quest for artistic self-realization is only one of the ironies behind his bizarre transformation.

III

To describe Gregor's animal form as it manifests itself in the narrative, one can best begin by noting what it is not: clothing. In Kafka's novel fragment of 1907, *Wedding Preparations in the Country,* we find an anticipation of Gregor Samsa's transformation. There Eduard Raban imagines himself split into two distinct selves: a giant beetle who stays in bed while his "clothed" human body is sent into the *Verkehr* of the world, "travelling" to the country to get married:

> I don't even need to go to the country myself, it isn't necessary. I'll send my *clothed body* . . . For I myself am meanwhile lying in my bed, smoothly covered over with the yellow-brown blanket . . . As I lie in bed I assume the shape of a big beetle, a stag beetle or a cockchafer, I think. (CS 55–6, my emphasis)[9]

What is surprising here is that Raban's grotesque form as a beetle con-notes protection and warmth. He feels no horror, surprise, or shame at his metamorphosis, but rather an odd kind of satisfaction, as if his hard beetle shell were simply one additional layer of protection from what-ever menaces him in the outside world. On the other hand his "clothed body" is sent like a messenger to take part in the "traffic of clothes," traveling to the country where he will perform the social rituals nec-essary for his impending marriage. This clothed body is clearly the unessential self: it "staggers out of the door," a movement that indicates not the body's fear but "its nothingness" (CS 55). And if it is not certain, as Walter Sokel maintains, that what remains behind in bed is Raban's "essential," "naked" self (protected by blanket, beetle shell, and the fetal position of his legs, Raban is everything but naked), it has been removed from the *Verkehr* of society. Raban's beetle self is unclothed and yet covered—"naked" in the sense that an animal is considered naked.

The fiction of *The Metamorphosis,* of course, is to turn Raban's dream into reality. "It was no dream," a disembodied narrative voice announces at the text's beginning. Here too clothing and *Verkehr* are intertwined. Previously Gregor worked as a travelling salesman, selling "cloth samples" for a large company; his collection of clothing lies open, like a suitcase, ready to be packed up for another day's journey. His metamorphosis signals first of all a break with this order of reality,

9. CS = Franz Kafka, *The Complete Stories,* ed. Nahum N. Glatzer (New York: Schocken, 1971). See above, p. 61 [*Editor*].

with the order of work, travel, clothing, and mortality, as is made clear in Gregor's first extended monologue:

> Oh God, he thought, what an exhausting job I've picked on! Traveling about day in, day out. It's much more irritating work than doing the actual business in the office, and on top of that there's the trouble of constant traveling, of worrying about train connections, the bad and irregular meals, casual acquaintances that are always new and never become intimate friends [*ein immer wechselnder, nie andauernder, nie herzlich werdender menschlicher Verkehr*]. (CS 89–90) [3–4][1]

Gregor's lament is directed not against work but against the "travelling" nature of his work, the movement that prevents him from realizing a truly "affectionate" relation to society, a "human" *Verkehr*. The irony of this phrase is the rhetorical reversal underlying the entire story, that of an "animal" who is more human than his human co-protagonists. "The devil take it all!", Gregor exclaims in a Faustian invocation, and immediately he senses the strangeness of his reptile body—an "itching up on his belly" which is now covered with small white spots, "the nature of which he could not understand" (CS 90) [4]. This "pact" with the devil seals Gregor's break with his human past, removes him from the "traffic of clothes," and prepares him for his existence as a radically singular, "animal" being, whose foreign body he must first learn to master.

The most striking counterexample to Gregor's grotesque form is the photograph that hangs in the Samsas' living room, depicting him during his military service as "a lieutenant, hand on sword, a carefree smile on his face, inviting one to respect his uniform and military bearing" (CS 101) [12]. This image of military authority, virility, and happiness depends on the effacement of individual singularity. Gregor wears the uniform that literally and symbolically establishes his participation in a social order whose identity is maintained by a common form of clothing. The "uniformity" of his military appearance coincides with the nature of his employment as a salesman who shows cloth "samples" (*Muster*) to his clients. Critics have often taken this word as a pun on *Musterknabe*, as if the text meant to say that Gregor was a "model child." He was, but only in the sense of being without any particular identity that would set him above or apart from the others—equivalent and interchangeable, like the cloth samples in his traveling kit. (Or, in an image whose uncanniness gives us a measure of Kafka's ambivalence toward the effacement of individual difference, like the three unnamed, indistinguishable men who later take lodging in the Samsa household.)

Kafka develops further the notion of the uniformization of work and social *Verkehr* through the father, who is forced to take a position as a

---

1. Norton Critical Edition page numbers appear in brackets.

bank messenger for which he wears a uniform with gold buttons and monogrammed cap. Herr Samsa thus enters the world of commerce as the transmitter of financial messages, a scarcely human vehicle in the circulation of commercial meanings. His uniform secures his identifiability in this network at the same time that it marks him as a prisoner and underling who has sacrificed his personal identity to an abstract order. Branded with the bank's mono-gram and uni-form, Herr Samsa's body functions only as a sign, a bearer of information in the *Verkehr* of the world's meaning; he even eats and sleeps in his uniform, "as if he were ready for service at any moment and even here only at the beck and call of his superior" (CS 123) [30]. As always in Kafka, this traffic signifies something irremediably base and unclean: "his uniform, which was not brand-new to start with, began to look dirty, despite all the loving care of the mother and sister to keep it clean, and Gregor often spent whole evenings gazing at the many greasy spots on the garment."

   Mother and sister also enter the world of *Verkehr*. Grete takes a job as a salesgirl and is learning shorthand to work as a secretary, thus serving as the transmitter of money, letters, information—a "vehicle" in social and economic traffic. Frau Samsa helps out by sewing "elegant underwear" for a fashion boutique, working late into the night (CS 123) [30]. With this covert reference to the fancy goods sold in his father's shop, Kafka depicts Gregor's mother as an unwitting madam *à distance*, mediating the *Verkehr* of elegant clothing, social ritual, and sexual couplings. At the end of the text the notion of traffic is literalized when the Samsas ride a streetcar to the country and envision their daughter's entrance into the sexual *Verkehr* of marriage: "It struck both Mr. and Mrs. Samsa [that their daughter] had bloomed into a pretty girl with a good figure. They grew quieter and half unconsciously exchanged glances of complete agreement, having come to the conclusion that it would soon be time to find a good husband for her" (CS 139) [42].[2]   *see Erич Fromm*

IV

Gregor's metamorphosis, then, makes a cut in his life, isolating him from the paternal and social order of work, clothing, business, "traffic." It defines him negatively: against the family's names he is nameless;

2. Kafka's depiction of the counter-metamorphosis that takes hold of the Samsa family reveals the extent of his ambivalence not only toward bourgeois sexuality and marriage but also toward the bourgeois notion of work. Since the Enlightenment, work in the public sphere had been seen as the key to individual self-definition; for liberal and Marxist philosophers alike, personal autonomy and freedom are guaranteed by one's profession or trade, through which individuals realize their identities and participate in the social collectivity. Kafka is closer to Max Stirner and other anarchist philosophers who see work and any participation in the *Verkehr* of the socio-economic sphere as a threat to individual identity. See especially the chapter entitled "Mein Verkehr" in Stirner's *Der Einzige und sein Eigentum* (1845), in which he emphasizes the individual's need to withdraw from the "traffic" of familial responsibilities.

against its human uniforms he has his singular animal covering; against its participation in the circulation of social or economic meaning, he remains cloistered in his room, cut off from human discourse. And yet the narrative does not limit itself to a merely negative definition of Gregor's identity. In opposition to this family "traffic" of clothing, it delineates an alternative, Utopian space of play, distraction, and child-like innocence that is curiously consistent with late nineteenth-century definitions of aesthetic experience. In fact, Gregor's metamorphosis fulfils the dream of every serious *fin-de-siècle* aesthete: to become not just an artist, but the artwork, the visual icon, itself.

The second paragraph of *The Metamorphosis*, immediately following the account of Gregor's transformation, describes a picture of a lady dressed in fur that, hanging on the wall opposite him, seems to mirror his newly transformed, animal self:

> Above the table . . . hung the picture which he had recently cut out of an illustrated magazine and put into a pretty gilt frame. It showed a lady, with a fur cap on and a fur stole, sitting upright and holding out to the spectator a huge fur muff into which the whole of her forearm had vanished! (CS 89) [3]

The picture clearly constitutes an aesthetic moment within the Samsa's petty bourgeois world. As we learn later, Gregor has himself fashioned the "pretty gilt frame" with his fretwork, a pastime or "amusement" that is explicitly contrasted with his work as a travelling salesman. "The boy thinks about nothing but his work," Frau Samsa explains to the chief clerk. "He just sits there quietly at the table reading a newspaper or looking through railway timetables. The only amusement he gets is doing fretwork. For instance, he spent two or three evenings cutting out a little picture frame; you would be surprised to see how pretty it is; it's hanging in his room" (CS 95–6) [8]. Here the mortality of *Verkehr*, evoked through the railway *time*tables and newspapers (*Zeitungen*),[3] is contrasted with Gregor's "amusement" or distraction (*Zerstreuung*) in making the picture; alienated labor is contrasted with a form of play that results in art, a framed image that is "beautiful" (*schön*).

Of course, one should be wary of idealizing what is after all a kind of pin-up—an erotic photograph cut out of a magazine that a lonely salesman hangs in his room. And what about the woman's fur clothing? Isn't it part of the same *Verkehr* of clothing, social intercourse, and mortality that defines the Samsa household? Fur was after all the clothing that Adam and Eve put on after being expelled from the Garden, as Kafka noted when he copied this passage from Genesis into his

---

3. Plural form of the German word for "newspaper"—*Zeitung*—which contains the word for "time" [*Zeit*] [*Editor*].

diary.[4] In fact, these furs function as emblems not so much of wealth and social status as of animality, which in this story symbolizes a liberation from specifically human problems of sin, guilt, mortality, even from pain and self-consciousness. This is the basic narrative movement to *The Metamorphosis*: after his initial transformation, Gregor will attempt to realize the promise implicit in this photograph, to merge with his mirror-image, to descend the evolutionary ladder into an animal state, to become the animal-artwork.

As several studies have pointed out, Kafka borrowed the image of the fur-clad lady as well as the basic plot structure for his story from a classic novel of *fin-de-siècle* eroticism, Leopold von Sacher-Masoch's *Venus in Furs* (1870).[5] The picture Gregor has cut out of a magazine thus functions as a coded reference to Kafka's own appropriation of Sacher-Masoch's narrative. This is not the place to rehearse the numerous and surprising similarities between the two texts, which include not only the fur clothing, but also uniforms, the name Gregor, and analogous "punishment fantasies," which, in Sacher-Masoch's text, turn the protagonist metaphorically into a "dog" or "worm" grovelling at his mistress' feet. Two points of contact between these texts are however worth stressing. The first is that in both works fur functions as a metonymy for sexual desire, either in the Freudian sense as a fetish recalling the mother's genitalia and pubic hair, or in the popular sense of "animal" passion and corporeality.[6] Secondly, in both texts desire is a product of images—paintings, sculptures, photographs, staged erotic encounters—in other words, art. One paradigmatic moment in *Venus in Furs* describes for instance the narrator's desire for a white marble copy of the Venus de Milo, which is draped in fur. The novel also opens with the

---

4. "And the Lord God made for Adam and for his wife garments of skins [*Röcke von Fellen*], and clothed them." (Diary entry for 19 June 1916.)

5. Sacher-Masoch's book has recently been reprinted in English with an extensive introduction by Gilles Deleuze (New York: Zone Books, 1989). On the relationship between Sacher-Masoch and Kafka see Ruth Angress, "Kafka and Sacher-Masoch: A Note on *The Metamorphosis*," *Modern Language Notes* 85 (1970), 745–6; F. Kuna, "Art as Direct Vision: Kafka and Sacher-Masoch," *Journal of European Studies* (1972), 237–46; and my own "Kafka and Sacher-Masoch," *Journal of the Kafka Society of America*, 2 (Dec. 1983), 4–19 (repr. in Harold Bloom (ed.), *Franz Kafka's The Metamorphosis*, Modern Critical Interpretations (New York: Chelsea House, 1988).

6. Freud writes: "fur and velvet—as has long been suspected—are a fixation of the sight of the pubic hair, which should have been followed by the longed-for sight of the female member." Cf. "Fetishism" (1927), in *The Standard Edition of the Complete Psychological Works of Sigmund Freud* (London: The Hogarth Press, 1961), xxi. 147–58. The fetish allows the subject to maintain his fantasy of a female penis, thus sidestepping the threat of castration. This interpretation seems to have validity for Sacher-Masoch's hero, who frequently fantasizes that the furs enclose some hard, erect object (such as a marble statue of Venus) or a source of violent energy. Masoch's emphasis on electricity, his image of the woman in furs as an "augmented electric battery," seems to suggest that the impersonality of the punishment is a key element in the masochistic experience of pleasure. (The apples that the father bombards Gregor with at the end of the second section roll about as if "electrisiert"; the machine in "In the Penal Colony" runs on electric power.) The image of the woman's forearm and fist in the fur muff also corresponds to Freud's notion of the (male) child's fantasy of the female member.

description of a painting of Venus to which it returns in the closing scene.

From Sacher-Masoch's novel one may hypothesize that masochistic desire is dependent on images because by definition the images preclude fulfilment. In between the opening and closing description of the painting, we witness the main protagonist orchestrate his desire in the guise of masochistic self-abasement, dressing his female partner in a variety of fur costumes, engaging her to act out pre-established scenarios of punishment and humiliation with him and other men, while all the time setting up formal obstacles to the consummation of his desire. In effect, the masochist turns his mistress into an actress, himself into her public. He "frames" her as art, establishing an inviolable line between his reality and material bondage on the one hand and her aesthetic freedom and power over him on the other. The image is merely a more radical form of this same inviolability, its inaccessibility as image guaranteeing the frustration of desire. The frame is so to speak the masochist's rope and chains.

This same dialectic of image, power, and desire is implicit in Gregor Samsa's unspoken relationship with his "pretty" picture. Unlike, say, Georg Bendemann in "The Judgment,"[7] Gregor has no mistress or fiancée, only the photograph, which through his own efforts he has inscribed as art, framing it and putting it behind glass. Already "only" an image, the woman is thus raised to the level of art, put into an ideal space that Gregor can aspire to but never truly enter. And this seems to be the source of its attraction and power. In the story's second section, Gregor's identity is threatened when his sister and mother begin cleaning out his room. He asks himself which object he should choose to rescue, considers (but rejects) his desk, then settles on the image of the woman in fur hanging on the wall. The encounter with art is explicitly erotic, the "cool" glass which separates Gregor from the image providing the actual "comfort."

> [H]e was struck by the picture of the lady muffled in so much fur and quickly crawled up to it and pressed himself to the glass, which was a good surface to hold on to and comforted his hot belly. This picture at least, which was entirely hidden beneath him, was going to be removed by nobody. (CS 118) [26]

What is unusual about Kafka's text and distinguishes it from Sacher-Masoch's racier but ultimately more conventional narrative, is that the movement toward "animality" and masochistic desire does not result in sin and guilt, but in a cleansing of these "human" remnants from Gregor's past. The animal is innocent. Thus his metamorphosis is akin

---

7. "The Judgment" was Kafka's breakthrough story, written in a single sitting during the night of September 22 until dawn, September 23, 1912, some two months before Kafka began writing The Metamorphosis [Editor].

to a rebirth, to a childlike awakening, to self-absorbed games and play. We are told for instance that Gregor's insect legs "dance . . . as if set free," that he learns to get out of bed by rocking himself to and fro— "the new method was more a game [*Spiel*] than an effort" (CS 94) [7]—and that, despite his grotesque form, he shows no hesitation in offering himself for public viewing. "He was eager to find out what the others, after all their insistence, would say at the sight of him" (CS 98) [10].[8] The sentiment voiced here is more than a comic device: Gregor is in the process of losing his capacity for self-judgment through the eyes of the world, of becoming an unself-conscious child-animal.

This reacquisition of an originary freedom and innocence coincides with Gregor's *Kunsttrieb*, his impulse toward art and self-display. Two moments stand out in this process. The first is the delightful interlude of unself-conscious play that takes place in the novella's second section. Despite the damage inflicted to his body by his father, Gregor enjoys a beatific state of distraction (*Zerstreuung*), innocent of memory, swinging like a gymnast from the ceiling, walking the walls, defying the material constraint of gravity much like the trapeze artists, circus riders, and floating dogs figured in Kafka's other writings. High above the furniture in his room, Gregor can breathe more "freely":

> He especially enjoyed hanging suspended from the ceiling; it was much better than lying on the floor; one could breathe more freely; one's body swung and rocked lightly; and in the almost blissful absorption induced by this suspension it could happen to his own surprise that he let go and fell plump on the floor. Yet he now had his body much better under control than formerly, and even such a big fall did him no harm. (CS 115) [23]

A happy state of distraction, easy breathing, the almost musical rhythm rocking his body—these are all privileged terms in Kafka's vocabulary. Capable of "falling" from a great height without harming himself, Gregor has achieved a state of innocent grace untroubled by his father's *Schulden*, the financial "debts" that are also, in German, the result of moral transgressions. But this "immortality" is achieved by the "artist" who has made his body into the vehicle of his art, a vehicle which performs, in these moments of unself-conscious play, as gracefully as the marionettes in Kleist's essay "Über das Marionettentheater."[9] If

8. This itinerary is essentially the opposite of that travelled by Red Peter in Kafka's later story "A Report to an Academy," an ape living in blissfully unself-conscious freedom on the "Gold Coast" who is captured and introduced into the *Verkehr* of human society: he learns to talk, wear trousers, drink schnapps, and fornicate with a trained (i.e. half-human) chimpanzee. By contrast *The Metamorphosis* describes Gregor's progressive acquisition of the freedom in his animal body, thereby returning to the "Gold Coast" of a childlike, prelapsarian innocence.

9. The work of Heinrich von Kleist (1777–1811), German author of dramas and short stories, has often been compared to Kafka's. "Über das Marionettentheater" [On the Marionette Theater] (1810) is an influential essay which asserts that gracefulness is to be found only in those bodies either without consciousness or with infinite consciousness—in marionettes or in God [*Editor*].

Luftmensch, as Günther Anders points out, connotes in German the artist who has no solid footing beneath his feet, Gregor is the *Lufttier*,[1] much like the floating dogs in the later story "Investigations of a Dog" who are animated by an uncanny, silent music, or the Japanese tumblers Kafka drew in his diary as an image of artistic freedom. Gregor literally floats above the traffic of human time, his consciousness absorbed by his dancing, though hardly *Jugendstilian*, body.

The second moment occurs in the third section of the novella and brings out the musical implications of Gregor's artistic self-realization. Gregor's sister Grete begins playing the violin for her parents and the lodgers while Gregor lies in his dirty, dark room. Animated by a corporeal *Kunsttrieb* or will to art, oblivious to the material consequences of his action, he creeps toward his sister or rather her "playing," her *Spiel*:

> Gregor's sister began to play; the father and mother, from either side, intently watched the movements of her hands. Gregor, attracted by the playing, ventured to move forward a little until his head was actually inside the living room. . . . [I]n spite of his condition, no shame deterred him from advancing a little over the spotless floor . . . Gregor crawled a little farther forward and lowered his head to the ground so that it might be possible for his eyes to meet hers. Was he an animal, that music moved him so? He felt as if the way were opening before him to the unknown nourishment he craved. (CS 130–1) [35–36]

Again Kafka's text insists on the ludic, innocent character of this encounter. Despite his animal condition, the filth that his body has accumulated, or even the evidently incestuous nature of his attraction to his sister, "no shame deter[s] him" on his path toward the "unknown nourishment" evoked by the music. We should note too the text's insistence on a lived, corporeal experience of the music: the boarders who read the musical notes over Grete's shoulder rather than experience music physically like Gregor are clearly portrayed as philistines.[2] Gregor, the innocent "child-animal" who wants to "play" with his sister, has access to the secret of art because his body is itself striving for a weightless, ethereal, musical condition. And this artistic impulse results, for the third and last time, in the body's self-display in a context of aesthetic performance.

Even the process of dying has an aesthetic, spiritual dimension. Like the initial rejection of clothing, cloth "samples," and the *Verkehr* of his employment, Gregor's progressive rejection of organic nourishment initiates a movement back to the innocence of childhood or, in biblical

---

1. Literally, *"animal* who lives on air"—a made-up word, a play on *Luftmensch* (literally, "airman") [*Editor*].
2. Aesthetically insensitive, materialistic bourgeois [*Editor*].

terms, to the moment in Eden before the eating of the apple. (The apple that Gregor's father throws at him interrupts this movement and ultimately seems responsible for the son's Christ-like death. But the apple originates with the father, not the innocent child, and as such represents the violent intrusion of the "traffic" of Gregor's previous life into his aesthetic paradise.) As the memory of his human past fades away, Gregor begins to "play" with his food like an infant, eventually renouncing it altogether for the pleasures of his home gymnastics: "he was fast losing any interest he had ever taken in food, so that for mere recreation he had formed the habit of crawling crisscross over the walls and ceiling" (CS 115) [23]. This fasting flattens and lightens Gregor's form, removing it from the circulation of human, organic life, "spiritualizing" it until it is completely empty. Grete, who shows a particular fascination for the corpse, remarks: " 'Just see how thin he was. It's such a long time since he's eaten anything. The food came out again just as it went in.' Indeed, Gregor's body was completely flat and dry." (CS 136–7) [40].

The Christian overtones of this death are clear and support the basic narrative of conflict between father and son. Herr Samsa makes the sign of the cross, for example, and Gregor is described as being "festgenagelt," "nailed fast" to the floor by the paternal apple bombardment. Yet Gregor is not only a fasting Christ or monk who has withdrawn from the world, but first of all the *fin-de-siècle* aesthete who "hungers" for music, the highest of the arts in Romantic and Symbolist poetics.[3] Within the corpus of Kafka's own writings, Gregor bears an unmistakable affinity with other artist figures. One thinks for instance of Georg Bendemann in "The Judgment" who performs his gymnastic "turn" over the bridge but then hangs to the railing "as a starving man clutches for food." Or of the famished musical dogs in "Investigations of a Dog," or the disappearing artist figures of the last stories, "A Hunger Artist" and "Josephine the Singer." But Gregor's metamorphosis into a dancing musical bug is the most astonishing of all Kafka's self-referential literary figures. Emptied of all organic substance, perfectly isolated from the paternal "traffic of clothes," he dies as a two-dimensional object, as "flat" and "dry" as the pages of printed characters on which he is now immortalized.

---

3. [The poetics of symbolism, a literary movement chiefly in France in the latter part of the nineteenth century, aims to express mysterious states of mind through evocative, refined, and ambiguous language—*Editor.*] Walter Pater's claim in *The Renaissance* that all the arts strive for the "condition of music" best sums up this tradition. Knut Hamsun's novel *Hunger* (1890) established the connection between fasting and the dedication to writing for an entire generation of German writers at the turn of the century, including Thomas Mann and Kafka. [Knut Hamsun (1859–1952) was Norway's greatest modern novelist; the stories and novels of the German writer Thomas Mann (1875–1955) frequently treat the artist as outsider to the bourgeoisie, itself caught up in decay and decline: his works include *Death in Venice* (1912), *The Magic Mountain* (1924), and *Doktor Faustus* (1947)—*Editor.*] Mann used the trope in his early story "Die Hungernden," Kafka most notably in "A Hunger Artist" and "Investigations of a Dog," where it is also related to music.

V

In the above remarks I have deliberately read Kafka's text against the majority of its critical interpretations, which see in Gregor's metamorphosis a tragedy visited upon an unsuspecting victim that ends with the "liberation" of the family through his ritualistic sacrifice. On the contrary, I see the family as enslaved and deindividualized by its re-entrance into the *Verkehr* of work, sexuality, and commerce (the realm of "clothing"), whereas Gregor carries out the project of self-definition, individual autonomy, and freedom implicit in his transformation into a "giant vermin." He takes off the "clothes of the world," to put it in the terms of this study, not to reveal an "essential self" or to retreat into religious seclusion, but, in line with the *fin-de-siècle* substitution of aesthetics for religion, to put on the grotesque mask of art, to retreat into the self-enclosed world of aesthetic play and freedom symbolized by his animal shell. Whether self-willed or not, a consciously Faustian transgression of human limits or a sudden eruption of repressed desire, Gregor's behaviour in his new form is sustained by a constant *Kunsttrieb*, an unconscious artistic will that prevents him from ever questioning the necessity of his metamorphosis or attempting to reverse it. Indeed, this consistent volition to *display* himself goes hand in hand with his "monstrosity" (etymologically related to *monstrare*, "to show"), which chases the chief clerk from the scene, puts the formerly parasitic Samsas to work, and dislodges the boarders, allowing Gregor to devote himself to narcissistic play, distraction, and innocent desire. Whatever the cause of his transformation, its implicit, unspoken *telos* is finally aesthetic: to turn the clothed, human body into a pure, autonomous artwork.

This is the place to stress Peter Cersowsky's insightful remark in his study of Kafka's relations to literary decadence that Gregor's metamorphosis into an animal can be seen as part of the traditional "melancholic disposition" and thereby linked to the melancholy of the *fin-de-siècle* decadent aesthete. Noting that Bourget had already defined the decadent as the isolated individual "unfit for the common labor of society," Cersowsky rightly stresses the parallel with Gregor's exclusion from family and society as an "unproductive" bug.[4] In this sense Gregor is a decadent "type" like Kafka's other bachelor figures—isolated, self-absorbed, ill adapted to work, melancholy, sexually impotent by definition (as the single example of his "species"), and therefore the endpoint of the Samsa family line. In essence Gregor's metamorphosis establishes the same opposition between aesthete self and bourgeois family that characterizes Thomas Mann's early novellas (which Kafka greatly admired), with all their connotations of health and vitality on one side, parasitism, decadence and death on the other. Gregor rep-

4. Paul Bourget (1852–1935) was a conservative French author who depicted the moral attitudes of his time by criticizing its writers [*Editor*].

resents the bizarre end of his "race," the tired, melancholy decadent who willingly departs from this life to make way for his "healthy" family.[5]

What this interpretation leaves out, however, is the positive, even aggressive countertendency in Kafka's text that insists on Gregor's form as the autonomous artwork. *The Metamorphosis* displays none of Mann's nostalgia for blond and blue-eyed *Bürgerlichkeit*.[6] Indeed, the petty bourgeois environment of the Samsa household—dirty, constricted, animated by a mean will for profit and social conformity—finally provokes the reader's disgust, perhaps the very disgust initially associated with the grotesque bug but which fades away as the story progresses and Gregor's "humanity" comes to the fore. As we have seen, the text's positive affirmations concern Gregor's form: its childlike aptitude for games, dance, music, and spiritual nourishment. And whereas Gregor's consciousness lags behind the radicality of his aesthetic form (even in death he seems tolerant and forgiving of his family), the body itself proclaims all the aggressive, even jubilant qualities of the avant-garde or modernist artwork: Art as an attack on Life, not just its impotent and nostalgic opponent; Art as the grotesque, abstract, ultimately incomprehensible object that has removed itself from the bourgeois social order.

But not outside the biological order of decay and death. Gregor's blissful state of "free breathing" and self-absorbed *Zerstreuung* while hanging from the ceiling in his room lasts only a brief while, eventually giving way to a melancholy yearning for an "unknown nourishment" he has never tasted. And the very refusal of organic nourishment that excludes him from the human, social realm and that augments his ethereal, *Lufttier* nature ultimately leads to his death and disappearance. The animal-artwork is not granted an unnatural physical permanence, but is effaced by the same cycle of life forces that is presumably responsible for its original transformation. On 9 December 1912, two days after finishing what would become his most famous story, Kafka sent Felice Bauer a postcard of Strindberg asking her if she knew his story "Alone," thus secretly revealing the meaning and aestheticist origins of his own text.[7] "That is finally what it means to be alone," Strindberg says at the end of his autobiographical narrative in reference to his isolation as an artist. "To spin oneself into the silk of one's own soul, to mask oneself in one's own cocoon, and wait for the metamorphosis, which never fails to come about." Kafka spun himself into his own literary cocoon and waited. Yet the metamorphosis that

---

5. See Cersowsky, "Mein ganzes Wesen," 74–6.
6. Middle-class conventionality [*Editor*].
7. Felice Bauer (1887–1960) was Kafka's fiancée during periods between 1913 and 1917; he corresponded extensively with her. August Strindberg (1849–1912) was Sweden's most important playwright and novelist; his work, containing supernatural elements, is often pessimistic [*Editor*].

took place in Prague in November 1912 did not produce the strange, beautiful butterfly of Strindberg's *fin-de-siècle* imagination, but a grotesque, primitive ornament of modernity: the "monstrous vermin."

HARTMUT BINDER

The Metamorphosis: The Long Journey into Print†

I. The Sons

On November 24, 1912, when Kafka was just beginning to write the middle section of *The Metamorphosis*, he read the first chapter aloud to his friends Oskar Baum and Max Brod.[1] Brod noted the event in his diary with the not quite apposite words that Kafka had recited his "splendid vermin novella." On December 15, 1912, and again on March first of the following year, Brod got to hear the entire story, which this time he characterized as the "bedbug thing" and the "insect story."[2] It is possible that Kafka did not immediately reveal the title to his friends even though [by early March 1913, when my narrative begins,] he had already written to his fiancée Felice Bauer, on November 23, 1912, that the little story still in progress was called *Metamorphosis*.[3] He had also already mentioned to Felice the reading of March first, which took place in the apartment of the newlywed Max Brod, noting: "I read myself into a frenzy with my story. But then we did let ourselves go, and laughed a lot."[4]

Just at this time Franz Werfel[5] was paying a visit to his native city of Prague, in the course of which he saw his friends Brod and Kafka.[6] On this occasion he must have heard about *The Metamorphosis*, because hardly had he returned to Leipzig than he called this new Prague production to the attention of Kurt Wolff. At the publishing house the decision had just been made to bring out a new series under the name of *Der jüngste Tag* [The Day of Judgment], which proposed to offer the works of progressive young writers at economical prices. Since the

---

† From the forthcoming *Kafkas "Verwandlung": Entstehung, Deutung, Wirkung* (Stuttgart: Metzler, 1996?). Trans. Stanley Corngold. Printed by permission of the author.

1. Franz Kafka, *Letters to Felice*, ed. Erich Heller and Jürgen Born, trans. James Stern and Elizabeth Duckworth (New York: Schocken, 1973) 62.

2. Joachim Unseld, *Franz Kafka: A Writer's Life*, trans. Paul F. Dvorak (Riverside, CA: Ariadne, 1994) 99.

3. *Letters to Felice* 58.

4. Ibid. 209.

5. In 1913 Franz Werfel (1890–1945), the well-known poet and novelist, was serving as an editor at the Kurt Wolff Publishing Company. Wolff (1887–1963) was until 1930 an important publisher of innovative works in Germany. In 1941 he migrated to the United States, where he founded Pantheon Books [*Editor*].

6. Cf. *Letters to Felice* 207.

first series was already supposed to be at the bookstores in the early part of the year, a list had to be drawn up swiftly. Authors suited to the new project were being sought, among whom it was hoped that Kafka, who had been highly praised by Werfel, could be recruited.[7] Hence Kurt Wolff's letter to Kafka on March 30, asking him to submit the new novella that Werfel had told him about, using the title *Die Wanze* [The Bedbug]. Kafka replied, "Pay no attention to what Werfel tells you. He does not know a word of the story. As soon as I have had a clean copy made, I will of course be glad to send it to you."[8] The next day a fleeting chance encounter occurred between Kafka and Kurt Wolff, in the course of which the publisher must have learnt that "The Stoker," the first chapter of Kafka's novel *Der Verschollene* [The Boy Who Sank Out of Sight]—another text suitable for publication—was available.[9] By April 2 Wolff had already asked Kafka "most cordially and urgently" to let him read "The Stoker" and the "bedbug story" "if possible *at once*."[1] Kafka answered by return mail, saying that he would send the first chapter of the novel "right away, since most of it has already been copied," and continued:

> My other story, *The Metamorphosis*, is not yet transcribed, since lately everything has combined to keep me away from writing and from my pleasure in it. But I will have this story, too, transcribed and sent to you as soon as possible. Perhaps later on these two pieces and the "The Judgment" from *Arkadia* will make up quite a decent book, whose title might be *The Sons*.[2]

After Wolff had read the manuscript of "The Stoker," he agreed to publish the text in *Der jüngste Tag*, at the same time proposing to Kafka the format in which it would appear. In his letter he does not mention *The Metamorphosis*, whose title in the meantime Kafka had augmented with the definite article. In his answer of April 11 Kafka declared himself "fully and happily in accord" but at the end repeated more expressly the request he had already formulated in his previous letter:

> "The Stoker," *The Metamorphosis* (which is one and one-half times as long as "The Stoker"), and "The Judgment" belong together, both inwardly and outwardly. There is an obvious connection among the three and, even more important, a secret one, for which reason I would be reluctant to forego the chance of having them published together in a book, which might be called *The*

---

7. Unseld, 102.
8. Kurt Wolff, *Briefwechsel eines Verlegers, 1911–1963* [Correspondence of a publisher, 1911–1963], ed. Bernhard Zeller and Ellen Otten (Frankfurt am Main: Scheffler, 1966) 28.
9. Most of this novel has been translated under the less correct title *Amerika*, trans. Edwin Muir (New York: New Directions, 1946 [*Editor*].
1. *Letters to Felice* 237.
2. Wolff, *Briefwechsel* 29. (Cf. *Letters to Friends, Family, and Editors*, trans. Richard and Clara Winston [New York: Schocken, 1973] 96.) *Arkadia* was a yearbook for new literature, edited by Max Brod. It appeared once, in 1913, at the Kurt Wolff publishing house—*Editor*.)

Sons. Would it be possible, then, for "The Stoker," apart from its publication in *Der jüngste Tag*, to appear eventually along with the other two stories in a book all their own, at some reasonable time which, however, I would leave entirely to your discretion? And would it be possible to include a statement of this pledge in the present contract for *The Stoker*. You see, I am just as much concerned about the unity of the three stories as I am about the unity of any one of them.[3]

As early as April 16 Wolff sent a "binding formulation" of the matter, for which, four days later, Kafka expressed his thanks.[4]

Thus ends the first phase of Kafka's efforts to have *The Metamorphosis* published. What is striking is not only that he felt a relation to exist between "The Judgment" and *The Metamorphosis* but that he also wanted to include "The Stoker" in the planned volume of novellas, although this text constituted the opening chapter of a novel as yet unfinished, a circumstance he expressly sought to underscore at the time of planning its separate publication by adding on the subtitle *A Fragment*. The reason for this decision lay in his conviction that of the portions of *The Boy Who Sank Out of Sight* that existed so far, only the opening part had substance, while all the other chapters deserved "to be rejected." Hence he wanted to publish only "The Stoker," which, moreover, he considered the best thing he had ever written.[5] Under the circumstances, the inclusion of this portion of the novel in an omnibus volume entitled *The Sons* was a good idea, because in actual fact all three stories contain correspondences in the plot, crucial details, and autobiographical background.

From a thematic point of view, the similarity consists in the fact that in each case a family conflict is depicted, in the course of which the sons involved in it—and who in corresponding constellations of images appear to be robbed of their human nature—are exiled, exposed, or condemned to death. In "The Judgment" this death is depicted as a summary execution; in *The Metamorphosis* one sees the decline of the hero over time as it passes almost seamlessly into his death; while in *The Boy Who Sank Out of Sight* the circumstances of the main figure Karl Rossmann develop so slowly that his possible death is indicated only hypothetically and even appears to take a turn for the better through a surprising reversal of his situation. Karl is "simply turned out" by his parents "just as you turn a cat out of the house when it annoys you." He was driven from his homeland to America "shamefully unprovided-for," where, "being thrown entirely on his own resources," he would in all probability have "come to a wretched end in New

3. Wolff, *Briefwechsel* 30. (Cf. *Letters to Friends* 96–97—Editor.)
4. Wolff, *Briefwechsel* 31.
5. *Letters to Felice* 218. Cf. 187.

York"[6] if the maid, who had plunged him into misery by seducing him
had not written a letter to his uncle in New York announcing his arrival
in the New World. Of course, this lucky stroke must be assumed only
to drag out the ultimate annihilation of the hero; for in his diaries, after
all, Kafka mentions that in the sections of *The Boy Who Sank Out of
Sight* that were as yet unwritten, Karl Rossmann was to be executed
"with a gentler hand," "more pushed aside than struck down."[7] Karl,
one could say, was *exposed* by his parents, under conditions that would
finally have had to doom him.[8] In contrast, Georg Bendemann in "The
Judgment" is eliminated as a member of the family when his father
sets himself up as his judge and *condemns* him to death on the grounds
that he is a devilish human being. Inwardly dependent on his father's
values, he assumes the verdict of guilt and without hesitation drops
from a bridge into the river that flows past the family house.

Finally, Gregor Samsa, as a family member, is *exiled* by the rest of
his family. He is locked up in his room and so mishandled by his father
that as a result he wastes away—until he dies. Here, too, the actual
moment of his death is jointly decided by the verdict of his sister, who
robs him of his right to live as her brother and declares him an animal
[*Untier*] with whom it is impossible to share a life.

An additional feature shared by the three texts, all of which were
written in close chronological proximity, consists in the fact that they
can be understood as the product of interrelated literary acts through
which Kafka "tries things out." They allowed Kafka to visualize on a
purely imaginative plane the possible effects of crucial life–decisions,
without his having to endure their consequences on his own flesh. By
attempting to play out in alternative conceptions, at first on the fictional
plane, the difficulties that had cropped up in his life, Kafka was able,
so to speak, to explore whether in this way acceptable chances of realization would arise. The process of literary creation and the stories
which thus arose can be seen in this optic as trials at problem-solving
aiming at the production of viable life–plans.[9] Here, in the case of the
three works that were supposed to be linked together under the title of
The Sons, the chosen solutions all lead to disaster.

In "The Judgment" Kafka fictively explores the possibility of marrying

6. *Amerika* 27.
7. *The Diaries of Franz Kafka, 1914–1923*, trans. Martin Greenberg (New York: Schocken, 1949)
   132. [This standard English translation contains an important mistake. Kafka's entire diary
   entry reads, in English: "Rossmann and [Joseph] K. [the hero of *The Trial*], the innocent and
   the guilty, both executed without distinction in the end, the guilty [*sic*] one with a gentler
   hand, more pushed aside than struck down." The German word which is translated as "guilty"
   toward the end of this sentence is *schuldlos*, which actually means "innocent." Karl Rossmann,
   the hero of *The Boy Who Sank Out of Sight*, though innocent, is executed—though with a
   gentler hand—*Editor*.]
8. Cf. Hartmut Binder, *Kafka-Kommentar zu den Romanen, Rezensionen, Aphorismen und zum
   Brief an den Vater* (Munich: Winkler, 1976), esp. 145–50.
9. Heinz Hillman, "Schaffensprozess," in *Kafka-Handbuch*, ed. Hartmut Binder, vol. 2, *Das
   Werk und seine Wirkung* (Stuttgart: Kröner, 1979) 28.

and taking over his father's business, something that his father had intended from the start. This life-plan adopts bourgeois values, turning the son into a recognized member of bourgeois society, which in the Jewish middle class in Prague was realized ideally by one's founding a family and becoming a successful businessman. In the course of "The Judgment" this possibility is crushed by the objection of the father, who, on the one hand, accuses the son of being a parasite who has disempowered him and assumed his position without really being able to fill it, but who, on the other hand, ridicules his attempts to marry by referring to base sexual motives. In this way the father certifies his son's inability to realize himself in bourgeois society. Georg accepts this judgment and draws the conclusion. The course of the plot of the story thus transposes onto the plane of narrative the resistance that Kafka had anticipated from his father or indeed had already internalized during his years of development whenever it came to his trying to shape a life of his own. In this way, the plot development reveals that there could be no future for him in the direction indicated, because here Kafka concedes to his father that he is not fit to be the father of a family and a businessman.

In fact Kafka's life reveals the rightness of the prognoses displaced here onto the fictional plane. On the one hand, as partner in an asbestos factory founded in 1911, he had had so little success that his father continually reproached him sharply for his business conduct. The correspondence between fiction and reality becomes all the more fitting when one realizes that Kafka's father was financially involved in this undertaking, for, after all, it is presupposed in "The Judgment" that Georg Bendemann and his father are involved in the same business venture.

The rest of the story can be viewed as the anticipation of expected paternal initiatives—something which the fearful author was especially equipped to register from the perspective of the other person and especially from that of his most important adversary. A few weeks after writing "The Judgment," Kafka in fact felt so bitterly attacked by the reproaches his father made to him about his alleged neglect of the factory that he was on the point of committing suicide. As far as the other thematic complex is concerned—Georg Bendemann's marriage—the main objection, which afterwards Kafka's father was to make against Kafka's planned marriage to Felice Bauer, was that as a husband he would so badly manage the financial side of things that he would soon fall into poverty. And Kafka's father insinuated, using almost the very same words as Mr. Bendemann, that his second fiancée Julie Wohryzek had dolled herself up in order to stimulate Kafka's sexual desires. Certainly Kafka saw his father's resistance to his plans to get married as a sign that he had in fact made the right decision, but in both cases, equally, he fell without ever having fired a shot.

In *The Metamorphosis*, which was begun shortly after the completion of "The Judgment," Kafka continues to probe, under changed presuppositions, the conditions of his own life. Here he begins with the premise that his father's business has collapsed and the son has to provide for the family by himself. Gregor Samsa breaks down under his duties. He masters them for only a limited time under the most extreme physical tension and against inner resistance, in order then—his human identity, so to speak, having been damaged—to become a burden to his family as someone requiring custodial care. The family in turn defends itself against the parasite, which it is soon no longer ready to acknowledge as its son and whose death it finally causes. This narrative action has roots in the thought perpetually in Kafka's head that in case his father should prematurely cease to be the family provider, he would have to take over his father's role. For according to the values prevalent at that time in the Jewish middle class in Prague, it was, as a matter of course, the son's duty in such a case to jump in and take over his father's business, whether or not the son was in any way active as a businessman or engaged in a different profession.

Such fears for the future were by no means unfounded. Kafka's father's health was unsatisfactory, his business had recently suffered severe reverses, and, finally, Kafka himself had financial responsibilities in connection with the founding of the asbestos factory in 1911, for as silent partner he had put up all his personal holdings as collateral. Recognizing that inwardly he was deeply dependent on his family, he was probably afraid that he would be unable to withstand the social pressure that would be applied to him in case the family's financial situation took a turn for the worse.

The trial at problem-solving in *The Metamorphosis* reveals the consequences for Kafka of following in his father's professional footsteps upon the collapse of the latter's business and the loss of his dominant position in the family. Such an exchange of roles, which would make him head of the family, would not signify any sort of improvement of his situation but instead lead ultimately to his death. His dependency on the other family members would be in no way diminished, for his working energy and achievement would have to be put so exclusively in their service that marriage would be impossible. These unbearable conditions would so unsettle him that he would be forced to return to the family group as parasite and, locked in combat with them, finally go to his ruin.[1]

Another significant common feature of the texts that Kafka wanted to publish under the title *The Sons* is the fact that the heroes cannot or cannot adequately come to an understanding with the world around

---

1. These reflections follow, in somewhat modified form, from Hillmann, *Schaffensprozess* 30ff.

them. This is, of course, most evident in *The Metamorphosis*, where Kafka has designed the plot in a way not absolutely required by the theme, so that immediately following the metamorphosis Gregor's voice is reduced to a chirping which the other members of the family cannot understand. And because his rigid body no longer permits mimicry and gesture in the usual sense, he can express his thoughts and wishes, if at all, only through his actions. The situation is furthermore severely aggravated by the fact that with one, hardly happy exception, the other members of the household never speak a word to him. This behavior is by no means obvious and not really something to be taken for granted, for one could also expect—since it is still Gregor, the son and brother, whose life is at stake, even if a creature sporting an animal shape—that his parents and his sister would at least make some attempt to come to an understanding with him, more or less the way one is accustomed to speak with dogs, cats, or canaries—that is, with the complete conviction that the creature addressed this way would understand what is said, at least through hints and clues. On the contrary, Grete, in her capacity, so to speak, as particularly well-qualified expert on the subject of Gregor, declares at the end of the story to her father, who in this matter has lost his bearings, that it is inconceivable that they could come to any sort of understanding with this animal, although she, unlike the cleaning woman, who from time to time does address a remark to Gregor, in attributing to him all manner of intelligence, has curiously failed really and truly to give it a trial run.

Besides correspondences between all three of the texts that Kafka wanted to publish in an omnibus volume *The Sons*, there exist features common solely to "The Judgment" and *The Metamorphosis*. In both stories, three stages in the development of a family are opposed to one another. In the first phase, which is projected as background history by the figure who establishes the narrative perspective, the father is an independent businessman. Along with this, both texts emphasize his striking importance, the negative counterpart of which is the son's feebleness in his profession. This connection is immediately apparent in "The Judgment," where Georg Bendemann, who is employed in his father's business, airs the suspicion with reference to his former position that up until the death of his mother, which had occurred ten years earlier, his father had resisted a genuinely independent activity on his son's part because in the business "he had insisted on having everything his own way."[2]

Similar conditions prevail in *The Metamorphosis*. At first the old man is the owner of a business, financially so closely tied up with the firm in which his son is employed that with the ensuing collapse of the

2. "The Judgment," in Franz Kafka, *The Complete Stories*, ed. Nahum N. Glatzer, trans. Willa and Edwin Muir (New York: Schocken, 1971) 78.

business, Gregor's boss becomes his creditor. Thus one could say that
Gregor's professional position as a little "stock clerk" [20][3] is to be
understood at least indirectly as the opposite pole of his father's position
at that time as an independent businessman.

But in both stories things don't stop with the dominant role of pro-
fessionally successful fathers. A turnabout occurs, which likewise still
belongs to the story's background, reversing at least externally the previous set of power relations. In "The Judgment" it is the death of the
mother, which has "hit the father harder" than it did Georg and hence
accelerated "the course of nature."[4] Old Bendemann becomes "less
aggressive"[5] in business, and he cedes more and more initiative
and responsibility to Georg. In *The Metamorphosis* it is the above-
mentioned business collapse and the financial disaster connected with
it that initially brings "everyone into a state of total despair" [20]. This
blow of fate does not, so to speak, hurtle the sons into ruin but
instead—and this is characteristic of the second phase of these family
histories—brings about their professional rise, which in respect of power
and influence puts them in the place of their fathers while the latter
are forced into a subordinate role comparable with the previous position
of the sons. "Almost overnight" Gregor Samsa is transformed from a
little employee to a commercial representative, who "earned enough
money to meet the expenses of the entire family and actually did so"
[20]. And Georg Bendemann now takes charge of the business with the
greatest determination and in this way can double the number of his
employees and increase volume fivefold. Responding to this situation,
his father, who is offended, characterizes him, even if ironically, as the
"boss," while the father himself, "old to the marrow of my bones"[6] and
racked by an increasingly faulty memory, has lost a general perspective
on the business and hence has gone almost entirely into retirement.

This turnabout is made vivid by numerous details. In "The Judgment" the position of the father as a senile old man is hinted at by the
fact that he lives in a badly lit back room in the apartment that they
share, sits in his dressing gown beside a closed window, although it is
almost noon on a beautiful spring day, peers at old newspapers whose
names Georg can't even recognize anymore, has hardly touched his
breakfast, wears underwear that is less than clean, and, like a baby, toys
with Georg's watch-chain as Georg carries him to bed. Similarly it is
said of Gregor's father that he drags out breakfast by reading various
newspapers for hours on end; indeed—in a detail that can be supplied
from another passage—he also wears a dressing gown [12, 28]. The old
man, who has gained a lot of weight, lies exhausted, buried in his bed,

3. Norton Critical Edition page numbers appear in brackets [*Editor*].
4. Ibid. 82.
5. Ibid. 78.
6. Ibid. 86.

when Gregor heads out on a business trip, receives him evenings in an armchair, because he is really not quite able to lift his bulk, and during walks must stop and gather the other members of his family around him whenever he has anything to say to them. Thus, in this story the physical deterioration of the father stands out more plainly, as well as that of the mother too, who suffers from asthmatic attacks and looks for relief to the open window.

The successful sons are depicted quite differently. Old man Bende-mann contrasts the withdrawnness of his own measly existence with Georg's abundant and luxurious social life: "My son [went] strutting through the world, . . . bursting with triumphant glee, and stalking away from his father with the closed face of a respectable business-man!"[7] In a corresponding moment in *The Metamorphosis* Gregor's happy vitality appears, if in a less aggressive manner, in the shape of a picture that hangs in the Samsa family living room, which depicts Gre-gor in a superior pose: "On the wall directly opposite hung a photo-graph of Gregor from his army days, in a lieutenant's uniform, his hand on his sword, a carefree smile on his lips, demanding respect for his bearing and his rank" [12]. Besides this confrontation in *The Meta-morphosis* between the withdrawn existence of the retiree and active worldliness, we encounter a striking contrast between useless parasitism and the kind of exhausting professional engagement requiring the use of all one's powers. The few evenings Gregor stays home he spends in the family circle, not going out. He reads newspapers or makes little objects with his fretsaw when he is not forced to devote even this hardly distinctive leisure-time activity to his job and with the help of timetables figure out the train connections that he plans to use on his next business trip. The counterpart to this form of life is provided less by his old parents than by his seventeen-year-old sister, who according to Gregor is still a child spending her days "wearing pretty clothes, sleeping late, helping around the house, enjoying a few modest amusements, and above all playing the violin" [21].

Now, however, in both stories a fundamental turn of the tide occurs in the family's affairs. In *The Metamorphosis* Gregor wakes up one morning as a vermin. The consequences for the other members of the family are remarkable. The invalid father takes a job as a bank messen-ger. Even though he must start work at six in the morning, he cannot be persuaded to go to bed before ten at night and refuses obstinately to take off his uniform at home, so that his dressing gown hangs "use-lessly" on the clothes hook [30]. The old mother, for whom formerly it was an ordeal even "to take a walk through the apartment" [21], now sews "delicate lingerie for a clothing store" [30]. And Gregor's sister gets a job as saleswoman and on top of this takes stenography and

7. Ibid.

French nights in order to qualify for a better job, perhaps, at some later time, while still having to look after her brother.

As we see, the previous conditions of life for the other members of Gregor's family are radically reversed. The father, who, unable to work, used to be still lying in bed when Gregor was heading out on a business trip, and who spent his days in his dressing gown reading newspapers and eating, now has to begin work very early, the way Gregor once had to, persisting in wearing his uniform until bedtime, as if to indicate by doing so that his new professional position requires just as much time from him now as the activity of traveling salesman used to require from his son. The mother, sick and exhausted, now takes on demanding sewing assignments, which require concentration and skill, and even the new life of the sister looks like the consciously structured antipode to her lifestyle hitherto: instead of being able to sleep till all hours, she now has to get up early, and instead of helping a little in the house, she is employed full-time and moreover must look after Gregor. Her little amusements have been replaced by advanced professional training, and in all the months since Gregor's metamorphosis, only once does she devote herself to her favorite pastime, playing the violin.

By means of the metamorphosis, however, it is not only the previous life–situation of the members of his family that turns into its opposite but also Gregor's own. Upon losing his job, he loses his dominant position in the family. If until now, as a consequence of their physical frailty, the parents had been chained, so to speak, to the apartment, now he is the one who is locked up and may not leave his room. If, earlier, Gregor supported his parents and his sister, now it is he who must be looked after like a child, while his sister, through the duties imposed on her, grows in self-confidence. And, indeed, by the end of the story, in spite of all the trouble, she has blossomed into a beautiful and voluptuous young woman, definitively leaving behind her the role of the child that previously, at least on Gregor's part, had been assigned to her.

Above all, however, it is the father who regains the position he has lost as head of the family, whereas Gregor loses respect and influence. This exchange of roles between father and son is reflected in characteristic details. If, before, it was Gregor, who, in his uniform, had demanded respect, now it is the father, who not by chance is introduced in his new service uniform: "Now however, he was holding himself very erect, dressed in a tight-fitting blue uniform . . . ; under his bushy eyebrows his black eyes darted bright, piercing glances" [28].

A corresponding turnabout occurs in "The Judgment" at the moment Georg visits his father in order to inform him that he has written to his friend in St. Petersburg of his impending engagement. This visit, which can be regarded as extraordinary simply by the fact that for months he has not stepped foot into his father's room, takes place at the moment

Georg, in the face of inner resistance, tries to acknowledge his engage-ment without any reservations whatsoever. The course of the ensuing conversation reveals that his friend, who lives as a bachelor, embodies the side of Georg's personality that his father approves of, whereas he stands inimically opposed to his son's marriage plans, attempting by every means to frustrate their realization. Given the opposing forces he has overcome by special effort, Georg cannot stand the test of this confrontation. As a result he experiences his father, who up until this moment has been fragile and like a child must be taken to bed and tucked in, as a "bogey," who now gains power over his inner world. While his gigantic father stands up in bed, "quite unsupported,"[8] prop-ping himself up with one hand against the ceiling and kicking out his legs, flaunting his superiority at his son, Georg loses his self-control and in the course of the encounter finally falls into such panic that he immediately takes over and executes the death sentence uttered by his father.

Both stories are furthermore marked by an ambivalence in the sons' behavior toward their fathers, apparently based on disturbed emotional relationships. Georg Bendemann relates to his father mainly in the business. Lunch is eaten, as is significantly noted, "at the same time"[9] and not, let us say, "together," at an "eating house"; whereas evenings, to the extent that Georg, "as mostly happened,"[1] is not out with friends or with his fiancée, they sit together "for a while, each with his news-paper, in their shared living room."[2] Intimate conversations—as these details are very likely meant to indicate—do not take place between father and son even when, after the business day is over, they spend time in their shared apartment.

The same holds true for *The Metamorphosis*. The family lets itself be supported by Gregor, receives the money "with thanks," yet before too long no special "feeling of warmth" goes along with it. [20]. This state of affairs is again illustrated in the way the evening is spent. In the late afternoon, while Gregor is still at work, his father is in the habit of reading aloud from the evening newspaper to the two women. To the extent that Gregor, upon returning from a business trip, is present in the evening, he sits beside the other family members at the living room table, "quietly reading the paper or studying train schedules" [8]. In the case of the Samsa family, too, things never get to the point where a real conversation takes place between the son and the other members of the family.

In "The Judgment" the superior strength of the father grows so strong

8. Ibid. 85.
9. Ibid. 81. The Muirs translate this phrase, incorrectly, as "together" [*Editor*].
1. Ibid.
2. Ibid. Translation modified [*Editor*].

that Georg unconsciously harbors the wish that his father would die. "Now he'll lean forward, thought Georg, what if he topples and smashes himself! These words went hissing through his mind."[3] In *The Metamorphosis* the hatred of the son for his rejuvenated father is not so directly expressed: nonetheless, it is present. In one passage, for example, Gregor is so filled with "rage" at his miserable fare that he considers whether he shouldn't just grab from the pantry what is "still" his due. The thought, too, of standing guard with the help of his "nightmarish looks" simultaneously at all doors of his room and "hissing and spitting at the aggressors" [36] who should dare to approach his sister, whom he thinks of as his consort, is aimed chiefly at his father, of course, even if this is not expressly stated. The same is true of his thoughts at the beginning of the story, in which he complains about the hardships of his job. He is sure that he would be fired "on the spot" if he ever lived like the other traveling salesmen, who are still sitting at the break-fast table when he returns to the hotel in the course of the morning to "write up" the orders he has gotten [4]. It cannot be overlooked that Gregor's dissatisfaction with the situation imposed on him is aimed at his own father, for whom breakfast is the most important meal of the day, which he drags out for hours, living literally like a harem woman.

In the same connection Gregor, dissatisfied with his treatment, ac-knowledges the fact that up until now he has not quit his job solely out of consideration for his parents, yet he still imagines the scene in which he could finally give in to his own desires and quit in a way that reveals a striking parallel to "The Judgment," in which the thought goes "hissing through" Georg Bendemann's head that his father, who is looking down on him from his bed, might topple and smash himself. For Gregor is driven by the desire to step up to his boss and speak his piece "from the bottom of his heart", so that his boss would have to fall off his desk and, one may add, in this way meet his death [4]. It does not seem far-fetched to see at work in this passage the depth-psychological Law of Displacement, which causes unconscious ideas censored from consciousness to be attached to unoffending objects. Thus, the boss who is in a close business connection with his father has stepped in as an ersatz for the hated father, against whom Gregor does not dare to rebel.

On the other hand, at the conscious level, the sons in *The Metamorphosis* and in "The Judgment" are still attached to their parents even in the hour of their death. As Georg Bendemann carries out the paternal judgment, he cries out: "Dear parents, I have always loved you";[4] and Gregor Samsa thinks back, while he is dying, with deep

3. Ibid. 86.
4. Ibid. 88.

emotion and love to his family, who in the course of events have brought about his death [39].

Furthermore, in individual details there are correspondences of theme between "The Judgment" and *The Metamorphosis*, which make convincing the conclusion that both texts arise from a common arsenal of prefabricated narrative building blocks. If it was the old Bendemann whose clothing was neglected as long as Georg conducted the business, now it is Gregor who exhibits himself "covered with dust" and drags around with him "fluff and hairs and scraps of food" [35], after his father has once again resumed the dominant position and sent him into retirement as the invalid which he had previously been. If in "The Judgment" the father, who finds himself banished to his memories in the back room of the apartment, is described as having eaten very little of his breakfast,[5] this loss of appetite carries over, in a sense, to Gregor, who, seriously ill, now has only his death ahead of him. In both instances the lack of interest in food appears as the long-term effect of family neglect, while within the system of *The Metamorphosis* the theme of food follows the principle of the exchange of roles between father and son: As commercial representative, who must get up at four o'clock in the morning, Gregor, unlike his father, does not have time to spend the morning at breakfast. After the metamorphosis, of course, he has a particularly keen appetite, and, in order to reflect on his situation, characteristically first wants to have a solid breakfast—like his father, one is inclined to add; at the same time it is forcefully emphasized that the other members of his family, confronted with the vermin, can hardly swallow a bite.

From the fact that in both stories each strengthening of the paternal position results in a weakening of the son's and vice-versa, one can draw the conclusion that Kafka wanted to portray an irreconcilable conflict between generations—one which stands out when the adversaries are present in a single family unit. In this respect a difference exists between the two stories only insofar as with Gregor's death the final obstacle to the renewed blooming of the other members of the family has been removed, while the judgment uttered by the old Bendemann, who, as one passage has it, has mobilized his final energies against his son, carries the judge to death along with Georg. Even while Georg rushes down to the bridge, in order to suffer death by drowning, he hears the "crash" with which his father falls onto the bed, perishing in the manner which he has secretly hoped for.

---

5. Ibid. 81.

II. The Title Page Illustration

Kafka had learned that the illustrator Ottomar Starke had been commissioned to draw a title–page illustration. For this reason on October 25, 1915, he wrote to his publisher:

> It struck me that Starke, as an illustrator, might want to draw the insect itself. Not that, please not that! I do not want to restrict him, but only to make this plea out of my deeper knowledge of the story. The insect itself cannot be depicted. It cannot even be shown from a distance. Perhaps there is no such intention and my plea can be dismissed with a smile—so much the better. But I would be very grateful if you would pass along my request and make it more emphatic. If I were to offer suggestions for an illustration, I would choose such scenes as the following: the parents and the head clerk in front of the locked door, or even better, the parents and the sister in the lighted room, with the door open upon the adjoining room that lies in darkness.[6]

A number of critics have tried to make use of Kafka's statement to interpret the story. * * * Jürg Schubiger [for example] intends to dematerialize *The Metamorphosis*.[7] He supposes that Kafka's prohibition against picturing the insect is rooted in a disparity existing between the figure of the metamorphosed creature and any insect that could be represented. Thus, Gregor's head ends in nostrils and strong mandibles, which are supposed to take the place of masticators in the human organism. The head is unusually mobile compared with that of familiar insects: Gregor can raise it and lower it, stretch it out and even twist it so far that he can see what is going on behind him. Gregor's weight, too, which Schubiger puts at at least sixty-five pounds, since it would take two strong persons to lift him out of bed, does not tally, according to Schubiger, with his later ability to wander over walls and ceiling. Information of this kind about Gregor's physical being, writes Schubiger, does not provide a rounded image of a living being but rather amounts to a mere inventory of possible forms of behavior, which come into their own only within concrete situations but which, however, must be discounted if the creature is to be truly characterized as an insect. As a result, he draws the conclusion that Gregor's bodily data should not be misunderstood as facts; rather, we have the case here of bodily–posed questions and answers in the beetle's dialogue with the world.[8]

Schubiger's conception is shaped by the desire to prove a direct correspondence between Kafka's idea that the insect cannot be grasped in a drawing and the manner of its representation in *The Metamorphosis*.

6. *Letters to Friends* 114–15.
7. Jürg Schubiger, *Franz Kafka: Die Verwandlung. Eine Interpretation* (Zurich and Freiburg i. Br.: Atlantis, 1969) 57.
8. Ibid. 56.

This project is not successful. For example, it is incorrect to want to fix the weight of the insect according to the self-conception Gregor has at the outset of the story. For at the point when he indulges in the thought that his father and the maid could scoop him up out of the sheets and set him on the ground, he has not grasped his change in any real way. Despite sensory evidence to the contrary, he considers himself the traveling salesman Gregor Samsa, while in reality he has been transformed into a vermin, whose body has shrunk to about half its size. Under these circumstances, it is only by calculating on the basis of the specific density of the human body that one arrives at a weight of sixty-five pounds. But insects, if only on account of their ability to fly, which often is the case, are in comparison with their extension much lighter than human bodies. Kafka must have proceeded from this assumption, or otherwise he would not have made the point toward the close of the story that the cleaning woman with her broom was able to shove the creature's cadaver, which of course as a consequence of an inadequate intake of nourishment has grown emaciated, "without any resistance to another spot" [39].

Nor is there anything to object to in the concept of Gregor's "jaws," for this is an expression customary both in the zoology of insects as well as in the anatomy of human beings and hence is precisely suited to this story. On the other hand, in mentioning Gregor's respiratory organs, Kafka had to make recourse to the expression "nostrils," which is used for the respiratory organs of animals, especially horses; after all, the story was not supposed to be oriented to a kind of natural scientific verisimilitude that would oblige Kafka to speak of "trachea."

Again, the truth is otherwise in the case of Schubiger's claim that in his story Kafka fails to provide a rounded representation of Gregor's form. Here, in fact, something correct has been noted while at the same time wrongly interpreted. It is quite true that at the beginning of the story Kafka does not lay out a coherent description of all of Gregor's individual physical peculiarities but rather reveals them piecemeal and always when they are of importance for the development of the plot—hence, as a rule, when Gregor, who only gradually becomes intimately acquainted with his new form of life, himself notes or uses them. Thus, for example, the reader learns of the sticky pads on his feet only when he uses them, for instance, to draw himself up against the clothes cupboard; of his feelers only at the moment when they are useful to him for orientation in the dark room, that is, at the beginning of the second chapter. But it is wrong to draw the conclusion from these facts that by means of this process Kafka wanted to prevent the metamorphosed being from being visualized as a representational whole. A close reading of *The Metamorphosis* would have been able to convince Schubiger that the process of giving information about existing relations in a successive manner applies not only to the main character but also, for example, to the representation of the living quarters. That in Gregor's room there is a chair and couch, that it contains a clothes cupboard, in which he stores his fretsaw and other tools, and that the table, on which he has spread out his fabric samples, is a writing table, which he had already used as a student, is by no means communicated in a coherent way at the beginning of the story, where Gregor, who has just awoken and is drugged with sleep, lets his eyes glide over the room in order to decide whether he is awake or dreaming. Rather, one learns about his furniture gradually in various later passages, and only then does one form a correct picture of the furnishings of this dwelling. The same thing is true of the data about the living room of the Samsa family. . . . Even the assumption that in a similar way the spatial dimensions of the story are, like Gregor, to be thought of as unreal, does not avoid embarrassment, for the Kafkan principle of narrative structure, foundational in every individual case, of so functionalizing the narrative stage that in each individual case only those components of the scenery are named which are needed precisely to advance the plot, is realized not only in *The Metamorphosis* but also in other texts of Kafka.

Seen in context, the employment and significance of this principle emerges as a consequence of the personal narrative situation favored by Kafka. It is not by any means supposed to express a particular degree of unreality of what is represented but rather to have the representation of external reality appear as the perception of the hero in a manner corresponding to the chosen perspective. When, however, the reader sees with Gregor's eyes, he or she may not expect any sort of standard exposition, with a description of the protagonist and his surroundings. For, on the one hand, the vehicle of the perspective as a rule has as little cause to visualize his familiar environment as a whole as he does himself and his body, so that the narrator, too, who conforms to him, has to renounce it when he does not for particular reasons in individual cases consider it advisable with the help of special tricks to get in under the guard of the given perspective-technical frame conditions. To this must be added the fact that the hero of *The Metamorphosis* acknowledges and registers his insect shape only in the course of time, as does the reader, who is limited to his vantage point.

But as what kind of creature did Kafka imagine this vermin, which he turns into the vehicle of the narrative events? The circumstance that Brod and Werfel often speak of a "bug" (*Wanze*)[9] is perhaps not entirely a coincidence; after all in Kafka's time in Prague the idea of vermin suggested first of all the image of a bug or a louse and much less so a beetle. For this insect's variousness of type, something known to ev-

---

9. "Bug" should not in any way suggest the cuteness of a bug snug in a rug or the daintiness of the ladybug, which in German is called "Marienkäfer [literally, Mary-beetle]"; note the allusion to the Virgin Mary in this word. The reader should think instead of a bug-infested mattress or a buggy summer night [*Editor*].

eryone, and the knowledge of its various habitats and lifestyles stand in the way of its wholesale denigration as parasite. Only some types, like the very widespread flour beetle, the most common sort of beetle, which has in common with Gregor the fact that it shuns dampness, counts without reservation as vermin. To this corresponds the fact that when in his "Letter to My Father," he characterizes himself as vermin, Kafka thinks of a stinging and bloodsucking insect that feeds parasitically on its host.[1] In truth the metamorphosed Gregor has important features in common with a bug—hence the strong stench that prevents his sister from staying even briefly in his room with closed windows. Even if Kafka at first may not have been familiar with this well-known fact, he was confronted with it at the latest on September 17, 1912, when a co-worker at the Workers Accident Insurance Institute[2] told him a story in the office which he reported in his journal as follows:

> His horror of vermin. In the army one night he had an itch under his nose, he slapped it in his sleep and crushed something. But the something was a bedbug and he carried the stench of it around with him for days.[3]

Furthermore, Gregor's brownish coloration and his shrinking from the light that makes his favorite spot the place under the couch and urges him to look out the window in darkness, as well as his inclination to crawl over the walls and ceiling, fit in better with a dun-colored house bug who is accustomed to staying in dark cracks during the day and unlike a beetle has sticky pads on the feet. Even Gregor's voice, which is reduced to a chirping [5], can be seen in this connection as an index of the fact that Kafka had in mind the model of a bug that can emit sounds, whereas beetles are mute. Of course, the fact that lice have only six legs causes some difficulty; and only on the assumption that Gregor's perception has gone fully haywire can it be squared with the "many" little legs which, upon his waking up, wave before his eyes.

Fundamentally, Kafka could not consistently maintain Gregor's vermin character, because in so doing he would have had to give him a sucking proboscis and the story would have turned into a Frankensteinian horror show because under these conditions he could have nourished himself only on the blood of the other members of the family or, in case his being held prisoner had prevented this, could not have stayed alive. But Kafka did not want to depict a monster whose feeding drive forced him to fling himself at the right opportunity on his family, the manager, the maid or the roomers—and in this way lose every gram of the reader's sympathy. For this reason, Gregor receives the masti-

1. *Letter to His Father*, trans. Ernst Kaiser and Eithne Wilkins (New York: Schocken, 1966) 123. See above, p. 71 [*Editor*].
2. Kafka's place of business in the years 1908–22 [*Editor*].
3. *Diaries, 1910–1913*, 133.

cators of a beetle which, of course, are in no way toothless—as Kafka erroneously presupposes—but which in any case allow him to open the door of his room and to feed on the rotted dishes which are typical for particular beetle types like the churchyard beetle. The cockroach, too, which has in common with Gregor a broad, flattened body, aversion to the light, and a preference for narrow hiding places, and which in nineteenth-century Russian literature, along with the louse, represents vermin purely and simply, has such masticators; and it is perhaps no accident that the hero of *The Metamorphosis*, dissatisfied with his provisions, is at one point tempted to raid the pantry and do a thorough job on it.

It moreover tallies with this classification of Gregor in the world of insects that Kafka, in his diary, at one point characterizes him as a black beetle and that the cleaning woman in one passage calls him an old dung beetle. The fact that Gregor can eat only with the cooperation of his entire body and that he thereby gets bigger, points in the same direction, for beetles are able to expand the size and length of their abdomen in order to breathe and take in nourishment.

Finally, in this connection, one could add that the hero of the work entitled "Wedding Preparations in the Country" at one point wants to be transformed into a giant stag beetle or cockchafer who, hibernating in bed, his legs pressed against his protuberant body, whispers orders to his body, wishing it to act for him while the body itself rests.[4] This scene is related in a certain way to the course of action of *The Metamorphosis*, for Raban, the hero of this early novel–fragment, does not feel himself equal to the demands of life in the outside world and plays in his thoughts with the solution that is actually inflicted on Gregor, who lives under comparable conditions.

Seen biologically, therefore, the insect represented by Kafka is a mélange of bug and beetle and—possibly—cockroach. It was designed to lend reality to his narrative intentions, even if a creature constructed like it cannot be found in the empirical world. At the same time, such a being is every bit as imaginable as any fabulous beast, especially as his physical build does not display any self-contradictory characteristics. Hence, it can certainly be drawn and be shown from a distance. It is not easy to see why Kafka rejected a graphic presentation of this sort of hybrid-insect while considering a verbal description possible. * * *

Neither the alleged disparity of the statements made about Gregor's external appearance nor the alleged dream-character of the story can therefore have caused Kafka to make his request that Ottomar Starke desist from drawing the insect. The reasons for his taking this position have to lie elsewhere and can only be surmised. Possibly he wanted to avoid the obvious misunderstanding that in the case of his story what

4. "Wedding Preparations in the Country," in *Dearest Father*, trans. Ernst Kaiser and Eithne Wilkins (New York: Schocken, 1954) 7. See above, p. 61 [*Editor*].

was at stake was a metamorphosis related to representations in classical literature or in popular fairy tales. In contrast with these, the peculiarity of Gregor's representation consists indeed precisely in the fact that he undergoes a transformation of only his physical shape. His human consciousness, however, and, with certain restrictions, his feelings remain intact throughout the whole story. A drawing that showed him as a vermin could not express this state of affairs: indeed, it would even obscure it. Kafka may thus have thought that a title-page illustration of this sort would produce a false preliminary understanding and thus create difficulties in the way of a correct reading of *The Metamorphosis*.

III. Punishments

After "The Stoker" had appeared in May 1913 in *Der jüngste Tag* and after a narrative text of relatively larger scope had arisen in October 1914 in the shape of "In the Penal Colony," which had to wait to be brought out under war conditions particularly arduous for publishers, a new situation arose with respect to Kafka's favored omnibus volume *The Sons*. He sought to deal with it by suggesting that under the title *Punishments* "The Judgment" be brought out together with *The Metamorphosis* and the new story. * * * Thus he excluded "The Stoker," which in the meantime had been published, from the corpus of the omnibus volume and put the unpublished "In the Penal Colony" in it, which necessarily led to a change of title.

From the fact that Kafka planned for a time to publish *The Metamorphosis* as part of a book that was supposed to bear the title *Punishments*, doubtful consequences for the interpretation of the story have been too swiftly drawn. Thus, the critic Norbert Oellers asserts that Gregor is punished for an offense arising from his relation to his father. Accordingly, old man Samsa has a part in the metamorphosis and punishes his son with death. Because while dying Gregor thinks back on his punisher, and hence, Oellers argues, accepts what has been inflicted upon him, the conclusion is drawn that there is truth, too, in the severity of the punishment, for Gregor's metamorphosis is understood here to be the high point of his ill-lived life. Since Gregor is never astonished that he has woken up as a creature unrecognizable as a human being, his development—so Oellers' thesis continues—has followed a logical course up until now, and the endpoint is a gesture of flight from the human condition. As a traveling salesman, under the pressure of his family connections and of the compulsion to work, Gregor has become an asocial human being, a disturber and corrupter of his family, namely: "In his hands, in his power, the other members of the family, drilled into helpless dependency, waste away in their relations to one another. Harmony is long a thing of the past: Gregor's sister, above all, is visibly alienated from the parents by Gregor."[5]

This interpretation, however, is wrong and contradicts the literal text of the story. Kafka remains completely silent as to the possible cause of the metamorphosis, so that it is impossible to make any well-founded assertions whatsoever about it. Certainly it is true that Gregor adjusts relatively swiftly to the new situation as soon as he has become convinced of its reality. The most that could be said is that in a certain sense his metamorphosis is welcomed by his own desires[6] while standing in opposition to the notions of his parents, who are convinced that as a dealer in fabrics Gregor had found a job for life. From this, however, one cannot conclude that Gregor is himself responsible for his animal shape, for then the first sentence of the story would have had to state that he had transformed himself, whereas Kafka writes that he *found* himself transformed into a monstrous vermin and so keeps silent as to the agency causing the event.

Even the background history of *The Metamorphosis* does not permit the insinuation that Gregor has committed a mortal offense. The claim that he has "drilled" the other members of the family into helpless dependency and got it in his power is at the very least untrue in its degree of generality, for his father and his sister are different cases. On the one hand, the relations dominating Gregor and his father can be so described that Gregor, although the sole support of the family, does not assume a position corresponding to his importance. The proof of this is provided by the highly remarkable circumstance that his father prevents him from gaining any insight into the financial circumstances of the family, an attitude which parents are normally in the habit of assuming toward their dependents in order to demonstrate superior authority. Corresponding to this, on the part of the son, is his inner dependence on the values of the parents, which reveal themselves in his conviction of having had to sacrifice himself for many years to the well-being of the family. The fact that in the hour of his demise he thinks back with deep emotion and love to the other members of his family, who have exiled him and brought on his death, is an expression of this inner dependency and thus does not point in any way at all to a feeling of guilt.

On the other hand, Gregor's relation to his sister has to be judged differently. When he regards this seventeen-year-old as a child, from whom he does not expect any work, tries to make her financially dependent on him by intending to pay for her music lessons, and when,

5. Norbert Oellers, "Die Bestrafung der Söhne: Zu Kafkas Erzählungen 'Das Urteil,' 'Der Heizer,' und 'Die Verwandlung,'" *Zeitschrift für deutsche Philologie* 97 (1978): 85.
6. Ingeborg Henel, "Die Grenzen der Deutbarkeit von Kafkas Werken. Die Verwandlung," *Journal of English and Germanic Philology* 83 (1984):71.

finally, after his metamorphosis, he wants to keep her in his room and defend against every aggressor, then the suspicion does indeed force itself upon one that he meant if not to oppress her nonetheless to keep her dependent on him. This is supported by the development which Grete undergoes. For the moment that Gregor has to give up his role as family provider, she breaks away from her former role. She undertakes responsible tasks and in the course of the story blossoms into a voluptuous young woman, whose marriage, soon to be awaited, rounds out the process of her maturation and acquisition of independence. The fact that the kind of relation that prevails between old Samsa and his son recurs in Gregor's relation to his sister may possibly be understood by the fact that Gregor passes on what he has suffered as his father's victim to his sister vis-à-vis whom he was the superior partner. Even the reader unwilling to explain Gregor's behavior in this way is still not entitled to charge him with an offense and on this account attribute a guilt to him that would justify his death, for it cannot be understood why Kafka would have considered such faulty behavior as worthy of punishment.

No less questionable is the position of the critic Ingeborg Henel, who does not situate Gregor's alleged offense before but instead during the metamorphosis. Through his transformation as a vermin, it is alleged, Gregor has gone from provider to parasite: instead of responsibility, he has heaped guilt upon himself, and this calls for punishment which is conciliated by death.[7] Here, however, one asks oneself why the father, who has lived for five years as Gregor's parasite and finally bears the responsibility for Gregor's faulty behavior toward his sister, isn't punished himself but instead appears as punisher. Furthermore, according to this view of things, Gregor could be culpable only if he could be made responsible for his transformation into a vermin, a notion which the text does not support. Finally, Ingeborg Henel would have had to explain why parasitism should be punished with death.

The main error in the positions of Norbert Oellers and Ingeborg Henel consists in this: Without more exact testing, they presuppose that Kafka depicts a righteous world in which crime and punishment stand in an ethically justifiable relation to one another, although various works of his show that this is not the case at all. The example of *The Boy Who Sank Out of Sight* can make clear that Karl's expulsion from his homeland, which in "The Stoker" [its first chapter] is expressly characterized as punishment, in no way turns him into a guilty party. To be sure, his punishment appears to correspond to guilt feelings, for in the initial chapter he believes that he has failed his parents as their son and now tries to make up for his failure by taking pains in the New World to uphold the values they represent. But, at the same time, these

---

7. Ibid. 83.

guilt feelings do not prove that Karl has in fact taken guilt upon himself. For, on the one hand, the uncle, who certainly cannot be suspected of wanting to trivialize any possible offense on Karl's part, says that Karl's offense "was of a kind that merely needs to be named to find indulgence."[8] On the other hand, one of Kafka's diary entries reveals that he meant to view the hero of *The Boy Who Sank Out of Sight* as innocent, while submitting him, however, at the same time, to the destiny of one who is "executed."[9]

In a related way, the same is true of the two other texts that Kafka wanted to bring together in *Punishments*. In "The Judgment" old Bendemann is able to bring forward a great many charges against his son: Georg goes "strutting through the world," bursting with "triumphant glee,"[1] with his intended marriage disgraces the memory of his mother, betrays his friend, and takes no heed of the grief of his old, sick, widowed father, whom he has stuck in bed so that he could not budge. These accusations can be only partly checked for their truth content in the body of the text and sooner lead to the conclusion that they do not correspond to the truth. But even if one were to consider them correct, they do not justify characterizing Georg as a devilish human being who must be condemned to death by drowning. No adequate reasons can be found to justify the inhuman severity of this punishment.

Still more absurd is the situation shown in "In the Penal Colony." Here Kafka describes an island penal settlement—one should not forget that he does not speak expressly either for or against it—where the principle is followed that guilt is never to be doubted and without exception to be avenged with death. This is true too of the case which is put before the explorer. The condemned man's neglect of duty is portrayed by Kafka in a manner that allows no room for doubt as to the injustice of conditions prevailing in the penal colony. For how can a soldier, who during his nightly watch in front of the door of his sleeping superior is supposed to salute every hour on the hour, but in this case is found sleeping, be punished with death for this offense? Thus, in "In the Penal Colony" a disproportion between offense and punishment is represented with a degree of caricaturing crassness that can scarcely be surpassed.

Kafka's "Letter to his Father" gives proof of the fact that this pattern expresses a basic experience of Kafka that shaped his feelings about life from early childhood on: After all, he always had the idea of having been punished in a terrible way by his father "for no reason at all."[2] Strange to say, these experiences did not lead to accusations of blame at the punishing father but rather produced guilt feelings in him that

8. *Amerika* 26.
9. *Diaries, 1914–1923* 132.
1. "The Judgment" 86.
2. *Letter to His Father* 17.

had no basis in the facts but arose from his parents' dissatisfaction with him. In this sense, for example, he wrote to Felice Bauer: "The family's harmony is really upset only by me, and more so as the years go by; very often I don't know what to do, and feel a great sense of guilt toward my parents and everyone else."[3]

In light of these connections, the assumption is obvious that in the three stories that Kafka wanted to publish together in *The Punishments*, he meant to depict precisely this psychic mechanism. It would therefore be quite wrong to want to conclude solely from the title of this omnibus volume that the punishments suffered by the figures who appear in them are just and are based on objectively determinable guilt. If Georg Bendemann and Gregor Samsa submit equally willingly to the punishments that have been imposed on them and depart from this life, their behavior allows one to conclude, certainly, that they feel themselves to be guilty even when this is not expressly said. But this guilt feeling governs them (to speak in the words of the first sentence of *The Trial*) without their having done anything wrong.

The middle position, which Kafka felt *The Metamorphosis* could occupy between "The Judgment" and "In the Penal Colony," is not based on its relation to the problem of punishment. For in this case one would have to assume that the disproportion between offense and punishment in *The Metamorphosis* is greater than in "The Judgment" and less than in "Penal Colony." But since this conception cannot be proved, it is more probable that Kafka had the formal structure more clearly in mind. He found "The Judgment" to be rather more lyric than epic, hence judged it to be a text in which a feeling of life is given conceptual and dialogical unfolding, which proceeds at the cost of epic successiveness. In contrast, "Penal Colony," with its long descriptive phases, represented a wholly different prose type. Finally *The Metamorphosis*, planned as a classic narrative, would be able, when placed between the others, to hinder, on the one hand the direct collision of the two formally different texts; on the other hand, however, to mediate between both sides: between "The Judgment," with which it shares a family conflict, and "In the Penal Colony," with which it shares the detailed description of someone marked for death, who goes to his ruin in a slow and agonizing way.

---

3. *Letters to Felice* 133.

ERIC SANTNER

Kafka's *Metamorphosis* and the Writing of Abjection†

I

The story of Gregor Samsa is an initiation into a universe of abjection.[1] Not only is Gregor transformed into a species of repulsive vermin, not only is he fed garbage, but his family gradually turns his room into a dumping grounds for all sorts of refuse—for what is refused from the family. Gregor's desiccated body is also finally expelled as so much trash, as if he had come to embody the waste products of the very family he had previously nourished with care and dedication. Although Kafka does not offer the reader anything like a causal account of Gregor's transformation, he does suggest a number of possible systemic or structural features that help make sense of it. In other words, Gregor's fall into abjection can be approached as a *symptom* whose fascinating presence serves as a displaced condensation of larger and more diffuse disturbances within the social field marked out by the text.

The story begins with a community—the Samsa family—in disarray. A strange, even miraculous, physical transformation has made it impossible for Gregor to perform the duties that had heretofore been the lifeblood of the family. The reader first encounters the members of this microcommunity as a series of *voices* recalling Gregor to his "official" responsibilities. Among the voices imploring Gregor to do his duty, the father's voice doubtlessly distinguishes itself as the most urgent and insistent one. This quasi-operatic *mise-en-scène*,[2] whereby characters are introduced as voices with distinctive vocal registers, may be, on Kafka's part, an allusion not merely to the world of opera in general but rather to a particular work whose cultural significance would not have escaped him: Wagner's final opera, *Parsifal*.[3]

In *Parsifal*, too, we find a community—the Grail Society—in disarray; there too the communal state of emergency is called forth by a son's inability to perform his official duties because of a bodily mutation or mutilation. Amfortas, the Fisher King, is unable to officiate over the Grail miracle. Seduced by Kundry—embodiment of Woman and Wandering Jew[4]—and wounded by the evil wizard Klingsor, Amfortas now longs only for the death that would put an end to his suffering. The

---

† By permission of the author.
1. Among the definitions of "abjection" offered by the *Oxford English Dictionary* are: the condition or estate of one cast down; abasement, humiliation, degradation; rejection; that which is cast off or away; refuse, scum, dregs.
2. Staging [*Editor*].
3. Richard Wagner completed *Parsifal* in 1882, a year before his death [*Editor*].
4. A figure in the legends of many countries who urged Jesus to hasten on the road to Golgotha and was thus doomed to know no rest himself [*Editor*].

gaping wound in his thigh materializes his liminal state between symbolic death—he is unable to assume his symbolic identity as King of
the Grail Society—and the real death he so powerfully desires.[5] Finally,
as in the early pages of *Metamorphosis*, the paternal voice—here, the
voice of Titurel—assumes a special status and urgency. Slavoj Žižek
has noted a more general analogy between *Parsifal* and the world of
Kafka's fiction:

> At first sight, Wagner and Kafka are as far apart as they can be: on
> one hand, we have the late-Romantic revival of a medieval legend;
> on the other, the description of the fate of the individual in con-
> temporary totalitarian bureaucracy . . . but if we look closely we
> perceive that the fundamental problem of *Parsifal* is eminently a
> *bureaucratic* one: the incapacity, the incompetence of Amfortas in
> performing his ritual-bureaucratic duty. The terrifying voice of
> Amfortas's father Titurel, this superego-injunction of the living
> dead, addresses his impotent son in the first act with the words:
> "Mein Sohn Amfortas, bist du am Amt?", to which we have to
> give all bureaucratic weight: Are you at your post? Are you ready
> to officiate?[6]

In *Metamorphosis*, the paternal injunction recalling the son to his
post is, however, marked by a peculiar ambiguity. In Kafka's story, we
are never quite certain about the status of the father as a source of
social power and authority, never sure of the degree of *imposture* informing that authority. Already in the short prose text "The Judgment,"
written months before *Metamorphosis*, Kafka had placed this uncertainty apropos of the father's potency in the foreground of his fictional
universe. No doubt the most breathtaking scene of that story involves
the father's sudden mutation from frail and childlike dependent to
death-bringing tyrant. With regard to that metamorphosis, Stanley
Corngold has remarked that its surreality "suggests the loss of even
fictional coherence; we are entering a world of sheer hypothesis."[7] A
careful reading of *Metamorphosis* suggests that the hypothesis in question refers to a change in the nature of patriarchal power and authority
that infects its stability, dependability, and consistency with radical
uncertainty.

The first indication of this uncertainty concerns not the father but
the other paternal master in Gregor's life, his boss. Reminding himself
that were it not for the family's outstanding, though curiously unspe-

---

5. We should recall that Gregor, too, becomes the bearer of a wound that refuses to heal, the
    product of an apple thrown by his father.
6. Slavoj Žižek, *The Sublime Object of Ideology* (London: Verso, 1989) 76–77.
7. Stanley Corngold, "Introduction," *"The Metamorphosis," by Franz Kafka*, trans. and ed. Stan-
    ley Corngold (New York: Bantam, 1986) xv. All subsequent quotations from *Metamorphosis*
    are cited parenthetically in the text. Norton Critical Edition page numbers appear in brackets.

cified, debt to his boss, he would have long ago given notice, Gregor muses about this master's ultimate imposture:

> He would have fallen off the desk! It is funny, too, the way he sits on the desk and talks down from the heights to the employees, especially when they have to come right up close on account of the boss's being hard of hearing. (4) [4]

This curious uncertainty about the force of institutional power and authority is, as it were, transferred to Gregor's father several pages later, in a single sentence: "But their little exchange had made the rest of the family aware that, contrary to expectations, Gregor was still in the house, and already his father was knocking on one of the side doors, *feebly but with his fist*" (6; my emphasis [5]). In each instance a male figure of authority seems to reveal a double aspect: a master's force and power is shown to contain an impotent, even laughable dimension. One of the most uncanny features of Kafka's literary universe is doubtless the way in which such impotence can suddenly reverse itself into awesome power, or better, the way in which impotence reveals itself to be one of the most disturbing attributes of power.

The inconsistencies and uncertainties informing patriarchal power get played out in *Metamorphosis* above all through the apparent and otherwise inexplicable reinvigoration of the father in the wake of Gregor's transformation. For the previous five years, i.e., since the collapse of the father's business, Gregor had lived a life of sacrifice and self-denial, becoming the sole means of support for his family and even securing its present lodgings. In the course of his early morning musings made possible by the forced interruption of normal activities, Gregor makes abundantly clear just how much he has suffered under the burdens of this sacrificial existence, burdens which have been, as noted earlier, aggravated by the parents' debt:

> "Oh God," he thought, "what a grueling job I've picked! Day in, day out—on the road. . . . I've got the torture of traveling, worrying about changing trains, eating miserable food at all hours, constantly seeing new faces, no relationships that last or get more intimate. . . . If I didn't hold back for my parents' sake, I would have quit long ago. . . ." (4) [3–4]

This sacrificial logic is reiterated and given a turn of the screw in the direction of middle-class sentimentality in the second part of the story:

> In those days Gregor's sole concern had been to do everything in his power to make the family forget as quickly as possible the business disaster which had plunged everyone into a state of total despair. And so he had begun to work with special ardor and had risen almost overnight from stock clerk to traveling salesman. . . . (27) [20]

In short order it is only Grete, Gregor's sister, who seems not to take Gregor's sacrifices completely for granted:

> Only his sister had remained close to Gregor, and it was his secret plan that she, who, unlike him, loved music and could play the violin movingly, should be sent next year to the Conservatory, regardless of the great expense involved. . . . (27) [20]

After his transformation, however, Gregor quickly learns that his family's financial situation was not nearly as grave as he had previously assumed. On the very first day of his new condition, he overhears his father opening a strongbox containing monies rescued from the failed business: "He had always believed that his father had not been able to save a penny from the business, at least his father had never told him anything to the contrary, and Gregor, for his part, had never asked him any questions . . ." (27) [20]. Although Gregor seems to be pleasantly surprised by this discovery, noting that his father had even managed to stash away some of Gregor's own salary, he also realizes that his father's "unexpected foresight and thrift" has also postponed the day on which the family debt could be paid off and he, Gregor, could quit his job and be free. But now, he concludes, "things were undoubtedly better the way his father had arranged them."(28) [21]

Just as Gregor has been mistaken about the state of his family's financial health, he appears to be equally deluded about his sister's warm and seemingly nonexploitative regard for him. It is hardly possible, for example, to take at face value Gregor's assumptions about his sister's motives when she locks the door behind her after bringing Gregor an assortment of half-rotten leftovers: "And out of a sense of delicacy, since she knew that Gregor would not eat in front of her, she left hurriedly and even turned the key, just so that Gregor should know that he might make himself as comfortable as he wanted" (24) [18]? How, then, are we to make sense of Gregor's apparent confusion and ignorance as to how things really stand in the family? And how is Gregor's original "innocence" and progressive initiation into the family's secrets related to his physical transformation and the father's (and family's) renewal and regeneration upon his death and decay?

It would seem that Gregor's new knowledge about the family is related to the rupture in the sacrificial logic by which he had previously organized his life. No longer able to live the life of the long-suffering son, he is compelled to perform what might be called the *sacrifice of sacrifice*. This radical act of sacrifice, i.e., of the very sacrificial logic that had given his life its doubtlessly bleak consistency, makes possible Gregor's discovery that the necessity of his former life, its apparent fatefulness, had been an artificial construction. His life of self-abnegation had been, it now appears, a kind of social game he had actively worked to perpetuate (one will recall that Gregor never asked about the father's finances, never asked what was in the strongbox). In this light, Gregor's condition anticipates that of the man from the country in the parable from *The Trial* who, after a lifetime of waiting at the gates of the Law, learns that its entrance had been designed for him all along and that his exclusion had been staged with his own complicitous participation. Gregor's metamorphosis might thus be understood as a sign of his abjuration of just such complicity, in this case with the "plot" imposing on him a life of self-sacrifice. His abjection would indicate his new position outside that plot, i.e., outside the narrative frame that had given his life meaning and value. This reading is, it turns out, supported by the etymological resonances of the words Kafka uses— *ungeheuere(s) Ungeziefer* ("monstrous vermin")—to introduce Gregor's transformation in the famous first sentence of the story. " '*Ungeheuer*'," as Stanley Corngold has emphasized, "connotes the creature who has no place in the family; '*Ungeziefer*,' the unclean animal unsuited for sacrifice, the creature without a place in God's order" (xix).[8]

To bring these findings to a point, I am arguing that Gregor's fall into abjection be understood as a by-product of his encounter with the ultimate *uncertainty* as to his place in the community of which his father is the nominal master. Gregor's mutation into an *Ungeziefer*, a creature without a place in God's order, suggests, in other words, not Gregor's unsuitability for sacrifice due to some positive, pathological attribute but rather a disturbance *within the divine order itself.* Gregor discovers one of the central paradoxes of modern experience: uncertainty as to what, to use Lacan's term, the "big Other" of the symbolic order[9] really wants from us can be far more disturbing than subordination to an agency or structure whose demands—even for self-sacrifice—are experienced as stable and consistent. The failure to live up to such demands still guarantees a sense of place, meaning, and recognition; but the subject who is uncertain as to the very existence

8. I am arguing, in effect, that we may observe two orders of abjection at work in Kafka's story. Abjection of the first order refers to Gregor's history prior to his metamorphosis, i.e., to his status as a sacrificial object *within* the family structure, and is thus linked to the introjection of the family debt or guilt. Abjection of the second order, a turn of the screw of the first, is the state of the metamorphosis: it signals precisely a radical separation from that family structure and the assumption of a position outside the texture of fate. From the perspective of this new position, what was concealed by the life of self-sacrifice, i.e., by the first order of abjection, becomes visible: the lack of a consistent and dependable Other from whom one could expect a determination of one's identity, whose gaze could guarantee one's recognition, even as *an object worthy of sacrifice.* From a structural point of view, Gregor's verminousness *is* the becoming-visible of this very lack, and that is why he provokes attempts not so much to sacrifice him as to *destroy* him. What must be destroyed is the object in which the inconsistency of the Other—and so of the sacrificial order itself—has become visible. The inconsistency of Gregor's own physical attributes, which makes it impossible to form a coherent image of the insect, is no doubt a crucial aspect of his monstrousness, i.e., what makes it possible for him to embody the dysfunction of the Other. Kafka converted this impossibility into a prohibition when he stipulated to his publisher, Kurt Wolff, that no illustration of the insect adorn the title page of the 1916 edition of the story.

9. According to the French psychoanalyst Jacques Lacan (1901–1981), the symbolic order is the field of language and culture—a system of symbols into which human beings are inserted and which becomes a law to them [*Editor*].

of an Other whose demands might or might not be placated loses the
ground from under his feet.[1] The mythic order of fate where one's lot
is determined behind one's back—in Kafka's story, as in ancient tragedy,
the force of fate corresponds to a familial debt or guilt—is displaced by
a post-mythic order in which the individual can no longer find his place
in the texture of fate. This distance from the mythic force of fate, this
interruption of the transference of a debt from generation to generation,
introduces into the world a new and more radical kind of guilt. As
Žižek has elsewhere argued,

> Therein consists the constitutive, fundamental guilt attested to by
> the neurotic symptoms which pertain to the very being of what we
> call "the modern man": the fact that, ultimately, there is no agency
> in the eyes of which he can be guilty weighs upon him as a re-
> doubled guilt. The "death of God"—another name for this retreat
> of fate—makes our guilt absolute.[2]

In *Metamorphosis*, the interruption of those entanglements we call fate
opens up a space within which monstrosities can appear. This interruption is figured in the story by means of a series of ambiguities pertaining to patriarchal power and authority.

Significantly, as in *Parsifal*, a disturbance in the domain of patriarchal authority is registered at the level of voice and staging. At the end
of the first part of the story, Gregor's father chases his son back into his
room, producing a strange and disturbing hissing noise: "Pitilessly his
father came on, hissing like a wild man . . ." (19) [15]. Gregor struggles
to comply but is distracted and unnerved by this curious vocalization:
"If only his father did not keep making this intolerable hissing sound!
It made Gregor lose his head completely. He had almost finished the
turn when—his mind continually on this hissing—he made a mistake
and even started turning back around to his original position" (19) [15].
During the final moments of this ordeal, the father's hissing achieves
an intensity such that *"the voice behind Gregor did not sound like that
of only a single father;* now this was really no joke anymore . . ." [(19)
[15]; my emphasis]. It is as if the father's voice had assumed the quality
of an uncanny chorus, signaling the dimension of an implacable and

---

1. Thus the office manager's negative evaluation of Gregor's performance as a salesman represents the lure of a consistent Other whose demands one can still struggle to satisfy. The failure
to meet those demands does not yet produce the extreme form of abjection which marks
Gregor's new condition.
2. Slavoj Žižek, *Enjoy Your Symptom! Jacques Lacan in Hollywood and Out* (New York: Rout-
ledge, 1992) 167. Žižek summarizes these two levels of guilt and sacrifice in terms that
elucidate the experience of Gregor Samsa: "The first level is the symbolic pact: the subject
identifies the kernel of his being with a symbolic feature to which he is prepared to subordinate
his entire life, for the sake of which he is prepared to sacrifice everything—in short, alienation
in the symbolic mandate. The second level consists in sacrificing this sacrifice itself: in a most
radical sense, we 'break the word,' we renounce the symbolic alliance which defines the very
kernel of our being—the abyss, the void in which we find ourselves thereby, is what we call
'modern-age subjectivity' " (167).

horrific paternal force exceeding that of any single individual. Our perplexity about this weird amplification and distortion of the father's voice is heightened in the third and final part of the story. At a moment when the family's rejuvenation is well underway, Kafka indicates that the father's reinvigoration may be nothing more than a pathetic imposture:

> Sometimes his father woke up, and as if he had absolutely no idea that he had been asleep, said to his mother, "Look how long you're sewing again today!" and went right back to sleep, while mother and sister smiled wearily at each other. (41) [30]

It is in the next sentence that the question of imposture is placed directly into the foreground:

> With a kind of perverse obstinacy his father refused to take off his official uniform even in the house; and while his robe hung uselessly on the clothes hook, his father dozed, completely dressed, in his chair, as if he were always ready for duty and were waiting even here for the voice of his superior. (41) [30]

The ambiguity of Kafka's diction makes possible the reading that the father has refused to remove his uniform not just at home but in public as well; his recent "investiture" with a kind of official status and authority, low though it might be, might, in other words, be a sham. Be that as it may, the father's clinging to the outward appearance—to the vestments—of institutional authority suggests just how precarious and uncertain this authority really is. Gregor's father achieves his new patriarchal authority, restores his damaged masculinity, by means of a kind of cross-dressing.

II

In a diary entry of September 23, 1912, Kafka registers the miraculous composition of "The Judgment" in the course of a single night's labor, one he would, the following year, characterize as a kind of *couvade*[3] in which his story emerged covered with the "filth and mucus" of birth. In the entry of September 23, he recollects various associations that passed through his head during the composition of the story and notes, "naturally, thoughts of Freud."[4] The year before the composition of "The Judgment" and *Metamorphosis*, Sigmund Freud published his only case study dealing with psychosis, his *Psychoanalytic Notes Upon an Autobiographical Account of a Case of Paranoia (Dementia Paranoides)*.[5] Freud based his study, as the title suggests, not on a clinical

---

3. A custom among many peoples, in which a father acts as though he had experienced the pains of giving birth to his newborn child [*Editor*].
4. Franz Kafka, *Tagebücher, 1910–1923* (Frankfurt a.M.: Fischer, 1990) 217; 215.
5. Sigmund Freud, "Psychoanalytic Notes Upon an Autobiographical Account of a Case of Paranoia (Dementia Paranoides)," *The Standard Edition of the Complete Psychological Works of Sigmund Freud*, ed. James Strachey, vol. 12 (London: The Hogarth Press, 1958) 9–79.

encounter with a patient but rather on a text: Daniel Paul Schreber's now famous account of his own mental illness, *Denkwürdigkeiten eines Nervenkranken* (*Memoirs of My Nervous Illness*), published in 1903 and written toward the end of nine years of confinement in various private and state psychiatric institutions. In these memoirs, Schreber, who, just prior to his mental collapse in 1893, had been named *Senatspräsident* (presiding judge) of the third civil chamber of the Saxon Supreme Court, tells a remarkable story of descent into a paranoid universe where body and mind are subjected to the often cruel, often merely mischievous, manipulations of doctors, spirits of the dead, and eventually God Himself. The nervous agitation generated by all this "nerve-contact"—Schreber's technical term for these multifarious influences and manipulations—resulted in a kind of cosmic disequilibrium, an apocalyptic state of emergency in God's order or what he calls the "Order of the World." The more agitated Schreber became, the more he began to undergo his own curious process of metamorphosis, not into an insect but rather into a woman and indeed one whose considerable forces of sexual attraction not even God was able to resist, thus endangering the normal relations between sacred and profane realms. It was this delusional experience of feminization that Freud placed at the heart of his interpretation of the case, reading it as the return, at a moment of extreme mental stress, of long repressed homosexual longings.[6] There is no direct evidence that Kafka read Freud's essay on Schreber or Schreber's own text; the parallels between Kafka's story of bodily metamorphosis and Schreber's are, however, quite stunning.[7] Indeed, the remarkable similarities of these stories allow us to turn to Schreber for illumination about Gregor Samsa.[8]

As with Gregor, Schreber's demise is correlated with a form of vocational failure: an inability to heed an official call, to assume a symbolic mandate, in this case as presiding judge in the Saxon Court of Appeals. After his mental collapse and forced withdrawal from his po-

---

6. Freud's emphasis on Schreber's ostensible homosexuality has been challenged by subsequent readers of the case material. It is clear from Freud's study, however, that he did perceive what I would call the modern or post-mythic nature of the disorder. The persecutory figure who pulls the strings behind the scenes and calls forth Schreber's metamorphosis is *not* an agency of fate in the usual sense. He is, rather, a figure who emerges precisely in the tear of the texture of fate.

7. A possible source of knowledge about Schreber on Kafka's part was an essay by Otto Gross, "Über Bewußtseinszerfall" ("On the Disintegration of Consciousness"), published in 1904 (*Monatsschrift für Psychiatrie und Neurologie* 15/1: 45–51; I am grateful to Dr. Zvi Lothane for drawing this essay to my attention, which very likely represents the first mention of Schreber in the psychiatric literature). Kafka met Gross for the first time only in 1917, but he very likely had some familiarity with his work prior to that. Kafka had studied criminology with Gross's father, Hanns Gross, at the University of Prague, and the latter's tyrannical treatment of his son was well known in intellectual circles in Central Europe.

8. Schreber's delusional universe, constituting a fantasy space that one could call his "own private Germany," might even be read as the secret mediator between the aesthetic projects of Wagner and Kafka. Schreber's memoir contains a number of references and allusions to Wagner's works. Schreber may be seen as providing us with a view of Kafka's mad universe as seen from the perspective of the *judge* rather than that of a supplicant to the Law.

sition in the courts, Schreber begins to suffer from what eventually becomes one of his core symptoms: the hearing of voices. These voices, which torment Schreber for most of the rest of his life, embody the excess of demands that made the administration of his office insupportable. Indeed, they seem to represent these demands purified of any instrumental value or meaning-content, a kind of pure and non-sensical "You must!" abstracted from the use value of any particular activity. At this zero-level of meaning, the voices eventually come to be heard as a steady hissing sound, i.e., the sound which for Gregor was that of a kind of wild and perverse paternal chorus: "But the slowing down has recently become still more marked and the voices . . . degenerated into an indistinct hissing."[9]

On one particular day, however, the voices that spoke to Schreber became overwhelmingly clear and distinct. On that day, Ahriman, one of the two (Zoroastrian)[1] deities that tormented him, appeared in the form of a booming, operatic voice:

> It resounded in a mighty bass as if directly in front of my bedroom window. The impression was intense, so that anybody not hardened to terrifying miraculous impressions as I was, would have been shaken to the core. Also *what* was spoken did not sound friendly by any means: everything seemed calculated to instil fright and terror into me and the word "wretch" [*Luder*] was frequently heard—an expression quite common in the basic language to denote a human being destined to be destroyed by God and to feel God's power and wrath. (124)

In spite of the rage and terror manifest in the *content* of this epiphany of divine power, the effects produced at the level of its enunciation turn out to be, as Schreber insists, strangely beneficial (here we are reminded of Gregor's momentary experiences of physical well-being):

> Yet everything that was spoken was *genuine*, not phrases learnt by rote as they later were, but the immediate expression of true feeling. . . . For this reason my impression was not one of alarm or fear, but largely one of admiration for the magnificent and the sublime; the effect on my nerves was therefore beneficial despite the insults contained in some of the *words*. . . . (124–25)

The most important of these words, *Luder*, has rich connotations both in the context of Schreber's torments and in *The Metamorphosis*. It can indeed mean, as Schreber's translators suggest, "wretch," in the sense of a lost and pathetic figure, but can also signify: whore, tart, or

9. Daniel Paul Schreber, *Memoirs of My Nervous Illness*, trans. Ida Macalpine and Richard A. Hunter (Cambridge: Harvard UP, 1988) 226. Further references will be made in the text.
1. Cf. Zoroastrianism, the religion of the Persians before their conversion to Islam, founded in Persia in the sixth century B.C. by Zoroaster, who was, according to Nietzsche, "the first moralist." Zoroaster (in Persian, "Zarathustra") asserts the ongoing struggle of the universal spirit of good (Ormazd) with the spirit of evil (Ahriman) [*Editor*].

slut; and finally, the dead, rotting flesh of an animal, especially in the sense of carrion used as bait in hunting. The last two significations in particular capture Schreber's fear of being turned over to others for the purposes of sexual exploitation as well as his anxieties, which would seem to flow from such abuse, about putrefaction, being left to rot. These latter anxieties merge at times with fantasies of being sick with the plague, leprosy, or syphilis. Schreber is, in other words, like Gregor Samsa, compelled to experience the world from the locus of abjection.

At this point another dimension of Schreber's metamorphosis forces itself on our attention. Not only does he experience himself being turned into a woman whose sexuality bleeds, as it were, into putrefaction, but also into the mythic figure of the Wandering or Eternal Jew. To become a *Luder* means, in Schreber's universe, to become a *Jude* (Jew).[2] According to the cosmic laws revealed to Schreber over the course of his illness, God might decide, in periods of extreme moral decadence and nervousness, to destroy mankind. "In such an event," Schreber writes, "in order to maintain the species, one single human being was spared—perhaps the relatively most moral—called by the voices that talk to me the '*Eternal Jew*' " (73). This Eternal Jew, Schreber continues,

> had to be *unmanned* (transformed into a woman) to be able to bear children. This process of unmanning consisted in the (external) male genitals (scrotum and penis) being retracted into the body and the internal sexual organs being at the same time transformed into the corresponding female sexual organs, a process which might have been completed in a sleep lasting hundreds of years. . . . (73–74)

How might we correlate these details of Schreber's metamorphosis into a feminized Wandering Jew—i.e., into a kind of Kundry-figure—with the fate of Gregor Samsa?[3]

Amidst the wealth of striking details that have preoccupied readers of Kafka's *Metamorphosis*, the one which situates Kafka's text most firmly within fin-de-siècle[4] obsessions with gender and sexuality is the brief indication of Gregor's erotic life suggested by a bit of interior decorating he had engaged in shortly before his verminous transformation:

2. Schreber remarks that the lower God Ahriman, who, of course, represents the evil principle in Zoroastrian theology, "seems to have felt attracted to nations of originally brunette race (the Semites) and the upper God [Ormuzd] to nations of originally blonde race (the Aryan peoples)" (53).
3. Schreber's feminization indicates that he shifts symbolic positions from that of Amfortas, the one unable to officiate as presiding judge of the Grail Society, to that of Kundry, the figure who, as composite of Woman and Wandering Jew, embodies in Wagner's ideological universe the blockage in the otherwise harmonious functioning of the community.
4. End of the nineteenth century [*Editor*].

> Over the table . . . hung the picture which he had recently cut
> out of a glossy magazine and lodged in a pretty gilt frame. It
> showed a lady done up in a fur hat and a fur boa, sitting upright
> and raising up against the viewer a heavy fur muff in which her
> whole forearm had disappeared. (3) [3]

The importance of this peculiar detail, alluding, very likely, to Leopold
von Sacher-Masoch's infamous novella, *Venus in Furs* (1870),[5] is underlined by its placement in the text: it appears in the second paragraph
following immediately upon the famous inaugural sentences announcing Gregor's metamorphosis and is introduced as if in answer to the
question with which the paragraph begins: "What's happened to me?"
The picture, most likely part of an advertisement, figures once more,
in the second part of the story, when Gregor is struggling to save some
piece of his former life from the efforts of his mother and sister to clear
his room:

> And so he broke out—the women were just leaning against the
> desk in the next room to catch their breath for a minute—changed
> his course four times, he really didn't know what to salvage first,
> then he saw hanging conspicuously on the wall, which was oth-
> erwise bare already, the picture of the lady all dressed in furs,
> hurriedly crawled up on it and pressed himself against the glass,
> which gave a good surface to stick to and soothed his hot belly.
> At least no one would take away this picture, while Gregor com-
> pletely covered it up. (35) [26]

The importance of this possession is further emphasized by Gregor's
willingness to attack his otherwise beloved sister rather than part with
his picture: "He squatted on his picture and would not give it up. He
would rather fly in Grete's face" (36) [26].

Gregor's peculiar attachment to this piece of pornographic kitsch is
obviously central to the text. Indeed, the entire story seems to crystallize
around it as an elaborate punishment scenario called forth by guilt-
ridden sexual obsessions. The indications of putrescence which prolif-
erate in the course of the story suggest fantasies of the consequences of
a young man's autoerotic activities. In this perspective, many hitherto
unintelligible details take on importance. When, for example, the maid
announces at the end of the story that she has removed *"das Zeug"*
("the stuff") from Gregor's room, this word connotes what would be
cut short or degenerated by compulsive autoeroticism, namely the capacity for *Zeugen*, the generation of offspring. The final sentences of
the story, which circle around Grete's sexual coming-of-age and prospects of imminent union with "a good husband," constitute the closure

---

5. One will recall that in Sacher-Masoch's story, the protagonist, Severin, receives a new name
once he enters into his contract with his dominatrix Wanda: *Gregor* (the term "masochism"
derives from the author's name).

made possible by the elimination of the perverse, i.e., nonreproductive, sexuality embodied in Gregor's abject, putrescent condition.

This reading is supported by a wide array of medical treatises and popular literature concerning the dangers of masturbation circulating in fin-de-siècle Europe; it presupposes, however, that the woman in furs must be understood as an object of heterosexual desire. But if we are to take the comparison with Schreber seriously, a different, more "perverse," reading becomes possible, namely, one in which the woman in furs is not an object of desire but rather one of (unconscious) *identification*. In other words, Gregor's picture of the woman in furs represents the unconscious "truth" of the other picture described in the story, the photograph of Gregor from his "army days, in a lieutenant's uniform, his hand on his sword, a carefree smile on his lips, demanding respect for his bearing and his rank" (15) [12]. Gregor's metamorphosis now becomes legible as a kind of feminization; his verminous state suggests the mode of appearance of a femininity disavowed under the pressures of a misogynist and homophobic cultural imperative shared by Kafka's Austria-Hungary and Schreber's Germany.[6]

This reading is supported by a detail pertaining, once again, to the voice. After missing the train on the first morning of his new condition, Gregor's mother calls to him from the other side of his locked door to remind him of the time. After noting the softness of his mother's voice, he notices a new quality in his own voice:

> Gregor was shocked to hear his own voice answering, unmistakably his own voice, true, but in which, as if from below, an insistent distressed chirping [*ein nicht zu unterdrückendes, schmerzliches Piepsen*] intruded, which left the clarity of his words intact only for a moment really, before so badly garbling them as they carried that no one could be sure if he had heard right. (5) [5]

Gregor's *Piepsen* suggests the mutation of the male voice in the direction of the feminine.

The importance of this birdlike vocalization is confirmed, once more, by an important detail in Schreber's memoir. At various moments, the voices that tormented Schreber miraculously took the form of little birds—*gewunderte Vögel*—who were understood by Schreber to be made up of residues of departed human souls which had, in his delusional cosmology, previously made up the so-called "forecourts of

---

6. Note that Gregor expresses his envy vis-à-vis his colleagues at work by noting that they get to live like "harem women" (4) [4]. For a discussion of the complex and wide-ranging political ramifications of the cultural anxieties about femininity and homosexuality in fin-de-siècle Europe, see George L. Mosse, *Nationalism and Sexuality: Middle-Class Morality and Sexual Norms in Modern Europe* (Madison: U of Wisconsin P, 1985), and John C. Fout, "Sexual Politics in Wilhelmine Germany: The Male Gender Crisis, Moral Purity, and Homophobia," *Journal of the History of Sexuality* 2/3: 388–421.

heaven." Schreber characterizes their chirpings as a series of mechanically repeated turns of phrase. Thanks to their purely repetitive and meaningless nature—their *deadness*—Schreber associates these vocalizations with putrescence or what he calls *Leichengift*, the poison of corpses. Freud, for his part, hears them as the voices of young girls: "In a carping mood people often compare them to geese, ungallantly accuse them of having 'the brains of a bird,' declare that they can say nothing but phrases learnt by rote, and that they betray their lack of education by confusing foreign words that sound alike."[7] Schreber confirms this interpretation when he gives some of the birds girls' names. But Gregor's *Piepsen* points also in the direction indicated by Schreber's other pole of identification: that of the Wandering Jew.

The fin-de-siècle culture of Kafka and Schreber was at many levels preoccupied with the peculiarities of the Jewish physical and mental constitution.[8] Central to these preoccupations was an obsession with the Jewish voice and Jewish language production. This obsession, already important in premodern Europe, was recoded in the nineteenth century in the idiom of racial biology and was conjoined with fantasies about Jewish sexuality. Jewish men, for example, were often regarded as exhibiting feminine characteristics, an association that placed them in the domain of a larger set of "impaired masculinities" that included the newly medicalized "homosexual" and came increasingly under the surveillance of various state, medical, and church-affiliated institutions.[9] Thus Otto Weininger's infamous treatise, *Sex and Charakter* (1903), reformulates many of Wagner's earlier theses apropos of the Jewish relation to language and music by consolidating the linkage of Jewishness and femininity.[1] If Jews lack a profound relation to music, as Wagner had claimed, it was, Weininger now argued, because they, *like women*, had an impaired relation to logic, ethics, and language (the preferred term for this impairment was, of course, *hysteria*). At the end of the nineteenth century, the faulty command of discourse attributed to Jews and condensed in the term *mauscheln*, meaning to speak (German) like Moses, was, in other words, coupled with femininity and, hence, homosexuality. To return to *Metamorphosis*, we might say that

7. Freud, "Psychoanalytic Notes," 36–37.
8. Sander Gilman's work has been crucial in revealing the intensity of these preoccupations. See, for example, Gilman, *Jewish Self-Hatred: Anti-Semitism and the Hidden Language of the Jews* (Baltimore: The Johns Hopkins UP, 1986), as well as more recently, *Freud, Race, and Gender* (Princeton: Princeton UP, 1993).
9. For a literary historical reading of fin-de-siècle German and Austrian literature under the sign of a generalized crisis of masculinity, see Jacques Le Rider, *Modernity and Crises of Identity: Culture and Society in Fin-de-siècle Vienna*, trans. Rosemary Morris (New York: Continuum, 1993).
1. Wagner first published these views in his essay "Judaism in Music" in 1850. For a rich, though polemical, discussion of the essay and Wagner's anti-Semitism more generally, see Paul Lawrence Rose, *Wagner: Race and Revolution* (New Haven: Yale UP, 1992).

the Jew's *Mauscheln* was recoded as a kind of feminized, queer *Piepsen*.[2]

Kafka's text, however, is more than a literary version of a kind of Jewish self-hatred, more than the narrative and poetic elaboration of a series of internalized anti-Semitic prejudices. For though Kafka is a writer whose work is at times burdened by negative conceptions about Jews, Judaism, and Jewishness, *Metamorphosis* is a text which indicates Kafka's profound awareness of the ideological role such conceptions played within the larger culture. In *Metamorphosis*, the cultural fantasies positioning the Jew, along with everything feminine, at the place of abjection, are led back to the deeper cultural crises and anxieties fueling them. These anxieties arise, as we have seen, from a fundamental dysfunctionality at the core of patriarchal power and authority. Kafka's story suggests, in other words, that at least in the modern period the domain of the abject and monstrous, or, to use the term that would prove so fateful and fatal during the Nazi period, the "degenerate," is linked to a chronic uncertainty haunting the institutions of power. The "redemption" of the Samsa family at the conclusion of Kafka's story thus represents the ultimate ideological fantasy, not unlike the conclusion of Wagner's *Parsifal*, where the restoration of the Grail Society is linked to Kundry's demise. With the destruction of Gregor *qua*[3] feminized Wandering Jew, the family can thrive, perhaps now for the very first time.

Kafka's story, however, offers an alternative to this Wagnerian scenario. It asks the reader to identify with Gregor's abjection as an imaginative support for the much more difficult task of staying with and working through the uncertainties that inform the subject's relation to institutional authority in the modern period. We might even say that the capacity and the will to risk such an identification is Kafka's own version of the heroism of modern life. This process of working through implies, however, an appreciation of the limits of any attempt to decipher Gregor Samsa, for interpretation is also, in the end, a form of redemption, an effort to heal the symptomatic blockages in the text. Any purely ideological reading of Kafka, whether as Jewish self-hater

---

2. On the cultural association of the male Jew and homosexual through the mediation of the queer voice, see Gilman, *Freud*, 164. For a compelling reading of Kafka's last story, "Josephine the Singer, or the Mouse Folk," through the prism of these cultural associations, see Mark Anderson's *Kafka's Clothes: Ornament and Aestheticism in the Habsburg Fin de Siècle* (Oxford: Clarendon Press, 1992) 194–215.

3. In his capacity as (Latin) [*Editor*]. The "redemptive" closure of story and family around the death and removal of Gregor is given a Christological coloration when the Samsas are first brought by the cleaning woman to Gregor's corpse: " 'Well,' said Mr. Samsa, 'now we can thank God!' He crossed himself, and the three women followed his example" (55) [40]. This passage reads as a conversion scenario, as if with Gregor's self-nullification the Samsas can enter into a new covenant free of the obligations of the old. Here we should recall the final lines of Wagner's essay "Judaism in Music," a chilling exhortation directed to all Jews: "But remember, that only one thing can bring about the redemption of the curse weighing down on you: the redemption of Ahasver,—destruction [*Untergang*]."

who has internalized the discourse of degeneration or, alternatively, as analyst of the very socio-psychological mechanisms behind such a discourse, will miss Kafka's most original contribution: the figuration of precisely that which dooms interpretation to failure, *even a correct one* (in this context, we should recall, once more, Kafka's explicit prohibition against the representation of the insect in any illustration [see p. 70]).[4] Gregor's abjection is, in other words, more than a symptom to be read and decoded, more than a condensation of social forces or contradictions, and thus more than a scapegoat figure. He remains a foreign body in the text and in any interpretation. Indeed, if there is anything that is completely foreign to Kafka's aesthetic and ethical imagination, it is the will to do away with such remainders.

This conclusion need not be taken as an argument against history or the importance of historicization. We can and should, for example, speculate as to the connections between Gregor's unreadability, i.e., the impossibility of forming a consistent and unified representation of him, and what Kafka would later characterize as an *impossibility of writing* which he in turn linked to the particular *historical* situation of German Jews at the turn of the century. In a now famous letter to his lifelong friend Max Brod, Kafka comments on Karl Kraus's critique of the *Mauscheln* he claimed to detect in the work of German-Jewish authors like Kafka's fellow Prague writer Franz Werfel. Before turning this charge against Kraus himself—"no one can *mauscheln* like Kraus"— Kafka confesses that he experiences the truth of Kraus's claims in a profoundly physical way. This physical dimension is reiterated later in this letter when Kafka retools the psychoanalytic notion of oedipal conflict to better fit the particular historical situation of Jewish families at the boundaries between traditional Eastern European and posttraditional Western European cultures. The image Kafka uses recalls Gre-

4. I am arguing, in other words, that the two orders of abjection we have discovered in the story correspond to two different orders of error to which any interpretation of the story is prone. The first order of error might be deemed "empirical" and refers to the reader's (always contingent) failure to interpret the details of the story in a way consistent with textual evidence or with an organizing thesis. This sort of error is always the reader's "fault" and is by definition correctable through harder and more careful work, i.e., through an act of self-sacrifice on the part of the reader. The second order of error might be deemed "ontological" and refers to the fact that the assumption of fictional coherence, of consistency on the part of the text, *has no guarantee*. As with the two orders of abjection, this second order of error has meaning only if it is encountered as a turn of the screw of the first, as the first order of error *in extremis*. These two orders or kinds of error pertain, in principle, to any text. What makes Kafka's text different is that he has, in the abject body of Gregor Samsa, figured the second order of error *within his own text*. Gregor's abjection is, in other words, the locus of a paradoxical knowledge of the chronic uncertainty of the hermeneutic enterprise. (This view is, of course, very close to Paul de Man's notion of an allegory of reading, i.e., of the way a text allegorizes the limits of its own readability: cf. *Allegories of Reading: Figural Language in Rousseau, Nietzsche, Rilke, and Proust* [New Haven: Yale UP, 1979].) By reading *The Metamorphosis* with Schreber's *Memoirs*, we have learned not only that such knowledge defines the position of the psychotic, but also that in the nineteenth century this position was coded as feminine, queer, and Jewish.

gor's inability, upon waking to his new condition, to coordinate the movement of his legs:

> Most young Jews who began to write German wanted to leave Jewishness behind them, and their fathers approved of this, but vaguely (this vagueness was what was so outrageous to them). But with their posterior legs they were still glued to their fathers' Jewishness and with their waving anterior legs they found no new ground. The ensuing despair became their inspiration.

Kafka goes on to link this—paradoxically—inspiring state of despair and desperation—of *Verzweiflung*—to what he characterizes as a life lived amidst a series of linguistic impossibilities: "These are: the impossibility of not writing, the impossibility of writing German, the impossibility of writing differently. One might also add a fourth impossibility, the impossibility of writing. . . ."[5] These "impossibilities," as Kafka notes at the end of the letter, keep the writer in a kind of perpetual *liminality*, a borderline-state between symbolic and real death, like that of a man who has written his will but not yet hanged himself. The story of the traveling salesman Gregor Samsa unfolds, in its entirety, within just such a liminal space between two deaths: between the exit from the sacrificial order of the family and the destruction of the body made monstrous by that first, symbolic, death.

Finally, the greatest mistake a reader could make would be to imagine that by historicizing this series of impossibilities, by locating their emergence within a particular historical state of emergency—that of German Jews at the turn of the century—that one has effectively distanced oneself from them and the painful disorientations that they imply. It is, rather, the ultimate strength of Kafka's aesthetic and ethical vision that he is able to take us through and beyond that fantasy—to reveal that the emergency, to cite another of his works, "cannot be made good, not ever."[6]

5. Franz Kafka, *Letters to Friends, Family, and Editors*, trans. Richard Winston and Clara Winston (New York: Schocken, 1977) 288–89.
6. Franz Kafka, "A Country Doctor," trans. Willa Muir and Edwin Muir, in *Franz Kafka: The Complete Stories*, ed. Nahum N. Glatzer (New York: Schocken, 1971) 225.

Franz Kafka: A Chronology

1883   Born in Prague on July 3, son of Hermann Kafka, a fairly
                affluent tradesman, and his wife Julie (née Löwy). Her-
                mann Kafka's father was a butcher; among Julie Löwy's
                forebears were several learned rabbis.
1885–87   Birth and death of his brother Georg.
1887–88   Birth and death of his brother Heinrich.
1889, 1890,   Birth of his three sisters—Gabriele (Elli), Valerie (Valli),
1892   and Ottilie (Ottla), his favorite. All three were murdered
                by the Nazis.
1889–93   Attends elementary school (German Boys' School) at the
                Fleischmarkt in Prague.
1893–1901   Attends the Old Town *Gymnasium*, together with mostly
                middle-class Jewish boys. First attested reading of Nie-
                tzsche in the summer of 1900.
1901–06   Studies law at the German University in Prague along
                with occasional courses in German literature.
1902   Vacation with Uncle Siegfried Löwy, a country doctor.
                Meets his lifelong friend and future editor Max Brod and
                participates in discussions on empirical psychology at the
                [Café] Louvre Circle, a reading group.
1904–05   Writes "Description of a Struggle."
1905   Vacation in Zuckmantel and first love affair. Meets reg-
                ularly with friends sharing literary and intellectual inter-
                ests, including Oskar Baum, Max Brod, and Felix
                Weltsch.
1906   Works in a Prague law office before graduating with a
                doctor's degree in law. Begins a year's internship in
                Prague, first at the penal court, then at the civil court.
1907   Writes "Wedding Preparations in the Country," part of
                a novel. Begins his first regular job, at the "Assicurazioni
                Generali," an Italian insurance company.
1908   Moves to the partly state-run Workers' Accident Insur-
                ance Institute for the Kingdom of Bohemia in Prague,
                where he will rise to a position of considerable authority
                (*Obersekretär*) until being pensioned in 1922. His first
                publication: eight short pieces under the title "Medita-
                tion" in the journal *Hyperion*.

1909   Spends vacation with Max Brod in Riva on Lake Garda
            in Austrian Italy. Publishes "Airplanes in Brescia" in the
            daily newspaper *Bohemia*, the first description of air-
            planes in a German newspaper. Further publication of
            two pieces from "Description of a Struggle."

1910   Begins keeping a diary. Sees a performance of a traveling
            Yiddish theater. Trips to Paris and Berlin.

1911   Repeatedly attends performances of another Yiddish the-
            ater troupe from Eastern Europe (Yitzak Löwy and his
            players). Studies hasidic tales and parables. Becomes in-
            terested in "alternative medicine": vegetarianism, sun-
            bathing, natural healing. Writes earliest drafts of the
            unfinished novel *The Boy Who Sank Out of Sight* (a.k.a.
            Amerika).

1912   Gives a public address in Prague "On the Yiddish Lan-
            guage." On the evening of August 13, with Max Brod,
            puts together his first published book *Meditation*, and
            meets his future fiancée, Felice Bauer, with whom he
            will correspond for five years. Writes "The Judgment"
            in a single night, September 22–23; in September and
            October, "The Stoker" and an early version of *The Boy
            Who Sank Out of Sight*; and from November 17 to De-
            cember 7, *The Metamorphosis*. Reads parts of the unfin-
            ished story aloud to friends on November 24 and in
            December gives a public reading of "The Judgment."
            Meditation published by Rowohlt.

1913   Reads the whole of *The Metamorphosis* aloud at Max
            Brod's. Meetings with Felice in Berlin. Publication of
            "The Stoker" (the first chapter of *The Boy Who Sank
            Out of Sight*). Publication of "The Judgment." Kafka
            visits Eleventh Zionist Congress in Vienna.

1914   In June, formal engagement to Felice Bauer in Berlin,
            followed, in July, by its being broken off. Outbreak of
            World War I as he begins writing *The Trial*. In October,
            work on *The Trial* having come to a standstill, he writes
            "In the Penal Colony" as well as the last chapter of *The
            Boy Who Sank Out of Sight*.

1915   Wins the Fontane Prize for literary achievement for
            "The Stoker." Reunion with Felice Bauer. In Prague
            lives for the first time in an apartment of his own. Pub-
            lication of *The Metamorphosis* in *Die weissen Blätter* and
            then in book form in November.

1916   With Felice in Marienbad. Public reading of "In the
            Penal Colony." Writes several of the stories collected in
            A Country Doctor.

1917	Lives in rooms in Alchemist's Lane, then in the Schönberg Palace. Further work on *A Country Doctor* and other stories. Second engagement to Felice Bauer shattered by the diagnosis of his tuberculosis in September. Takes leave from his office and joins his sister Ottla in Zürau. Writes a series of aphorisms. In December the engagement is dissolved.
1918–19	Studies Kierkegaard. Meeting with Julie Wohryzek. Appearance of *In the Penal Colony* and *A Country Doctor*. Engagement to Julie Wohryzek. Writes the never-mailed "Letter to His Father."
1920	Conversations with Kafka allegedly recorded by Gustav Janouch. Correspondence with the Czech literary personality Milena Jesenská. End of the engagement to Julie Wohryzek. Resumes literary work after a pause of more than three years.
1922	Beginnings of *The Castle*. Writes "A Hunger Artist" and "Investigations of a Dog." Last conversations with Milena. Lives with his sister Ottla in Planá in the Czech provinces, where he continues work on *The Castle*.
1923	Meets Dora Diamant (Dymant), his last consort, and from September on lives with her in Berlin-Steglitz. Inflation and cold. Writes "The Burrow." At Kafka's behest Dora Diamant burns several of his manuscripts. The collection *A Hunger Artist* goes to press.
1924	Very ill from tuberculosis of the larynx, writes "Josephine the Singer" while attempting to recover in his parents' apartment in Prague. Visits various hospitals and sanatoria, finally Kierling near Vienna, where he is accompanied by Dora Diamant and his doctor, Robert Klopstock. On June 3, at the age of forty-two, Kafka dies, and on June 11 is buried in the New Jewish Cemetery in Prague. Milena writes in an obituary: "His stories reflect the irony and prophetic vision of a man condemned to see the world with such blinding clarity that he found it unbearable and went to his death." Posthumous publication of *A Hunger Artist*.
1925	Posthumous publication of *The Trial*.
1926	Posthumous publication of *The Castle*.
1927	Posthumous publication of *The Boy Who Sank Out of Sight*.

Selected Bibliography

• Indicates works included in or excerpted for this Norton Critical Edition.

Adams, Robert M. *Strains of Discord: Studies in Literary Openness.* Ithaca, N.Y.: Cornell UP, 1958. 168–79.

Adorno, Theodor W. "Notes on Kafka." *Prisms.* Trans. Samuel and Shierry Weber. London: Spearman, 1967. 245–72.

Albrecht, Erich A. "Kafka's *Metamorphosis—Realiter.*" *Homage to Charles Blaise Qualia.* Lubbock: Texas Tech P, 1962. 55–64.

Anders, Günther. *Franz Kafka.* Trans. A. Steer and A. K. Thorlby. London: Bowen and Bowen, 1960.

Anderson, Mark. "Kafka and Sacher-Masoch." *Journal of the Kafka Society of America* 7.2 (1983): 4–19.

• ———. *Kafka's Clothes: Ornament and Aestheticism in the Habsburg Fin de Siècle.* Oxford: Clarendon Press, 1992. 123–44.

Angress, Ruth K. "Kafka and Sacher-Masoch: A Note on 'The Metamorphosis.'" *MLN* 85 (1970): 745–46.

Angus, Douglas. "Kafka's 'Metamorphosis' and 'The Beauty and the Beast' Tale." *Journal of English and Germanic Philology* 52 (1954): 69–71.

Asher, J. A. "Turning-Points in Kafka's Stories." *Modern Language Review* 57 (1962): 47–52.

Barry, Thomas. F. "On the Parasite Metaphor in Kafka's 'The Metamorphosis.'" *West Virginia U Philological Papers* 35 (1989): 65–73.

Beck, Evelyn Torton. *Kafka and the Yiddish Theater: Its Impact on His Work.* Madison: U of Wisconsin P, 1971. 135–46.

Beicken, Peter. "Transformation of Criticism: The Impact of Kafka's *Metamorphosis.*" *The Dove and the Mole: Kafka's Journey into Darkness and Creativity.* Ed. Ronald Gottesman and Moshe Lazar. Malibu, CA: Undena, 1987. 13–34.

Beissner, Friedrich. "Kafka the Artist." Trans. Ronald Gray. *Kafka: A Collection of Critical Essays.* Ed. Ronald Gray. Englewood Cliffs, N.J.: Prentice-Hall, 1962. 15–31.

Benjamin, Walter. "Franz Kafka. On the Tenth Anniversary of His Death." *Illuminations.* Ed. Hannah Arendt. Trans. Harry Zohn. New York: Harcourt Brace, 1968. 111–40.

Bennett, E. K. *A History of the German Novelle.* Revised and continued by H. M. Waidson. Cambridge: Cambridge UP, 1961. 267–68.

• Binder, Hartmut. *Kafkas "Verwandlung": Entstehung, Deutung, Wirkung.* Forthcoming.

Binion, Rudolf. "What the *Metamorphosis* Means." *Symposium* 15 (1961): 214–20.

Blanchot, Maurice. "The Diaries: The Exigency of the Work of Art." Trans. Lyall H. Powers. *Franz Kafka Today.* Ed. Angel Flores and Homer Swander. Madison: U of Wisconsin P, 1964. 195–220.

Bloom, Harold, ed. *Franz Kafka's "The Metamorphosis."* New York: Chelsea House, 1988.

Boa, Elizabeth. "Creepy-Crawlies: Gilman's *The Yellow Wallpaper* and Kafka's 'The Metamorphosis.'" *Paragraph: A Journal of Modern Critical Theory* 13.1 (1990): 19–29.

Booth, Wayne C. *The Rhetoric of Fiction.* Chicago: U of Chicago P, 1961. 281–82.

Bouson, J. Brooks. "The Repressed Grandiosity of Gregor Samsa: A Kohutian Reading of Kafka's *Metamorphosis.*" *Narcissism and the Text: Studies in Literature and the Psychology of Self.* Ed. Lynne Layton and Barbara Ann Schapiro. New York: New York UP, 1986. 192–212.

Brod, Max. *Franz Kafka—A Biography.* Trans. G. Humphreys Roberts and Richard Winston. New York: Schocken, 1960. 134.

Brown, Russell E. "A Mistake in 'Die Verwandlung' of Kafka." *Germanic Notes* 16.2 (1985): 19–21.

• Bruce, Iris. "Elements of Jewish Folklore in Kafka's *Metamorphosis.*" Orig. "Kafka's *Metamorphosis*: Folklore, Hasidism and the Jewish Tradition." *Journal of the Kafka Society of America* 11.1/2 (June–December 1987): 9–22. Rev. 1994.

Camus, Albert. "Hope and Absurdity." Trans. William Barrett. *The Kafka Problem.* Ed. Angel Flores. New York: New Directions, 1946. 251–61.

Cantrell, Carol Helmstetter. "*The Metamorphosis*: Kafka's Study of a Family." *Modern Fiction Studies* 23 (1977–78): 578–86.

Corngold, Stanley. *The Commentators' Despair: The Interpretation of Kafka's "Metamorphosis."* London and Port Washington, N.Y.: Kennikat, 1971.

• ———. *Franz Kafka: The Necessity of Form.* Ithaca: Cornell UP, 1988. 47–80.

Danto, Arthur C. "Review of Kafka's *Metamorphosis* on Broadway." *Journal of the Kafka Society of America* 11.1–2 (1987): 61–63.

Deleuze, Gilles/Guattari, Félix. *Kafka—Toward a Minor Literature.* Trans. Dana Polan. Minneapolis: U of Minnesota P, 1986. 3, 14, 34, 39, 47, 54, 64, 67, 77, 87.

D'Haen, Theo. "The Liberation of the Samsas." *Neophilologus* 62 (1978): 262–78.

Duroche, Leonard L. "On Reading Kafka's 'Metamorphosis' as a Masculine Narrative." *U of Dayton Review* 18.2 (1986–87): 35–39.

Eggenschwiler, David. "*Die Verwandlung*, Freud, and the Chains of Odysseus." *Modern Language Quarterly* 39 (1978): 363–85.

Empson, William. "*A Family Monster*" [a review of *The Metamorphosis*]. *The Nation* 162 (1946): 652–53.

Emrich, Wilhelm. *Franz Kafka: A Critical Study of His Writings.* Trans. Sheema Z. Buehne. New York: Ungar, 1968. 132–48.

Erlich, Victor. "Gogol and Kafka: Note on 'Realism' and 'Surrealism.' " *For Roman Jakobson: Essays on the Occasion of His Sixtieth Birthday.* Ed. Morris Halle et al. The Hague: Mouton, 1956. 102–04.

Fleissner, Robert E. "Is Gregor Samsa a Bedbug? Kafka and Dickens Revisited." *Studies in Short Fiction* 22.2 (1985): 225–28.

Foulkes, A. P. *The Reluctant Pessimist: A Study of Franz Kafka.* The Hague: Mouton, 1967. 107–11.

Fraiberg, Selma. "Kafka and the Dream." *Partisan Review* 33 (1956): 47–69.

Freedman, Ralph. "Kafka's Obscurity: The Illusion of Logic in Narrative." *Modern Fiction Studies* 8 (1962): 61–74.

Friedman, Norman. "Kafka's 'Metamorphosis': A Literal Reading." *Approach* 49 (1963): 26–34.

———. "The Struggle of Vermin: Parasitism and Family Love in Kafka's *Metamorphosis*." *Ball State U Forum* 9.1 (1968): 23–32.

Gilman, Sander L. "A View of Kafka's Treatment of Actuality in *Die Verwandlung*." *Germanic Notes* 2.4 (1971): 26–30.

Goldstein, Bluma. "The Wound in Stories by Kafka." *Germanic Review* 41 (1966): 206–14.

———. "Bachelors and Work: Social and Economic Conditions of 'The Judgment,' 'The Metamorphosis,' and 'The Trial.' " *The Kafka Debate: New Perspectives for Our Time.* Ed. Angel Flores. New York: Gordian, 1977. 147–75.

Greenberg, Martin. "Gregor Samsa and Modern Spirituality." *The Terror of Art: Kafka and Modern Literature.* New York: Basic Books, 1968. 69–91.

Gunvaldsen, K. M. "Franz Kafka and Psychoanalysis." *U of Toronto Quarterly* 32 (1963): 266–81.

Hartman, Tom. "Kafka's *The Metamorphosis*." *Explicator* 43.2 (1985): 32–34.

Hawkins, Desmond A. "Fiction Chronicle." *Criterion* 18 (1938): 506–08.

Hibberd, John. *Kafka: "Die Verwandlung."* London: Grant and Cutler, 1985.

Holland, Norman N. "Realism and Unrealism: Kafka's 'Metamorphosis.' " *Modern Fiction Studies* 4 (1958): 143–50.

Honig, Edwin. *Dark Conceit: The Making of Allegory.* New York: Oxford UP, 1966. 63–68.

Jacobs, Jerry. *Getting By: Illustrations of Marginal Living.* Boston: Little, Brown, 1972. 145–48.

Janouch, Gustav. *Conversations with Kafka: Notes and Reminiscences.* Trans. Goronwy Rees. New York: New Directions, 1969.

Jofen, Jean. " 'Metamorphosis.' " *American Imago: A Psychoanalytic Journal for Culture, Science, and the Arts* 35 (1978): 347–56.

Kafka, Franz. *The Metamorphosis.* Ed. and trans. Stanley Corngold. New York: Bantam, 1972.

Klubach, William. *Franz Kafka: Challenges and Confrontations.* New York: Peter Lang, 1993. 89–101.

Kuhn, Ira. "The Metamorphosis of *The Trial*." *Symposium* 26 (1972): 226–41.

Kuna, Franz. *Franz Kafka: Literature as Corrective Punishment.* Bloomington: Indiana UP, London: Elek, 1974. 49–63.

Landsberg, Paul I. "The Metamorphosis." Trans. Carolyn Muehlenberg. *The Kafka Problem.* Ed. Angel Flores. New York: New Directions, 1946. 122–33.

Lawson, Richard H. "*Ungeheures Ungeziefer* in Kafka's *Die Verwandlung*." *German Quarterly* 33 (1960): 216–19.

Levine, Michael G. "The Sense of an *Unding*: Kafka, Ovid, and the Misfits of Metamorphosis." *Writing Through Repression.* Baltimore: The Johns Hopkins UP, 1994. 149–77.

Luke, F. D. "The Metamorphosis." *Franz Kafka Today.* Ed. Angel Flores and Homer Swander. Madison: U of Wisconsin P, 1964. 25–43.

Madden, William A. "A Myth of Mediation: Kafka's *Metamorphosis*." *Thought* 26 (1951): 246–66.

Mann, G. Thomas. "Kafka's 'Die Verwandlung' and Its Natural Model: An Alternative Reading." *U of Dayton Review* 15.3 (1982): 65–74.

Margolis, Joseph. "Kafka vs. Eudaimonia and Duty." *Philosophy and Phenomenological Research* 19 (1958): 27–42.

Martin, P. A. M. "The Cockroach as an Identification; With Reference to Kafka's *Metamorphosis*." *American Imago* 16 (1959): 65–71.

Mendoza, Ramón G. *Outside Humanity: A Study of Kafka's Fiction*. Lanham,: UP of America, 1986. 89–105.

Moss, Leonard. "A Key to the Door Image in 'The Metamorphosis.' " *Modern Fiction Studies* 17.1 (1971): 37–42.

Munk, Linda. "What Does Hegel Make of the Jews?: A Scato-logical Reading of Kafka's *Die Verwandlung*." *History of European Ideas* 18.6 (1994): 913–25.

Murphy, Richard. "Semiotic Excess, Semantic Vacuity, and the Photograph of the Imaginary: The Interplay of Realism and the Fantastic in Kafka's *Die Verwandlung*." *Deutsche Vierteljahrsschrift für Literaturwissenschaft und Geistesgeschichte* (1991): 304–17.

Nabokov, Vladimir. "Franz Kafka (1883–1924): 'The Metamorphosis' (1915)." *Lectures on Literature*. Ed. Fredson Bowers. New York: Harcourt Brace Jovanovich, 1980. 251–83.

Natarjan, Nalini. "Man into Beast: Representations of Metamorphosis." *Bestia: Yearbook of the Beast Fable Society* 5 (1993): 117–22.

Neider, Charles. *The Frozen Sea: A Study of Franz Kafka*. New York: Oxford UP, 1948. 77–78, 180–81.

Noy, Ruth S., and Sharron, Avery. "Child Abuse in Kafka's Eyes: The Victim's Invisible Metamorphosis." *Victimology* 9.2 (1984): 296–303.

Pascal, Roy. *Kafka's Narrators: A Study of His Stories and Sketches*. Cambridge: Cambridge UP, 1982. 32–59.

Pfeiffer, Johannes. "The Metamorphosis." Trans. Ronald Gray. *Kafka: A Collection of Critical Essays*. Ed. Ronald Gray. Englewood Cliffs, N.J.: Prentice-Hall, 1962. 53–59.

Poggioli, Renato. "Kafka and Dostoyevsky." *The Kafka Problem*. Ed. Angel Flores. New York: New Directions, 1946. 102–04.

Politzer, Heinz. *Franz Kafka: Parable and Paradox*. Ithaca, Cornell UP, 1962. 65–84.

Rahv, Philip. "Franz Kafka: The Hero as Lonely Man." *Kenyon Review* 1 (1939): 60–74.

Rolleston, James. *Kafka's Narrative Theater*. University Park: Pennsylvania State UP, 1974. 52–68.

• Santner, Eric. "Kafka's *Metamorphosis* and the Writing of Abjection." Norton Critical Edition, 1996.

Schepers, Gerhard. "Images of Amae in Kafka: With Special Reference to *Metamorphosis*." *Humanities: Christianity & Culture* 15 (1980): 66–83.

Seyppel, J. H. "The Animal Theme and Totemism in Franz Kafka." *Universitas* (English ed.) 4.2 (1961): 163–72.

Sharron, Avery. *See* Noy, Ruth S.

Simka, Margit M. "Kafka's *The Metamorphosis* and the Search for Meaning in Twentieth-Century German Literature." *Approaches to Teaching Kafka's Short Fiction*. Ed. Richard T. Gray. New York: The Modern Language Association of America, 1995. 105–13.

Sokel, Walter H. "Kafka's 'Metamorphosis': Rebellion and Punishment." *Monatshefte* 48 (1956): 203–14.

———. *The Writer in Extremis: Expressionism in Twentieth-Century Literature*. Stanford: Stanford UP, 1959. 45–48.

———. *Franz Kafka*. Columbia Essays on Modern Writers. New York: Columbia UP, 1966.

———. "From Marx to Myth: The Structure and Function of Self-Alienation in Kafka's *Metamorphosis*." *The Dove and the Mole: Kafka's Journey into Darkness and Creativity*. Ed. Ronald Gottesman and Moshe Lazar. Malibu, CA: Undena, 1987. 1–12.

Spann, Meno. *Franz Kafka*. Boston: Twayne, 1976.

Sparks, Kimberly. "Kafka's *Metamorphosis*: On Banishing the Lodgers." *Journal of European Studies* 3 (1973): 230–40.

Spilka, Mark. "Kafka's Sources for *The Metamorphosis*." *Comparative Literature* 11 (1959): 289–307.

———. *Dickens and Kafka: A Mutual Interpretation*. Bloomington: Indiana UP, 1963. 77–79, 252–54.

• Straus, Nina Pelikan. "Transforming Kafka's *Metamorphosis*." *Signs: Journal of Women in Culture and Society* 14.3 (1989): 651–67. Rev. 1994.

• Sweeney, Kevin W. "Competing Theories of Identity in Kafka's *Metamorphosis*." *Mosaic* 23.4 (1990): 23–35.

Tauber, Herbert. *Franz Kafka: An Interpretation of His Writings*. Trans. G. Humphreys Roberts and Roger Senhouse. New Haven: Yale UP, 1948. 18–26.

Taylor, Alexander. "The Waking: The Theme of Kafka's *Metamorphosis.*" *Studies in Short Fiction* 2 (1965): 337–42.

Thiher, Allen. *Franz Kafka: A Study of the Short Fiction.* Boston: Twayne, 1990. 33–50.

Tiefenbrun, Ruth. *Moment of Torment: An Interpretation of Franz Kafka's Short Stories.* Carbondale: Southern Illinois UP, 1973. 111–35.

Urzidil, Johannes. "Meetings with Franz Kafka." *Menorah Journal* 40 (1952): 112–16.

———. "In the Prague of Expressionism," "Brand." *There Goes Kafka.* Trans. Harold A. Basilius. Detroit: Wayne State UP. 18–19, 82–96.

Waldeck, P. B. "Kafka's 'Die Verwandlung' and 'Ein Hungerkünstler' as Influenced by Leopold von Sacher-Masoch." *Monatschefte* 64 (1972): 147–52.

Webster, Peter Dow. "Franz Kafka's 'Metamorphosis' as Death and Resurrection Fantasy." *American Imago* 16 (1959): 349–65.

Weinstein, Arnold. "Kafka's Writing Machine: Metamorphosis in *The Penal Colony.*" *Studies in Twentieth-Century Literature* 7.1 (1982): 21–33.

Weninger, Robert. "Sounding Out the Silence of Gregor Samsa: Kafka's Rhetoric of Dyscommunication." *Studies in Twentieth-Century Literature* 17.2 (1993): 263–86.

Wexelblatt, Robert. "The Higher Parody: Ivan Ilych's Metamorphosis and the Death of Gregor Samsa." *Massachusetts Review: A Quarterly of Literature, the Arts, and Public Affairs* 21.3 (1980): 601–28.

Winkelman, John. "The Liberation of Gregor Samsa." *Crisis and Commitment: Studies in German and Russian Literature in Honor of J. W. Dyck.* Ed. John Whiton and Harry Lowen. Waterloo: U of Waterloo P, 1983. 237–46.

Witt, M. A. F. "Confinement in 'Die Verwandlung' and *Les séquestrés d'Altona.*" *Comparative Literature* 23 (1971): 32–44.

Wolkenfeld, Suzanne. "Christian Symbolism in Kafka's 'The Metamorphosis.'" *Studies in Short Fiction* 1 (1973): 205–07.

Norton Critical Editions